Conversations with Malcolm Cowley

Literary Conversations Series

Peggy Whitman Prenshaw
General Editor

Conversations
with Malcolm Cowley

Edited by
Thomas Daniel Young

University Press of Mississippi
Jackson and London

Books by Malcolm Cowley

Racine. Paris: Privately Printed, 1923.
Blue Juniata. New York: Cape, 1929.
Exile's Return. New York: Viking, 1934.
After the Genteel Tradition. New York: Norton, 1937.
The Literary Situation. New York: Viking, 1954.
Black Cargoes (with Daniel P. Mannix). New York: Viking, 1962.
Blue Juniata: Collected Poems. New York: Viking, 1968.
Think Back on Us. Carbondale: Southern Illinois University Press, 1970.
A Many Windowed House. Carbondale: Southern Illinois University Press, 1970.
—And I Worked at the Writer's Trade. New York: Viking, 1972.
A Second Flowering. New York: Viking, 1973.
The Dream of the Golden Mountains. New York: Viking, 1980.
The View from 80. New York: Viking, 1980.
The Flower and the Leaf. New York: Viking, 1985.

Copyright © 1986 by the University Press of Mississippi
All rights reserved
Manufactured in the United States of America
89 88 87 86   4 3 2 1

The paper in this book meets the guidelines for permanence and durability
of the Committee on Production Guidelines for Book Longevity
of the Council on Library Resources.

Library of Congress Cataloging-in-Publication Data
Cowley, Malcolm, 1898–
    Conversations with Malcolm Cowley.

    (Literary conversations series)
    Bibliography: p.
    Includes index.
    1. Cowley, Malcolm, 1898–   —Interviews.
2. Authors, American—20th century—Interviews.
I. Young, Thomas Daniel, 1919–   II. Title.
PS3505.O956Z463 1986   811'.52 [B]   85-26484
ISBN 0-87805-290-9 (alk. paper)
ISBN 0-87805-291-7 (pbk. : alk. paper)

For

Ruth Nuzum
Who helped and helped and helped

Contents

Introduction   ix

Chronology   xix

The Art of Fiction LXX: Malcolm Cowley   *John McCall
and George Plimpton*   3

Statement Made in the Investigations Office, OEM
George J. Gould   19

The Teaching and Study of Writing: A Symposium
Western Review   28

An Interview with Malcolm Cowley   *Fresco*   30

An Interview with Malcolm Cowley   *William F. Dawson*   34

An Interview with Malcom Cowley   *L. L. Graelle*   42

Thirty Years Later: Memories of the First American Writers'
Congress   *Daniel Aaron, Malcolm Cowley, Kenneth Burke,
Granville Hicks, and William Phillips*   53

An Interview with Malcolm Cowley   *Page Stegner
and Robert Canzoneri*   92

Malcolm Cowley: Literature Was a Substitute for Religion
in the '20s   *Joseph Haas*   105

The Importance of Knowing Ernest   *Denis Brian*   113

PW Interviews: Malcolm Cowley   *Roy Bongartz*   118

I Wish It Were 1900   *Arthur S. Freese*   123

Excerpts from "Two Gentlemen on Literati Road"   *Tom Wood*   129

Malcolm at Eighty   *Patrick Hynan*   138

A Conversation with Malcolm Cowley   *Diane U. Eisenberg*   151

An Interview with Malcolm Cowley   *Warren Herendeen
    and Donald G. Parker*   164
An Interview with Malcolm Cowley   *Randell Watson
    and Michael T. Guinzburg*   175
Malcolm Cowley: Countryman   *Robert Cowley*   182
Malcolm Cowley Talks about William Faulkner
    Dorys Crow Grover   193
A Conversation with Malcolm Cowley
    Donald W. Faulkner   201
Cowley: He Found the Lost Generation   *John King*   213
Index   218

Introduction

Born on a farm near Belsano, Pennsylvania, seventy miles south of Pittsburgh, on 24 August 1898, Cowley attended public school in Pittsburgh. After he was graduated from Peabody High School in 1915, he matriculated at Harvard University, and although he ranked second in a freshman class of seven hundred, he withdrew in the spring of 1917 to volunteer for the American Field Services. After driving a munitions truck in France for a year, he reenrolled at Harvard but withdrew shortly thereafter to enlist in the American Army. After the conclusion of the war he married Marguerite Frances Bairds and moved to Greenwich Village. In the fall he returned to Harvard for his final semester and was graduated Phi Beta Kappa in the winter of 1920 (though he was officially classified as a member of the class of 1919). After his graduation he returned immediately to Greenwich Village and began his long career as a free-lance writer, reviewing books for a cent a word (and the editor usually limited the number of words he could write about each book to one hundred. He soon saw that he could not support his wife on the meager income he could earn from book reviewing so he took a minor position on the staff of *Sweet's Architectural Catalogue.*

In 1921 Cowley was awarded an American Field Service Fellowship, which was renewed for the next year; therefore he was able to study in France for two years. As he remarked later the fellowship was for $1,000 a year and during his two years in France he was able to earn about $1,000 from his contributions to American and French magazines. He and his wife lived modestly but comfortably on $1,500 a year in France immediately after World War I, and he had enough money left for his fare back to New York and a month's rent on an apartment in Greenwich Village. As he has commented many times, it was the fact that one could live so cheaply in France, not to mention the easy accessibility of the leading French artists, that prompted so many American writers to settle in and around Paris in the early twenties. The Cowleys lived in Giverny, about fifty miles west of Paris, and came to know well many of the Dadaists, especially André Breton Tristan Tzara and Louis Aragon. He also contributed to and performed editorial chores for several little magazines, especially *Broom* and *Secession.* Among the distinguished contributions to the magazines were E. E. Cummings, Marianne Moore, Wallace Stevens, Jean Toomer, William Carlos Williams, and, of course, Malcolm Cowley.

In 1923, Cowley returned to New York. He later remarked that he found an apartment "ridicuously cheap"; however, he could not pay the rent and other necessary expenses by writing notices of new books for a penny a word so he returned to his old job of writing advertising copy for *Sweet's.* In 1929 he gathered some of the poems he had been writing for the past ten years and published *Blue Juniata* (named for the river that flows by his hometown). That year, Cowley later commented, "was my breakthrough" because not only was his book well reviewed (Allen Tate wrote that "as a document of the first postwar generation it is unique"), but he also was appointed to succeed Edmund Wilson as literary editor of the *New Republic,* a position he held for almost twenty years.

In a letter to Kenneth Burke (a schoolmate and lifelong friend), written at the time, he states his "personal philosophy." But, he said years later, that he was "using a big word," his philosophy was "really an attitude, or at best a collection of beliefs":

> I believed, first of all, that the only respectable ambition for a man of letters was to be a man of letters—not exclusively a novelist, an essayist, a dramatist, but rather one who adopts the whole of literature as his province. . . .
> I believed that the man of letters, while retaining his own point of view, which was primarily that of the poet, should concern himself with every department of human activity, including science, sociology, and revolution.
> I believed that more writers were ruined by early success than by the lack of it, and was therefore willing to make a fool of myself in order to avoid being successful. . . . I was highly moral but in a fashion acquired from my Dadaist friends. A writer could steal, murder, drink, or be sober, lie to his friends or with their wives: all this I said, was none of my concern; but my tolerance did not extend to his writing, from which I demanded high courage, absolute integrity and a sort of intelligence that was in itself a moral quality. (*Exile's Return,* pp. 160–61.)

In 1931 Cowley and his wife were divorced. The next year Cowley became involved in the mining strikes in Kentucky (the experiences are recounted in *The Dream of the Golden Mountains*). Later that summer he became concerned with the elections, trying to assist the Communist Party as much as he could, and in June he married Muriel Maurer, to whom he is still married. The next year he visited the Tates in Tennessee and Kentucky and met many of the Agrarians. To his great surprise he found that many of the ideas of that conservative group were more convincing than he had expected them to be. "Listening to the Agrarians," he wrote in 1965, "I felt they were trying to make a Northern convert, and for all my radical opinions I agreed with them on many points."

In his position at the *New Republic* Cowley had a profound effect on the literary community. Writing of Cowley in *Starting Out in the Thirties* (1965), Alfred Kazin comments: "The lead review in the *New Republic*, a single page usually written by Cowley himself, brought the week to focus for people to whom this page, breathing intellectual fight in its sharp black title and solid double lines of argument, represented the most dramatically satisfying confrontation of a new book by a gifted, uncompromising critical intelligence." Cowley was also in a position to assist unknown writers trying to find a publisher. Although he denies "discovering" John Cheever, he admits that his reaction to Cheever's first story "was as close to discovery as an editor can hope for."

> I was the junior editor on the *New Republic* in 1930. A manuscript came in marked for my attention; it was a story on yellow copy paper called "Expelled from Prep School." I read it with great interest and carried it to Bruce Bliven, the managing editor. Bruce said, "Well, it's a little long. Cut it down by half and we'll take it." A couple of months after that, John Cheever himself appeared. He was eighteen. His brother had given him an allowance of ten dollars a week to try to be a writer in New York. That memoir was the first I read of John's. He began writing stories—published in small magazines that didn't pay—always stories about seven thousand words in length, always fresh and very good, too, but with no hope of their being published by magazines that paid money.
>
> One Friday night when John was at our house for dinner, I told him, "Tomorrow, write a story of one thousand words. Sunday write another, and Monday write another, three and a half pages, and do the same thing on Tuesday." Wednesday was my day at the *New Republic* for seeing contributors, so I said, "Bring them all in on Wednesday and I'll see if I can't get you some money."
>
> Well, this sounds like wise old Nestor telling a young author what to do.

But I knew John; nobody else could have invented four stories in four days. But on Wednesday he brought in four thousand-word stories. The *New Republic* didn't print fiction but I thought one of them could be considered local color. So I got one accepted, and I sent the other three stories to Katherine White at the *New Yorker.* She took two of them, and John was launched on his career as a professional writer. (*Paris Review* interview)

Exile's Return, now considered Cowley's most important book, did not fare well with the reviewers. In 1934, when the book was first published, many readers, critics and writers were concerned with matters other than those written about by Hemingway, Fitzgerald, and the other artists of the so-called "Lost Generation." In the depth of the greatest depression the country had ever known, many were convinced that capitalism was no longer the economic system that would best serve the citizens of a democratic nation. Bernard De Voto just about summed up the critical reaction to *Exile's Return* in his statement that the writers Cowley was surveying were "ignorant, inaccurate, foolish—or frivolous and corrupt." Because of its critical reception, the book sold fewer than a thousand copies in its first year and only a few hundred more during the next ten years. When he revised it nearly twenty years later, Cowley says, "it was almost universally praised, and it has since gone through twenty or more printings." Then he adds, "of all the writers De Voto praised as being better and more morally uplifting than those I wrote about, not one of them is read today."

During the 1940s Cowley edited a number of *Portables* for Viking, the best known of which is undoubtedly the one he did on Faulkner. Before its appearance Faulkner was virtually unknown and many of those who had read him knew only *Sanctuary* and "A Rose for Emily," both of which were included among the most scandalous works of fiction ever published in America. When Cowley first suggested the idea of a collection of Faulkner's stories and excerpts from the novels, Viking was not interested in undertaking the venture. But Cowley, who had almost finished a long introduction, divided it into several essays and published them. Suddenly Viking concluded there was enough interest in Faulkner to justify publishing the *Portable,* a conclusion apparently reached because of the impression created by Cowley's essays. When the book appeared a short time later, Cowley states its purpose clearly in the introduction: "there in Oxford Faulkner performed a labor of imagination that has not been equalled in our time, and a double labor: first to invent a Mississippi county that was like a mythical kingdom . . . second to make his story of Yoknapatawpha County stand as a parable or legend of all the Deep South." Then Cowley presents seven hundred twenty-five pages of Faulkner's fiction to demonstrate the truth of the statements made in the introduction. Cowley's book was followed by important essays by Robert Penn Warren and others, and Faulkner's reputation was made. He soon became the most widely read and written about author in American literature.

After Cowley left the *New Republic* he became an advisor to the Viking Press where he not only edited the *Portables*—Faulkner, Whitman, Hemingway and Hawthorne—he also supported the publication of some of the "beat generation" fiction, principally Jack Kerouac's *On the Road*. Although he did not copyedit the book, he did strongly support its publication, and he affected the form in which the novel was finally published. "I had no great interest in changing commas or words," he said in 1980, "but I thought that in the structure of the book he'd done a weak thing by having it swing back and forth across the country like a pendulum. One suggestion was that he should telescope two-thirds of the trips across the country and have a simpler movement. I think he did that. He certainly didn't rebel against anything I told him. After I finished with the manuscript it went to a copy-editor and the copy-editor had ideas about commas, sentences, and so on, and changed some of Jack's precious prose. He was furious."

Although Cowley is very explicit in describing the manner in which he made his way in the literary world—as a free-lance writer and book reviewer as opposed to the modern practice of teaching creative writing—in recent years he has taught in some of the most prestigious universities in the country. One of the most productive and talented classes he has taught was at Stanford in 1960. In this class he had, among others, Ken Kesey and Larry McMurtry, and from its students have come more than seventy volumes. Cowley has also been a prolific writer, publishing seven books since the reissue and enlargement of *Blue Juniata: Collected Poems* in 1978.

It is only when this last work is considered that one can give a just estimate of Cowley's contribution to American letters, and even then, it is difficult to place Cowley's work in definite categories, as George Core points out in his essay on Cowley in *American Writers* (New York: Scribner's, 1981)—one of the most helpful essays on Cowley's literary career:

> The most obvious modes are the personal essay and the autobiographical memoir, criticism formal and informal, literary history, editorials, poetry, translation. In practice it is difficult to sort out the published work aside from the book review, editorials, poems and translations, putting a given piece in this bin or that. But one can make general distinctions that hold true for the most part. *Exile's Return* and *A Second Flowering* belong together as critical and autobiographical accounts of American literary modernism, especially the figures of the lost generation. *The Literary Situation* and—*And I Worked at the Writer's Trade* are books about the literary profession and the state of publishing;—*And I Worked . . .* has a more critical aspect than *The Literary Situation. . . . The Dream of the Golden Mountain* is . . . a reminiscense about the 1930's. . . . *Think Back on Us . . .* and *A Many Windowed House* show Cowley the editorialist and the book reviewer and Cowley the critic and literary historian. . . . The *Faulkner-Cowley File* is a unique chapter in literary relations as an author and editor respond to each other. (141)

Although Malcolm Cowley was busily engaged in what he called "the writer's trade" for more than half a century, there is little of the real Cowley in what he wrote. In the first place in much of his writing it was important that the writer remain invisible. Too, he is a very modest, unassuming man, and this is the way he appears in the interviews. It is this unpretentious critic, however, who has been acknowledged for reviving critical and popular interest in Faulkner. William Faulkner's literary career by the beginning of World War II was seemingly over. Many of his books were out of print or the publisher had allowed them to go out of print and melted the plates for the war effort. Faulkner's few readers had either forgotten him or remembered him as the author of *Sanctuary* or "A Rose for Emily." Even though Cowley's *Portable Faulkner* resurrected the literary career of one of our most significant novelists, he always said that Faulkner was too good a writer to be neglected for long. He said in interview after interview that Faulkner would have been rediscovered, that his book had merely moved that rediscovery ahead a few years. "What I did," he said many times, "was to make him teachable." The

academics discovered Faulkner and began to teach him and thus the
demand for Faulkner's works grew.

In the late 1940s when the *Portable* was first published, was the
fastest selling book around and used in many classrooms all over
America, Robert Penn Warren in a review of that book wrote that
Cowley's view of Faulkner was too limited. Cowley had claimed in his
introduction that "Faulkner had created a legend of the deep South."
Warren argued, however, that Faulkner's basic concern was the
condition of modern man everywhere, "the plight and problem of us
all." Soon after Warren's review Cowley made a public statement in
which he agreed with Warren completely.

Another of many incidences that might be cited to demonstrate
Cowley's modesty is the well-known episode in the career of John
Cheever cited earlier. Credited with discovering Cheever, Cowley's
response was "John was such a naturally talented writer that all he
needed was a little direction and a little time. Someone was bound to
recognize that he was born a writer."

In addition to his modesty, these interviews reveal that Cowley is a
congenial, caring, and accommodating man. He is always saying that
he is deluged with requests that keep him away from the typewriter.
Yet I know of no instance in which he has failed to grant an interview,
often coming from his home in Sherman, Connecticut, to the
Harvard Club in New York City, to keep the interviewer from having
to come to Sherman and to be sure the interview is held in the most
appropriate place he can provide. Once the interview gets underway,
he responds in a serious professional manner and always allows it to
proceed as long as anything worth while is being accomplished.
Although he has said many times that he resents the time consumed
in answering questions from students or scholars interested in the
literary twenties, I know of few times he has failed to answer a query.
I know the dozens of letters he wrote me—helping me to locate
sources, to identify interviewers, assisting me in editing interviews that
have never been published, and even aiding in the process of
procuring permissions to publish interviews—are not isolated inci-
dents.

We know that Cowley has lived and worked in a rennovated barn
in Sherman, Connecticut, and that he has always tried to prevent
interruptions that would keep him from writing and editing. That he

has been remarkably successful in this endeavor is demonstrated by the number of books he has published, particularly in his later years when he could devote most of his time and energy to writing. Yet there is a placard in his living room awarded to him for twenty years of devoted service to the Zoning Commission of Sherman, of which he served as chairman. He was willing, he said, to do what he could to preserve the fields, woods, and the open space around the village. Most of all he wanted to prevent as long as possible Sherman from becoming just another bedroom community serving New York City. "The side of my father," Robert Cowley wrote me, "that I brought out in that interview ['Malcolm Cowley: Countryman'] is the one that people tend to overlook. They shouldn't. It's the key to the way he regards the world. That's why I want to be in your book." There are few more charming, helpful, and genuinely honest people than the person revealed by these interviews.

The interviews in this collection cover all aspects of Cowley's long and varied literary career. Except for the first—and Cowley requested that the *Paris Review* interview be the one the reader would likely read first because in his opinion it gives the best overview of his entire career—the interviews are arranged chronologically. Except for Cowley's interview with George J. Gould of the Office of Emergency Management, the conversations are presented as they appeared in their first printed version. Some of the interviews, those that existed only on tape, have been edited, by the interviewer and Mr. Cowley, for smoothness and clarity. All the entries in this collection are conversations although a few of them do not follow strictly the interview form. Full bibliographical information concerning each interview is given on the first page. Footnotes are held to a minimum in order not to divert the reader's attention, although in a few cases identification of a person or event seemed advisable.

Many persons have assisted me in numerous ways in the preparation of this book. First of all I owe a special debt of gratitude to Malcolm Cowley for the many hours he spent answering my queries and for the promptness with which he responded to my numerous letters. I am also grateful to Bonnie Orick and Gail Davis Read for their expert typing of the several versions of the manuscript. I am especially grateful that Seetha Srinivasan, executive editor of the

University Press of Mississippi, invited me to compile this volume. Most of all I am indebted to the gracious lady to whom this book is dedicated for her invaluable assistance in identifying and locating many of the conversations that appear in this volume.

TDY
September 1985

Chronology

1898   Malcolm Cowley is born on a farm near Belsano, Pennsylvania, on 24 August.

1904–11   Attends Liberty School in Pittsburgh.

1911–15   Attends Peabody High School in Pittsburgh.

1915   Enrolls in Harvard University.

1917   In April withdraws from Harvard and goes to France to drive an ambulance for the American Field Service.

1918   Back at Harvard for spring semester; withdraws in spring to join American Army.

1919   Mustered out of army and moves to Greenwich Village; in August marries Marguerite Frances Baird; returns to Harvard in the fall and graduates in the winter of 1920 (but is listed as graduating in the class of 1919). Graduates with honors and Phi Beta Kappa.

1920–21   Free-lance writer in Greenwich Village; earns money by working as advertising copy writer for *Sweet's Architectural Catalogue.*

1921–23   Attends University of Montpellier, France, on a fellowship from the American Field Service.

1923   Returns to New York; resumes free-lance writing in Greenwich Village and working for *Sweet's Architectural Catalogue.*

1924   Resigns from *Sweet's* and moves to Staten Island; tries
            again to earn his living from free-lance writing.

1925   Moves to Sherman, Connecticut.

1928   Buys farm in upstate New York. His neighbors are Allen
            Tate and Caroline Gordon Tate, Matthew Josephson,
            Robert M. Coates and Hart Crane.

1929   *Blue Juniata,* his first book of poems is published; begins
            work for *New Republic.*

1930–40   Serves as literary editor of *New Republic.*

1931   Divorced from Marguerite Frances Baird (Peggy) Cowley.

1932   Involved with mining strikes in Kentucky; in June marries
            Muriel Maurer.

1933   Spends summer with Allen Tate and Caroline Gordon
            Tate in Kentucky; meets many of the Agrarians and works
            on the manuscript of *Exile's Return.*

1934   *Exile's Return: A Literary Odyssey of the 1930s* is pub-
            lished; son Robert is born.

1936   Moves into a remodeled barn in Sherman, Connecticut,
            where he and his wife still live.

1937   Attends World Congress of Writers in Madrid; *After the
            Genteel Tradition: American Writers Since 1910* is pub-
            lished.

1942   Works briefly in federal Office of Facts and Figures;
            questioned about his political activities during the 1930s
            by the Office for Emergency Management; appears be-
            fore the Dies Committee of the U.S. Congress.

1943–48   Receives a Mellon Fellowship to work on American writ-
           ers.

1944   Edits *The Portable Hemingway*.

1946   Edits *The Portable Faulkner*.

1948   Edits *The Portable Hawthorne;* becomes literary consul-
           tant to Viking Press.

1949   Testifies at the trial of Alger Hiss; elected to the National
           Institute of Arts and Letters (served as president 1956–59
           and 1962–65).

1950   Walker-Ames Lecturer at Washington University

1951   Edits *The Short Stories of F. Scott Fitzgerald*.

1954   Publishes *The Literary Situation;* edits *Winesburg, Ohio*.

1956–65   Teaches at Stanford University on four occasions.

1957   Teaches at University of Michigan.

1958   Edits First Series of *Paris Review Interviews*.

1959   Edits *Leaves of Grass: First Edition*.

1960   Teaches at Stanford.

1962   Publishes *Black Cargoes: A History of the Atlantic Slave
           Trade* (with Daniel P. Mannix); teaches at the University of
           California at Berkeley.

1966   *The Faulkner-Cowley File: Letters and Memories 1944–
           1962 is published;* Cowley is named chancellor of the
           American Academy of Arts and Letters (1966–76).

1967   *Think Back on Us: A Contempory Chronicle of the 1930s* is published.

1968   *Blue Juniata: Collected Poems* is published.

1970   *A Many-Windowed Room: Collected Essays on American Writers and American Writing* is published.

1971   *Lesson of the Masters: An Anthology of the Novel from Cervantes to Hemingway* (edited with Howard E. Hugo) is published.

1973   *A Second Flowering: Works and Days of the Lost Generation* is published; teaches at the University of Warwick, England.

1978   *—And I Worked at the Writer's Trade: Chapters of Literary History, 1918–1978* is published.

1980   *The Dream of the Golden Mountains: Remembering the 1930s; The View from 80* are published.

1985   *The Flower and the Leaf: A Contemporary Record of American Writing Since 1941* is published.

Conversations with Malcolm Cowley

The Art of Fiction LXX: Malcolm Cowley

John McCall and George Plimpton/1982

This interview was conducted in two places dear to Malcolm Cowley, and which suggest the two main areas of his literary life. One conversation took place in the Harvard Club's Card Room, a cubbyhole in the New York Club's upstairs warrens. Cowley often lunches at the club on the days when he comes into New York from his Connecticut home to perform his editing duties at the Viking Press. Although Cowley refers to himself only as a writer in his *Who's Who* biographical data, he enjoys a great reputation as an editor and critic—especially for a championing of William Faulkner in the late '40s which was largely responsible for the renewed interest in the author. Second talks were held at Cowley's Connecticut home where he is freer to do his own writing.

Cowley has twice been President of the National Institute of Arts and Letters and Chancellor of the American Academy of Arts and Letters. His demeanor these days (he is 84) suggests that he could take up these tasks again with ease. His manner is brisk, his voice hearty. He wears a hearing aid, but that is his only visible concession to his years.

Thomas H. Guinzburg, who was Cowley's former publisher and employer at the Viking Press, wrote the following upon reading this interview: ". . . fellow readers will gain the strong impression Cowley is determined to resist the constant invasions of his time. Do not believe him. Malcolm has always given ample time to any of us who were perceptive enough to seek it, frequently delaying his own more valuable projects in the process. Cowley missed the golden pay day when editors suddenly became stars and found themselves negotiating *their* names onto book jackets and title pages. Nor did he ever adopt the 'New York' scene. He and his wife, Muriel, continue

to live and work in Sherman, Connecticut, and from his
one-man assembly line there continues to pour out our
most accurate impressions of the life and times of American twentieth-century writing and publishing."

Interviewer: How would you compare the lot of writers today with
when you started?

Cowley: In many ways things are easier now for writers. Sixty
years ago there were no such things as writing fellowships; there were
no Guggenheims . . . very few prizes. There were almost no teaching
posts for writers. So the would-be writers came to New York and
tried to get a job on a newspaper. Usually they ended up in an
advertising agency, or they starved in the Village. Freelance work was
paid for at the rate of about a penny a word for reviews. The *New
Republic* and the *Dial* paid two cents; that was high, and besides, you
were always glad to be printed in those magazines.

The only chance for higher pay was with fiction, in the glossies.
These had enormous circulations for that time, and they were paying
good rates for fiction. The *Saturday Evening Post* went up to $4,000
per story with F. Scott Fitzgerald, and I don't think that was absolutely
their top rate. A couple of other writers earned up to $50,000 every
year writing short stories. Fiction was the field and remained so until
the disappearance of the family magazine in the 30's and 40's, one
after the other going, until now it is the devil's own job to get fiction
published, even for people who are very good at it. But still, by the
large, the writer has an easier time of it than a few decades ago.

Interviewer: What about the poets?

Cowley: There's been an enormous change. As late as 1930 there
were only a few men and women who supported themselves as
poets. One was Robert Frost and another was Oscar Hammerstein II.
We had great respect for e. e. cummings because he lived as a poet,
but even he got a little money from his mother. T. S. Eliot was a bank
clerk, and then with Faber & Faber, the publishers. Robert Frost
managed to support himself after *North of Boston* by readings, and
by lecturing at universities. He rather blazed a trail in that respect.
Now, a lot of poets are not poets primarily. Many of them may teach

or read their poetry to keep up, but probably two or three hundred people in the United States if asked their trade would say "poet."

Interviewer: Do you regret not having concentrated more fully on your poetry?

Cowley: Yes, I have regretted it very much. The shift, for me, was the essential middle-class feeling that I had to support myself.

Interviewer: What were you paid for *Blue Juniata?*

Cowley: I got an advance of $125 and no further payments.

Interviewer: That was why you didn't go on?

Cowley: I wanted to go on writing poetry, but I always had the feeling that I couldn't write any poem that didn't come to me. I didn't say to myself, "Go spend two hours and write a poem." Perhaps I should have. Of course, if I'd had a few more dollars I would have written more poetry. Book reviewing didn't help. Odd: being an editor didn't interfere with my writing; it was being an editor *and* a book-reviewer. You find that you put everything you've got into anything you write. There may not be so much left over.

Interviewer: There are many excuses for not writing.

Cowley: Pipes are one of the best. I can use one even to keep from talking. And there's always a letter to be written. One of the great penalties of having been around for a long time is that there is hardly a genuine letter in the mail I receive. It's rare that one of my letters isn't a request for information about somebody on whom the requester is doing a dissertation. Jesus! Well, at least I don't have Edmund Wilson's great arrogance of sending back a printed card saying that he won't do it. I do reply. I generally refer them to other sources.

Interviewer: You're probably considered a soft touch.

Cowley: I keep hoping I'll be compensated in some way. Once I wrote a piece that tried to sum up the joys and vexations of being eighty, but I left out one of the worst vexations—which is to become a national scholarly resource, I never expected to become a national scholarly resource—but you can't escape the destiny of your dotage. Simply by having outlived your great contemporaries, you find that you have a field all to yourself; or if you don't have a field, at least you have a stable in one corner of the field. Hundreds of scholars then come into the field who are writing dissertations, monographs, biographies—all sorts of things—and for each one they want to have a little reinforcement, a little supplement; they want to have a word straight from the horse's mouth. So they come to me and say, "Well, you are the horse—won't you please share your memories? Won't you please answer this little questionnaire of five single-spaced typed pages?" or, "Won't you let us put your memories on tape?" There is no enrichment from this sort of thing. Not one of them thinks of filling the horse's feedbox with oats or of putting a little hay in the manger. They assume, I guess, that a horse can just forage for himself—if he has time; certainly nobody gives him an offer to earn an easy living by putting himself out to stud.

Interviewer: You're making us feel guilty. Do you mind if we ask you about Gertrude Stein's remark, "You are all a lost generation"?

Cowley: Oh, it's simple as all get-out. Gertrude Stein was having her Model-T Ford repaired at a garage in the south of France. The mechanics weren't very good; they weren't on the job—in fact, I think they were on strike. The proprietor said to Miss Stein, "These young men are no good—they are all a lost generation"—*une génération perdue*. So an unknown French garage man should get credit for that remark. Of course, Miss Stein deserves credit for picking up on the phrase.

Interviewer: Is it possible the garage man was referring to "a lost generator"?

Cowley: Her French was better than that.

Interviewer: Was there a special sense, a feeling, about being an artist, or writer at that time?

Cowley: The writers had an odd advantage in being born around 1900. The century had turned, so as they grew older they began to feel that it was their century—new, unprecedented. This doesn't mean that they all thought they were wonderful people, but they did think that their lives represented the fate of the new world, no less. That feeling is very strong in Scott Fitzgerald, for example, and in other writers, too; there's something of it in Dos Passos and cummings.

Interviewer: What were some of the English-speaking magazines in Europe when you arrived?

Cowley: The first one that I ran into in Paris was *Gargoyle*, edited by two characters from Greenwich Village, Arthur Moss and Florence Gilliam. Then, in 1921, Gorham D. Munson and Matthew Josephson arrived, and they got out *Secession*. Matty became a friend of the French Dadaists; he was wonderful at making acquaintances. Next he got a job on *Broom*, which Harold Loeb had started and published in Rome; then, with Matty as managing editor, the magazine moved to Berlin, where everything was fabulously cheap. Matty had a salary of $100 per month, for which he had a triplex apartment and riding lessons for his wife.

After that came the other magazines. The great Paris magazine was Eugene Jolas's *Transition*. There was an extremely vivid sense that a new type of writing was coming along. Something had to change after the war that had shaken civilization; here were all these people who regarded the older magazines as stuffy, commercial, not giving a voice to younger people. So the magazines were started partly with the idea that a new generation was coming onto the scene, and that they should have periodicals that spoke for them and introduced new talents. Ernest Walsh did that in *This Quarter*. Ford Madox Ford started *The Transatlantic Review* and was very much interested in the younger Americans.

Interviewer: Did you ever see Pound in Paris?

Cowley: I went to see him a couple of times, but I was a little uneasy with him. Pound always had some new discovery or enthusiasm; he was always finding the lowdown on something. On one of my visits to his little apartment, he announced loudly, "I've got the lowdown on the Elizabethan drama! It was all cribbed from these books," and he carried out two huge volumes of the Venetian State Papers. Well, it *was* a real discovery: the plots of several Elizabethan plays *did* come out of the Venetian State Papers.

Interviewer: Why did Hemingway have such an apparent dislike for Ford Madox Ford?

Cowley: Hemingway had the bad habit of never forgiving anyone for giving him a hand up. That may have been the problem between them. Ford was a character; he was a liar, not for his own profit, but just because he had a very faint hold on actuality. He told beautiful stories of English literary life, in which he knew everybody, had a hand in everything, and his hand grew larger as he told the story. He had a roving eye for younger women, whom he especially liked to fascinate. He came to this country after the breakup of his marriage to Stella Bowen. I can remember on one occasion he came up to

Robber Rocks—a place back in the woods near the New York-
Connecticut line which was the country headquarters for Allen Tate,
Hart Crane, and others—where a lot of young wives were around at
the party. They would be fondled by Ford, and then escape him up
the stairs. Ford, heavy and wheezing by that time, would follow them
to the head of the narrow stairs, and the door would close in his face.
He would wheeze back down, and a while later he'd follow another
young woman until she took refuge behind a locked door.

Interviewer: Do you think collecting in such colonies is of value to
a writer? It doesn't seem to be done as much these days.

Cowley: Perhaps that is true. But I think young writers always
collect, and that is a good thing, because the persons they learn from,
their real professors, are other writers of the same age. That particular
neighborhood, near Robber Rocks, was cheap. The Rocks was
owned by Slater Brown, but others rented rooms from a woman
called Aunt Addie Turner, who lived in a great barn of a house that
had once been a boys' school. She rented out parts of it for eight
dollars a month. A few miles over the Connecticut line was another
group—Josephine Herbst, John Hermann, Nathan Asch, and a
couple of others.

Interviewer: What sort of a boarder was Hart Crane?

Cowley: He was rather difficult. You forgave Hart a great deal
because he was so kind and helpful. But then he'd get drunk and
start throwing furniture out of the window. Or he'd stagger around
the house with a lighted kerosene lamp.

Interviewer: I take it that for him alcohol acted as a stimulus to
the creative process?

Cowley: One of the reasons why Hart, and many writers, turn into
alcoholics is that early in their lives they find that getting drunk is part
of the creative process, that it opens up visions. It's a terrible sort of
creative device, because three out of four who involve themselves in
it become alcoholics. But it does open up doors in the beginning.
Hart Crane would even make a first draft when he was drunk; he'd
come out and read it, and say, "Isn't this the greatest poem ever
written?" It wasn't. But then he would work over it patiently, dead
sober, for several weeks, and it would amount to something. Not the
greatest poem ever written, but still extraordinary.

Interviewer: Did Crane get any help from his family?

Cowley: Hart's father had been quite wealthy until 1929. He invented the Lifesaver-candy with a hole in it. "Crane's Chocolates" used to advertise in *The Saturday Evening Post.* But Hart was estranged from his father after his parents were divorced. The father remarried after the Crash and started a quite fashionable country restaurant named Canary Cottage in Chagrin Falls, outside of Cleveland. Still, he couldn't have helped Hart much.

Interviewer: Did Faulkner write under the influence of alcohol?

Cowley: I rather think he did in his early years. He always hesitated to admit it, but I'm sure that a good many of his things were written when he'd been drinking. It didn't break him. And he did an extraordinary amount of revision, but he would try to preserve the integrity of that orginial vision, so that his rewritting was not so much line for line as it was shifting episodes and characters.

Interviewer: What did his manuscript pages look alike? Did he make many corrections on the galleys?

Cowley: He made them in the case of one book, *Sanctuary.* Otherwise his corrections were usually made in typescripts.

Interviewer: Writers so often complain about the horrors of writing.

Cowley: Almost all of them are certainly procrastinators, but a few people really like to write. Kay Boyle used to say that she loved the smell of paper. Anthony Trollope trained himself to turn out forty-nine pages of manuscript a week, seven pages a day, and he was so rigorous about keeping to that exact number of pages that if he finished a novel halfway through the last day, he'd write the title of a new book and "Chapter One" on the next page and go right on until he'd done his proper quota of seven pages.

Interviewer: Do you think American writers are more prone to procrastinate than British writers?

Cowley: American authors are more self-conscious than the British . . . a little more preoccupied with what the critics will say. The writer's problem is largely one of self-esteem. He thinks, "Is what I am writing worthy of the picture I have formed of my talent?" A lot of writers have only one book in them. Margaret Mitchell wrote *Gone with the Wind*—then she never even tried to write another book. A lot of writers keep publishing what are essentially the same books with a different title.

Interviewer: Can success be harmful?

Cowley: They tell me that success is a terrible test of people. Thank God I've never had to undergo it. But nationwide success with money pouring in will kill lots of writers. Ross Lockridge, who wrote *Raintree County*, and Thomas Heggens, the author of that novel about a ship, *Mr. Roberts*, both committed suicide. It was always said that Gilbert Seldes's review of *The Great Gatsby*, which was ecstatic, probably damaged Scott Fitzgerald. The trouble is that after something like that, every work has to count . . . every word has to live up to this marvelous praise. The poor author gets stage fright.

Interviewer: Are the creative impulses involved in writing poetry and essays vastly different?

Cowley: There a is different process involved: the poem has to start with an emotion. After that, you call on the same parts of your mind during the creative process, but the beginning is quite different. With the essay you start out with a given or chosen subject. The poem comes to you.

Interviewer: Are there mnemonic devices to get you going on a day's work?

Cowley: A lot of people use walking. I wonder if the decline of walking will lead to a decline of the creative process.

Interviewer: Do you see a relationship between unhappiness and poetic creativity?

Cowley: To the extent that poems may be born from a straining of one's senses and imagination to a degree to which they couldn't be strained in ordinary life. I was reading F. Scott Fitzgerald's correspondence the other day. Scott and Zelda's difficulties were ones I never had to face; I never had to drive myself to drink in order to get my imagination working. Actually, I found my imagination worked best on fatigue. That's another form of intoxication . . . to set yourself writing, and keep on writing until after two or three hours the subconscious takes over. It's certainly safer than alcohol. The trouble with alcohol is that you can't keep it up.

I went to visit the Fitzgeralds when they were living outside of Baltimore—a place called "La Paix." Scott said to me, "I'm on the wagon, but I got you a pint of whiskey from my bootlegger; I'm on water." So we talked, or mostly *he* talked, and every once in a while he'd go out to the kitchen to get another glass of water. His talk became more belligerent, sometimes incoherent, until finally he said, "You know, that water I've been drinking all evening—it's half grain alcohol." I said to myself, "Oh . . . surprise!"

Interviewer: So alcohol is of no use?

Cowley: Sometimes Edmund Wilson said a glass of whiskey would get him started on a piece—would help with the start and perhaps the finish. But usually the writer is sober when he writes. He had better be. John Cheever used to say he could tell from a writer's work if he'd had a drink. . . .

Interviewer: Who worked with William Faulkner at Random House?

Cowley: A succession of people, but they didn't really work with him at first. I don't think they always read proofs of his novels, at least in the late thirties, because some of them are marred by errors in grammar that Faulkner would have been glad to have pointed out to him, and would have fixed up. But he absolutely could not have stomached receiving a critique on the whole concept of a book—the sort of thing that Maxwell Perkins at Scribner's might have put together—and he certainly would not have written a book to order.

Interviewer: And yet he spent those years in Hollywood.

Cowley: Cynically. He didn't think he was actually any good in Hollywood. He was able to work consistently with only one director, and that was Howard Hawks. One thing that has never been published about Faulkner is that he thought his best movie was *The Southerner,* the Jean Renoir film, for which he did not get movie credit. He was under contract to Warner Brothers and could not let it be known that he had worked for another studio.

Interviewer: What about your own remarkable identification with Faulkner's work?

Cowley: I shouldn't be given all the credit for rescuing Faulkner from neglect. There were always men of letters in this country— Conrad Aiken, Robert Penn Warren and a couple of others, Caroline Gordon, especially—who were enthusiastic about Faulkner's writing. But it is true that public estimation of his books sank so low that by the middle of the War, only one book, *Sanctuary,* was not out of print; his publishers donated the plates of other novels to the war effort to be melted down and to make copper jacketings for bullets. The publishers were very patriotic. So at that time I had the strong feeling that Faulkner had to be brought back. I had done a Hemingway *Portable* for the Viking Press, a book that came early in their series of Portables. I had suggested, "Why not a Faulkner *Portable?*" Viking replied, "We don't think Faulkner has sufficient public to justify a *Portable.*" That wasn't enough for me. Fortunately, through Matty Josephson I had been offered a contract to write a history of American literature. I always hated big undertakings—the sort of thing he suggested—so I thought I'd break it down and do one author at a time. Since I'd been reading Faulkner and believed that among the writers of his generation his public reputation was one most out of line with his extraordinary talent, the choice was compulsive. I took about ninety single-spaced pages of notes. Then I began writing an essay which got to be too long for any magazine to print as a whole. So I "beefed" it—I got that phrase from George Milburn, a writer and a good one, too, who came from the back country in Oklahoma. He told me that he had beefed a novel by cutting it into steaks and selling them to the *New Yorker.* I beefed the essay on Faulkner and sold chunks of it to three magazines.

At the time I was helped financially by an extraordinary piece of good luck. It was during the war. The phone rang, and the voice at the other end said, "This is Stanley Young. How would you like to be supported for five years?" I said, textually, "Well, I'd like that fine, but I'm getting along all right. Why don't you make that offer to Kenneth Burke?"—who was my oldest friend. Stanley said, "Oh, no. We'll think about Kenneth later. In the meantime, we'd like you to figure out how much it would take you to live for five years." He went on to explain. "This is an idea of Mary Mellon's, of the Pittsburgh Mellons. You come in and have lunch with Mary and if you pass muster this idea of hers will go through."

So I had lunch with Mary Mellon. I think I drank too many martinis. I talked very much and excitedly. So it went through. For five years I received, under contract with Mary Mellon, $5,500 per year, which seemed a great deal of money to me.

Four other people got this arrangement. Then it was decided the plan wasn't working. When Mary Mellon died, Paul Mellon closed out all the contracts, which he was quite right to do. As a matter of fact, I was the only one of the five authors who carried through on the aim of the plan. It enabled me to do a great deal of work on authors, including Faulkner, while at the same time being rather standoffish about publication.

Of course, it could have been an opportunity to write poetry, but I kept remembering that the arrangement was only for five years. At the end of that time I would still have to live mostly by writing for magazines. So I "beefed"—cut steaks and roasts from—the long Faulkner essay and published them.

One day Marshall Best of the Viking Press called and said, "It seems to us that Faulkner's work is attracting a good deal of attention in magazines. We're thinking of going ahead with the Faulkner *Portable*." I said, modestly, "Yes. It is attracting a good deal of attention." I had this idea of putting together an outline of the Yoknapatawpha County saga in the *Portable*. I also had an idea that Faulkner might help me on this with advice. It turned out he was most eager to do so.

So we worked through this, discussing by letter what should go in and what should stay out—a correspondence published in a book called *The Faulkner-Cowley File*. At the end of it Faulkner wrote and added a biographical dictionary of the Compson family. When the *Portable* came out, Faulkner inscribed a copy to me, writing, "Damn you, you've done what was supposed to be the occupation of my declining years." Apparently, that's what he had wanted one day to do himself.

Interviewer: Was the Faulkner *Portable* an immediate success?

Cowley: The *Portable* couldn't have started a renewed interest in Faulkner's work if it hadn't been for Caroline Gordon, who did a frontpage review for the *New York Times,* and Robert Penn Warren, who reviewed it for the *New Republic* in an article so long that it had to be published in two issues. From that time on, Faulkner, who had been completely beneath the dignity of English departments to talk about, began to be studied by graduate students.

Interviewer: What was your personal relationship with Faulkner?

Cowley: Beginning in 1944 we had quite a correspondence. I wrote him a letter saying I wanted to do a piece about his work. I hoped to meet him. After four or five months he answered from Hollywood. He explained that when he got letters from strangers, first he opened them to see if there was return postage. If there was, he used the stamps. As for the letters, he'd drop them in a drawer and then, he said, every six months or so he'd open the drawer and begin to read the letters. Mine had been luckier; it had only waited in the drawer three or four months. He wrote me that the idea of finishing his career without having attracted any more attention that he had done so far was painful and, yes, he would be grateful to have a long essay written about him, but he didn't want any personal details included. He wanted to live anonymously. He wrote me in one of his letters that he wanted his tombstone inscribed, "He wrote the books and he died."

Interviewer: Did you know that there is an odd typographical error on his tombstone in Oxford, Mississippi? It reads, "Belove'd Go to God." It was probably supposed to say, "Belovèd Go to God," but the carver misread the accent mark for an apostrophe.

Cowley: I think he would have smiled at that.

Interviewer: Was he a good storyteller in person?

Cowley: He would tell a story very much as stories were told on the "gallery," as they call it, of a little one-room store in Mississippi—men squatting on their heels in overalls and chewing tobacco. He didn't chew tobacco, but he told stories the way backwoods storytellers told them, which was very entertaining. He wasn't one of them, but he fit in. In Oxford they called him "Count No Count."

Interviewer: Did Faulkner know Hemingway?

Cowley: Hemingway and Faulkner never met, but they read each other and profited by the reading, Faulkner epecially. It's largely a question of emulation that causes writers to appear as if in groups. Even if they never meet, they read each other.

Interviewer: Hemingway's life has always been closely linked to his work. Now that his private letters have been published, what effect do you think they'll have on his reputation?

Cowley: His reputation as a man will go down because there's a great deal of malice, rivalry, and plain falsehood in his letters. All his weaknesses of character come out, and in the published letters they're not balanced or driven from your mind by his tremendous personality. He had a gift for charming people by giving them his undivided attention. As he said, so few people know how to listen. That's one way he charmed people, by listening. At the same time he was always suggesting expeditions and adventures, so that in personal relations he had an enormous charm that doesn't come through in the letters.

Interviewer: It's difficult to reconcile this charm with the impression one gets from the letters.

Cowley: Well, he wrote those letters very often late at night when he couldn't sleep. Frequently he wouldn't mail the letters because they told too much. But I think if you sit back from that collection of printed letters and consider what he's saying, you can begin to get a picture of his charm, because for each of the persons he was writing to he had adopted a different story. He was projecting himself into their different personalities.

Interviewer: I recall Selden Rodman's comparing Hemingway to Byron and saying that Hemingway's genius was essentially comic.

Cowley: Comic isn't the word. He was never a comic writer. He was often a satirist, and a cruel one.

Interviewer: What would you say was the essence of his genius?

Cowley: A sort of restoration to literature of various primal qualities. There's almost the quality of a medieval lyric in much of Hemingway's writing. It's fresh. If you read *Le Mortre D'Arthur,* the chapter that begins with the month of May at King Arthur's court, there's a freshness in it that one finds again in Hemingway.

I think he is a lyric writer, more or less. He always had trouble with plot because he wasn't so much filling out a plot as he was making a journey or progression, day by day. Later he would try to fit that into a plot. If it came out well, it came out very well indeed. At other times he stumbled off the path, as in two or three of his unpublished manuscripts.

Interviewer: Despite these difficulties with plot, he was a very good storyteller?

Cowley: As a storyteller in company he was amazing. He was even more amazing in the matter of simple vitality. When he came into a room, he filled it, as people say.

Interviewer: Were his ethics as great as his vitality?

Cowley: As a writer his ethics were very strong . . . that is, his ethics governing the relationship between his "me" and the product of "me"; it would be hard to find any higher. But as a man in relation to other writers—Dos Passos, for instance—his ethics were lower than a snake's belly.

Interviewer: This question of ethics in relation to fiction seems to be a current critical concern. What is your opinion of John Gardner's contention, in *On Moral Fiction,* that fiction must point out a moral, or that the worth of fiction can be assessed in terms of the ethic it espouses?

Cowley: He's got hold of a half-truth. Any fiction should be a story. In any story there are three elements: persons, a situation, and the fact that in the end something has changed. If nothing has changed, it isn't a story. Almost every story, therefore, becomes a fable, because the change is usually for better or worse. And if the reader extends the applicability of this change from a particular set of events to another, then he's drawn out of the story a fable with a moral. And, of course, every work of fiction involves moral judgments concerning the characters . . . judgments that the author reveals by his style or his choice of details, if in no other fashion.

There is another sense as well in which not only fiction, but all kinds of writing are moral. Almost every work set on paper involves a choice. The writing of one page might involve hundreds of moral decisions. "Shall I use this word, which easily comes to hand, or shall I stop and search my mind for a slightly better word?" Those are aesthetic decisions which almost always have a moral element. Choosing the hard over the easy is already a moral choice.

Interviewer: Faced with moral considerations, can you as a critic render a positive judgment of a book's aesthetics while at the same time disliking its meaning?

Cowley: I can do that, yes. I might wish that the author had a different set of morals. And I can also make my judgment by not reading the book—a very easy way to get around it.

Interviewer: What do you find yourself reading nowadays?

Cowley: I too often pick up magazines. I read the *Nation,* the *New Republic,* the *New York Review,* and sometimes the *New Yorker,* against which my complaint is that the articles are too long. If I get hooked on one, the evening is shot.

Interviewer: Has there been a change in the character of the publishing houses?

Cowley: It's always been a strange profession; publishers and editors seem to change jobs more than men in other professions. They go from house to house like baseball players . . . except they're not sold, or traded. Those who really change places are the publicity directors . . . musical chairs!

Interviewer: What about the relationship between the editor and the author?

Cowley: These days there's a good deal more directed writing in which bright young publishers or editors dream up an idea for a book and then think of somebody to write it. Part of the creative process, at least in nonfiction, has moved over from the writer to the editor.

Interviewer: What would someone like Maxwell Perkins have made of this trend?

Cowley: Perkins wasn't much interested in nonfiction. But with fiction, he took a tremendous hand . . . concerned with motivation, the handling of scenes, and the overall picture of a book . . . so much so that he was capable of writing ninety pages of directions and suggestions. He did this for Marcia Davenport's *Valley of Decisions.* She put Max's directions to the left of her typewriter and her original manuscript on the right; she looked at Max's directions, then at the manuscript, and she retyped the book. It subsequently became very successful.

Interviewer: What are the distinguishing attributes of a good publishing house editor?

Cowley: The first ingredient would be a nose for good writers. And then loyalty to the writer once he found him. The most loyal editor in the whole game was Pat Covici at the Viking Press, who was loyal to his authors in a way that made the authors completely loyal to him. He did this with his interest, his confidence, his offer of whatever help they needed. Steinbeck wrote a whole volume of letters to Pat when he was working on *East of Eden.*

Interviewer: What about an editor's attitude toward public taste?

Cowley: If an editor begins to let the concept of catering to the public weigh on him he becomes, to me, a bad editor. An editor should have an idea of what meets his own taste; that should provide the criterion. The whole notion of divining the public taste has been one of the deadliest ideas of publishing. When *True Confessions* was at the height of its success, a new fiction editor was picked up every month. She would be one of the typists in the office, preferably the youngest, because it was felt that if she followed her own honest feeling about what was good, that was what the public wanted. After a month or so, she would become too sophisticated and then they would fire her as the fiction editor and take on another typist. That was cynicism carried to the extreme, but it may well have produced better results than an editor guessing at what the public might like.

Interviewer: What has been the most rewarding aspect of your long career in literature?

Cowley: Writing becomes its own reward. What do you need from others—except a little money—if you have satisfied the stern critic in yourself? For me the most rewarding moments have been those when I knew that a book was finished at last and ready to be printed. I remember one such moment; it was when I finished the revised edition of *Exile's Return,* in 1951. I had worked on the revision happily, being a revisionist by instinct, and most of the manuscript had gone to the printer. But there was a necessary appendix still to come, and it had to reach the Viking Press by a certain date or else the book would be postponed to another season. I have the story in an old notebook. [There is a long pause while Cowley finds and pages through the notebook.]

The date for Viking was March 30, 1951. I finished and sealed and addressed the appendix at half-past eight in the evening of March 29. In those fortunate days there was a mail car on the train that left Pawling at 9:05, and letters given to the clerk were delivered in New York the following morning. Pawling was a dozen miles from our house, over back roads. I drove there with Muriel and our son Rob and missed the train by three minutes. Then I raced it fifteen miles south to Brewster, at the risk of wiping out the family. This time the train was pulling out of the station just as we pulled in. I raced it again to Croton Falls, where Rob ran hard and gave my big envelope to the mail clerk just as the wheels of the engine started to turn. At last the book was out of my hands, finished to my satisfaction, and I was exultant. We drove home slowly while I sang old songs in a cracked voice.

Statement Made in the Investigations Office, OEM

George J. Gould/1942

Cowley was interrogated by George J. Gould, chief of the
Office of Emergency Management, on 5 February 1942
because for a brief period at the beginning of World War
II he was a writer in the Office of Facts and Figures, a
position that made available to him what the government
regarded as "sensitive information." The purpose of this
interrogation, obviously, was to try to determine the extent of Cowley's pro-Communist activities during the
1930s. The interrogation, which has been much abbrevi-
ated here because it appears to go over the same or
similar territory many times, was not released to Cowley
until 1985. Reprinted with the permission of Malcolm
Cowley.

Gould: What is your name?

　Cowley: Malcolm Cowley.

　Gould: Do you live in Washington, Mr. Cowley?

　Cowley: At present. My permanent residence is Sherman, Connecticut.

　Gould: Where are you employed?

　Cowley: Office of Facts and Figures.

　Gould: What are your duties, Mr. Cowley?

　Cowley: I am a writer there.

　Gould: What type of writing do you do?

　Cowley: It is hard to answer that question in one sentence
because I might be called upon to do any sort of writing that is
desired by the Director of the organization.

　Gould: When you were being considered for the position that you
now have, were you informed that all appointments were made
subject to investigation?

Cowley: Yes.

Gould: As a result of our investigation, Mr. Cowley, certain things were uncovered that I think you should have an opportunity to explain and, for that reason, we called you to the office. Do you mind relating your various employment?

Cowley: When I got out of college I was first regularly employed by Sweet's Catalogue Service, publishers of *Sweet's Architectural Catalogue* and an engineering catalogue. I had a year there. I won a fellowship to France given by the American Field Service, which was renewed the second year. Coming back to this country in '23 I went back to work for Sweet's Catalogue Service, staying there for about one and one-half years. Then I was a free-lance writer for various magazines. I was taken on the staff, in October 1929, of the *New Republic,* where I remained until I came to work in the office here. Since 1929 I have not been employed by any organization except the *New Republic.*

Gould: Did you ever belong to the Authors Union?

Cowley: No. I might add, I do not even know what it is. Or was.

Gould: Did you belong to any authors' organization that you discovered was communistically inclined and then resign?

Cowley: Yes. To the League of American Writers, beginning 1934 until the summer of 1940. I resigned in the summer of 1940. The League of American Writers was not a Communist organization. There were Communists in the membership. When war began in the fall of 1939, after the Hitler-Stalin Pact, there was a continual quarrel in the Executive Board of the American Writers as to the course the League should take, which was between non-Communists and Communist sympathizers. The non-sympathizers were in a considerable majority in the Executive Board, but unfortunately, instead of sticking together and swinging the organization, they resigned, one by one. I stayed in the organization for a year on account of the fact that non-Communists had the majority. Finally, I found we had lost the majority, due to the resignations. I went out myself with several other writers.

Gould: Which group did you belong to, Mr. Cowley?

Cowley: Group in what?

Gould: On which side of this—(Interruption by Mr. Cowley)

Cowley: On, the non-Communist side distinctly.

Gould: Are you, or were you, a member of the League for Professional Groups for Foster and Ford?

Cowley: Yes.

Gould: Is it still in existence?

Cowley: They only stayed in existence until the spring of '33.

Gould: How did you happen to become a member of that group?

Cowley: It would be a long story. That period was the time when everything was at the bottom of the depression. I was extremely worried by the critical situation of this country at the time, and it seemed to me that none of the measures which were being recommended for getting the country out of the depression went far enough. I was attracted at that time by the Marxian theory. Although I had no thought at all that the Communist system of government would ever prevail in this country, I believed that discussion of Communist theories would broaden out and loosen up the thinking here. Accordingly, I joined with about fifty other people of whom I doubt more than two or three were Communists.

Gould: Were you an active member?

Cowley: Yes.

Gould: How long did this organization stay in existence?

Cowley: About eight months.

Gould: Were you one of the organizers?

Cowley: That is a hard question to answer because you cannot think of the personnel. That I was an active member would be a good way of putting it.

Gould: What was the program of this group?

Cowley: You have me stumped by that question. You are asking me about events of ten years ago. As I remember, the pamphlet stated that none of the means offered for the solution of the depression would be effective and that the only solution would be a working class government in this country. The pamphlet would not have called for revolution. It did call for an election of the Communist candidate.

Gould: It called for an election of a Communist candidate?

Cowley: It did.

Gould: You subscribed to it at that time?

Cowley: Yes. I signed the pamphlet without wholly agreeing with it.

Gould: Are, or were you, a member of the Citizens Committee for the Election of Israel Amter?

Cowley: What year was that?

Gould: 1938.

Cowley: I think I probably was. May I add to this? I want to explain what this joining of committees involved, because my name, unfortunately, was widely used for a while. I worked at the *New Republic* and anybody would could put a nickel in the coin box would get me on the telephone and say they were sending somebody to see me. They would ask me if I would give my name to such and such a committee. If I said no, there would be somebody else the next day, and the day after that. If I said yes, there was an end to it. I would often say, I will give my name to your committee if you can promise it won't involve any work on my part, such as going to meetings, speaking for it, or anything else. Thereupon my name appeared on many letterheads. I am anxious to tell you the whole story. I think that this Citizens Committee for the Election of Israel Amter was one I permitted to use my name. I do not actually remember. I do not have any documentary evidence in Washington. I did not vote for Amter. I voted the straight Democratic ticket.

Gould: Who was Israel Amter?

Cowley: He was a Communist. He still is, as far as I know.

Gould: Were you active in that group?

Cowley: No.

Gould: You took no part at all?

Cowley: Absolutely none at all.

Gould: But you may have permitted your name to be used in connection with it?

Cowley: Yes.

Gould: Did you sign a statement by the American Progressives on the Moscow trials? Were you one of the signers?

Cowley: What statement was this?

Gould: It was around April 1938.

Cowley: I think I did. Again I must apologize for saying I think, but without the documents here it is very hard to tell.

Gould: Who was sponsoring that movement?

Cowley: I think that Corliss Lamont was the chief sponsor.

Gould: In addition to signing this statement, did you take an active part in the activities of this organization?

Cowley: No. I do not think there was any organization connected with it.

Gould: What was the purpose of it?

Cowley: There was, as I remember it, a letter stating that the people felt and believed that the testimony given at the Moscow trial had been substantially correct. It was circulated for signatures, and that was all.

Gould: Were you a sponsor of the American Relief ship for Spain?

Cowley: I don't think so. That would be in 1938, too?

Gould: Your name was on their letterhead.

Cowley: Well, then I was. If so, it has slipped by mind. But I might add that I had nothing to do whatsoever with the organization.

Gould: Do you know anything at all about the organization?

Cowley: I don't even know anything about the organization.

Gould: Did you become a member of the National Committee for People's Rights in 1938?

Cowley: I don't know what it is or was.

Gould: Do you recall that organization?

Cowley: No, I do not. I have no wish to say I didn't if I did. Perhaps the proper way to phrase that question is: Did you allow your name to be used in connection with that organization? My answer to that would be: I do not remember.

Gould: Were you one of the signers who called the Congress of American Revolutionary Writers together at the convention or whatever kind of a meeting they held?

Cowley: I was one of the signers that called for the first American Writers' Congress. It was in 1935.

Gould: Were you active?

Cowley: Yes I was active.

Gould: What were the functions of this organization?

Cowley: They wanted to form an organization of American writers interested in social problems and of a liberal or radical tendency.

Gould: Was it dominated by Communists?

Cowley: There were Communists in the organizing committee.

Gould: Did that word revolutionary in the name have any significance?

Cowley: Very little at the time. Thousands of people were calling themselves revolutionary. It comes around to a definition of the word revolutionary as describing any shift in power toward the working class; people called themselves revolutionary if they meant they were simply pro-labor. I might add that I never called or considered myself revolutionary. . . .

Gould: Were you a Contributing Editor of *Soviet Russia Today*?

Cowley: As far as I know, I was on this Advisory Board and on nothing else. I never made any contributions to *Soviet Russia Today*. By 1938 the magazine was berating me for being skeptical about the Soviet Union.

Gould: Can you tell us anything about the National Writers' Congress which you were one of the signers in 1937?

Cowley: It was the second American Writers' Congress, the one mentioned before, and it was mostly devoted to calling for aid for Spain. The chief speakers at Carnegie Hall were Ernest Hemingway and Vincent Sheean.

Gould: How about 1939?

Cowley: The Third Writers' Congress was a very non-Communist affair. I can't remember who was the principal speaker at the first meeting in Carnegie Hall—Thomas Mann, I believe. I spoke on the last day about the European Refugees in this country. It was a very interesting Congress, chiefly concerned with the technical problems of writing. . . .

Gould: Do you recall what this meeting was at the Madison Square Garden at which you spoke as an editor of the *New Republic?*

Cowley: A meeting against Hitler in the spring of 1933.

Gould: Who sponsored that?

Cowley: At the present I do not know.

Gould: How about this meeting that you spoke at Newark on February 17, 1937?

Cowley: I did speak once in Newark, but I don't remember when or where it was or what I said. I remember I spoke there because I remember eating in a restaurant afterwards with the people who had attended the meeting. But if it was in 1937, it must have been about Spain.

Gould: Did you live at 49 West 44th Street in Manhattan, Mr. Cowley?

Cowley: Yes. It was a hotel.

Gould: In 1936 did you sign a Communist Party petition for the 1936 city and state New York election?

Cowley: No. Not to the best of my knowledge.

Gould: The records show that Malcolm Cowley did sign a Communist Party Petition for the 1936 city and state New York elections. Would that be you?

Cowley: I was living at that address. What would signing a petition be?

Gould: It would probably be signing a nomination petition for candidates. In the lack of information that is what I assume it would be.

Cowley: They wouldn't have needed nominating petitions in 1936. They were on the ballot.

Gould: Doesn't every candidate have to have so many names on the petition before his name can be placed on the ballot?

Cowley: I wasn't living at that address in April 1936. I was living at that time at 69 West 11th Street. So the whole thing is out there. The Communist Party would not have needed a nominating petition. You get on the ballot by being a nominee of a recognized party. I suppose I allowed myself to get into the position of the young lady who had forgotten how to say no. In most of these areas I find that I have little or no recollection of the organizations of which I am supposed to be a prominent member.

Here, to the best of my knowledge, is a list of all the organizations to which I actually belonged:

The League of Professional Groups for Foster and Ford, founded in 1932 and dissolved in 1933.
    The National Committee for the Defense of Political Prisoners, founded, I think, in 1932. I ceased to attend meetings in 1934. The Committee still exists, I believe, but it has changed its name. I don't know what the present name of it is.
    The American League Against War and Fascism, along with a previous

Committee to Organize a Congress Against War. I have not attended any
meetings of this organization since 1934. This was the predecessor of the
American League for Peace and Democracy, which was dissolved in the
autumn of 1939.

The League of American Writers founded in 1935, of which I was a
vice-president until I resigned from membership in 1940.

The North American Committee to Aid Spanish Democracy, the
Medical Bureau—later affiliated with that Committee—and the Committee for Technical Aid to Spanish Democracy. I never attended any
meetings of these but I spoke for them.

Since 1938 I have belonged to nothing but the League of American
Writers. Since 1940 I have belonged to no political organization of
any sort except the Democratic causus of the town of Sherman,
Connecticut.

To set the record straight—and I want to keep it straight, making
the issues absolutely clear—let me say that I could have been
described as a radical in 1932. My ideas had been very deeply
affected by the depression and I believed that radical steps would
have to be taken if the country was to avoid disaster. It was in 1932
that I joined the Communist Party or let it do my thinking for me or
participated in any of its private meetings whatsoever. I never
engaged in any activities that were not in the open.

Beginning in 1935 my political opinions began gradually to be
more conservative. I felt much more reassured about the state of the
country and was much more disturbed by the foreign danger,
especially the growth of Fascism. In all my political writings—though I
haven't written much on politics—and even in my book reviews I
kept calling attention to the growing menace of Fascism and to the
fact that the United States could not hope to stand untouched. I
worked with some organizations in which there were Communist
members, but I did this for one compelling reason, and one only—
namely, that the Communists were Hitler's enemies. That cooperation
ceased on the day of the Stalin-Hitler Pact. It has not been and will
not be renewed. Since that time I have been frequently and violently
attacked in the *Daily Worker*, the *New Masses* and other Communist
organs. If the Communists ever seized power here—they never will—
I would be among the first to be jailed.

I have never worked on the staff of any Communist publication. I
do not believe in the Russian system of government or in any other

system except our own. I have tried to act for its best interests. I do believe that the United States now is in the midst of the worst crisis in its history as a nation. It can call on its citizens for undivided loyalty and service in any capacity, and the citizens should and must respond. This nation has given birth to me, fed me, educated me and has been my home for all my life. Anything that I can give the nation in return will be too little to pay the debt.

The Teaching and Study of Writing: A Symposium
Western Review/1950

From *Western Review*, XIV (Spring 1950), 165, 174–75.

In the spring of 1950 a writer for *Western Review* submitted the following questions to a number of writers and critics for their reaction:

1. How much of the art of writing (the writing of serious poetry or fiction) can be taught?
2. Can anything be taught through regular college programs in literature?
3. In your opinion, does the setting up of separate curricula, special courses, etc., represent an opportunity to the young writer? Are there dangers in such programs?
4. Do you prefer the procedure of the occasional writers' conference, the setting up of separate programs within an English Department, or a combination of both? Do you have special objections to any of these programs?
5. How should the faculty for such programs be selected?
6. Should credit be given and degrees awarded to students who have completed such programs?
7. What, in your opinion, is the relative importance of (a) literary history, (b) literary criticism, (c) creative writing courses in such a program?
8. From your own experience, what do you consider the most important advice to give a young writer who wants to know how best to prepare himself for a possible career as (a) a poet, (b) a writer of fiction?

Malcolm Cowley

I don't feel myself qualified by sufficient experience to answer some of the more technical questions in your symposium: for example (5) How should the faculty for such programs be selected? and (6) Should credit be given and degrees awarded to students who have completed such programs? On the other hand, I do have decided feelings about the first question, How much of the art of

writing can be taught? and it might be that the answer would cast
some light on the answers to other questions.

The art, properly speaking, of writing cannot be taught, and neither
can the other arts. But the craft of writing can be taught, like the
crafts of painting and sculpture, and the craft is a necessary foundation for the art. The craft consists of all past experience and
achievement that can be reduced to rules. The art consists of the
personal contribution that goes beyond the rules and may some day
become a rule in itself. Painters go to schools of painting; even
Cezanne spent his years in a Paris atelier. Why shouldn't writers go to
schools of writing, where they can produce trial works under skilled
supervision, before they are ready to work for and by themselves?

There need be no conflict between the craft and the art. Sometimes there *is* a conflict, in teaching, when the instructor gives his
class the wrong rules, those which will ensure the sale of stories to the
pulps or the slicks, instead of the rules that apply to writing in general.
I suppose that a few promising students have been ruined by such
instruction, but others have survived it. The classical example of a
writing course in this country was George Pierce Baker's English 47
and 47a at Harvard, in which he taught a selected group of students
to write plays for Broadway theatres. Most of them learned that
lesson, and no more, but Eugene O'Neill was also a student in
English 47, and made theatres produce the plays he wanted to write.

Yes—to answer question 2—a great deal can be taught through
regular college programs in literature. Most of the older writers today
followed those programs and no others. And yes again—to answer
question 3—the setting up of separate programs does offer an
opportunity to young writers. They shouldn't be allowed to enter
such programs, however, until their junior year at the earliest, and
then only if they have given proof of marked ability.

My chief advice to a young writer today, if he wants to be really
good, is to cut loose and take chances. Too many youngsters of the
present generation are playing safe and taking courses in creative
writing. I can imagine no better way for a creative writing program
such as you are discussing to become inbred and worthless. The
instructors in the course should be writers and not graduated students
of writing.

An Interview with Malcolm Cowley
Fresco/1957

From *Fresco,* 7 (Spring–Summer 1957), 18–21. Reprinted by permission of the University of Detroit.

Q: Mr. Cowley, would you comment on *Life* magazine's charge of "negativism" against the more important contemporary novelists and the suggested remedy of "positivism"?

A: Now, you want to ask me about negativism and positivism in the novel. You have to go far back into history for that. You know, the American novelist has always been in opposition. He has always been a critic; even Emerson, who finally became a spokesman for one side of American society, offered some very bitter criticism of American business, and before that time, for example, his Harvard Divinity School lecture—in what year was that? I think 1839—was so badly received that he wasn't invited back to Harvard for twenty years after that.

And so it has been with almost all our novelists right through. I don't know what that is, but we haven't been able to produce an official literature, what I would call a Vergilian literature, of any value at any time. Now, with *Life* magazine leading the way, there have been certain attempts to do that lately. Authors like Herman Wouk, or however you pronounce his name, and the author of *The Man in the Gray Flannel Suit,* and so on have been writing what I would call "all-right-nik" books. . . . "All-right-nik" is a wonderful Yiddish word.

I do not think that these novels have had the power and the intensity of the American novelists who have written from the more or less opposition point of view.

The strange thing is that these novelists writing in opposition have been the ones who created the picture of American society in Europe—insofar as the movies didn't create it. And actually it has been a more favorable picture than is sometimes admitted because they created a picture of this country as a very interesting and dramatic place. I gave that example in the lecture, you know, of the

Grapes of Wrath, when Hitler tried to use it as anti-American propaganda and found it was going out of his hands. [Mr. Cowley, discussing the novel as a propaganda weapon, made the observation that the propaganda value of a given work is quite difficult to evaluate. He told of Hitler's ban on all American novels except John Steinbeck's *Grapes of Wrath,* which was, supposedly, an excellent example of capitalistic exploitation of the poor. However, the reaction of the typical German was, "What! In America, even those poor farmers have automobiles?" And soon that novel, too, was banned.]

But there are other things about negativism and positivism. Dos Passos wrote a book called *Manhattan Transfer,* which when it was first written was taken as a piece of negative criticism, as indeed it was, of American society in New York. I reread it a couple of years ago and part of it seemed very old-fashioned, but some of the rest of it seemed rather charming and youthful and exuberant. The negative quality had disappeared in the thirty intervening years.

Q: Do you believe that Hemingway's *The Old Man and the Sea,* which *Life* magazine published, is a conscious attempt to be positive or is it traditional Hemingway fiction?

A: No, no! He would never attempt at positivism. It isn't traditional Hemingway fiction, but it is Hemingway at nearly sixty speaking for himself; a man of nearly sixty has different ideas from a young man of thirty.

Q: Since Faulkner has treated both the "Old South" and the "Modern South" and has used the Negro as an important factor in his novels, the question of his attitude toward integration necessarily arises. Can this attitude be related in some way to his growth as an artist and an observer of humanity?

A: He has always been, whatever he said, a lover of man and of human dignity. He is a tremendously proud person, probably the proudest person I have ever met. And a mixture of pride and humility and love and hatred for fellow man has always been strong in him. Early in his career he wrote a lot of books to shock people. Certainly he wrote *Sanctuary* with that intention. Now, he isn't much interested in shocking people. He has always had a strong feeling of the decay of the South. I would say that Faulkner was a Southern nationalist— not a regionalist, a nationalist. He loved the South as a nation and he felt that his nation was going to pieces, and had been attacked from outside by Northern industrialism and from the inside by this new tribe of the Snopeses. And so he did express his sense of decay in most violent images, in the most violent that anybody could find.

The Negro or the Poor White comes off very well in his novels when he is staying to the land. He paints some of the most sympathetic pictures of Poor Whites and Negroes that you could find anywhere. Of course, Faulkner too has grown older and one feature of growing older is to be more interested in permanence and a little bit less in change.

His novels aren't a reasoned statement of his position. They come much closer to being an expression of his emotions and his imagination and he has two sets of contradictory emotions. On one hand he is a Southern nationalist, and the Southern nation today has chosen the wrong flag. The flag that it has chosen is white superiority. And that isn't necessarily the real flag of the South, which is rather that of a society of traditional values, a more or less agricultural society with traditional values. That is the real flag, but through a series of historical accidents it turned around to having white superiority as its slogan. So Faulkner, who is emotionally committed to the South, has to say, "Well, I'll wave this flag, too," but at the same time he deeply feels that the South has been unjust to the Negro, that the South must make amends to the Negro, and the only compromise he can arrive at is the idea that the South must do it itself instead of being forced to do it by the North.

It is a very difficult and contradictory position, and it led Faulkner to almost simultaneously write that letter in *Life* to which you refer and at the same time write the article for the Negro magazine *Ebony*, taking a different position.

Q: Would you give your opinion of possible changes in Faulkner's ranking of the five leading contemporary American novelists? (1. Wolfe, 2. Faulkner, 3. Dos Passos, 4. Caldwell, 5. Hemingway.)

A: I had an answer to this question and it was perfect. I decline to answer on the grounds that my answer might tend to incriminate or degrade me. But I'll go into this. I think the two most important American novelists of that particular generation, which was mine, are Faulkner and Hemingway. Both of them produced a body of works that stands through.

After them, I don't know. Though I haven't liked his recent work, I think Dos Passos, perhaps for his early work, would rank third in my estimation. Perhaps, Fitzgerald fourth. And after that, I don't know, after that . . . Thornton Wilder ranks higher in my estimation than in his general American reputation, it would seem, and I think on the whole—well—I don't know—he is so different. He might turn out to be more important than Wolfe. And he might not. Wolfe I have very mixed feelings about.

And Caldwell I like for his early works. He wrote some extra-ordinary stories in his early days which are known little now—and I think, too, some of his early novels. He wrote crazy books like *Journeyman, The Bastard,* that are not known at all.

His first book of stories called *American Earth* had wonderful stories in it and another book called *Georgia Boy* had very good stories. But his later stuff, though, has been written, it seems to me, without sufficient thought or growth from his early stuff.

Q: Finally, in the light of these remarks, would you have for the college writer advice essentially different from that which *Life* infers?

A: I don't think college writers should pay the least attention to that editorial in *Life*. I don't think it has anything sensible to do with American literature and I think that if college writers set out now to express what might be called their own sense of life, things as they actually see them, not as they learned how to see them through reading books, you might get something very new, because I think there is something new in the present generation that hasn't been yet expressed.

Now in that respect the English are getting ahead of us. There are young people in England who are doing quite new work. Kingsley Amis, I was thinking of; of course, nobody has done that sort of work for this country yet. Oh, perhaps a little, perhaps Norman Mailer and Saul Bellow—and Salinger possibly. I should have mentioned him.

An Interview with Malcolm Cowley

William F. Dawson/1957

From *Artesian Way,* (May–June 1957), 11–14. Reprinted by permission of William F. Dawson.

Haven Hall is mostly offices for professors at the University of Michigan. The English department is on the third floor, and down at one end of the corridor, last door on the right, is the tiny office of the visiting lecturer. This semester the name stenciled on the glass in little black letters is Malcolm Cowley.

I was late for a 2 o'clock interview with him so I ran up the stairs and down the hall like any good student who isn't quite sure about offending the teacher who marks him. Still panting from my run, I knocked on the door and it was opened by Cowley, a big handsome man with a medium-sized mustache and lots of sandy-gray hair. He was dressed in a brown herringbone tweed sport jacket. He was smoking a pipe. "Come on in, Buck," he said, and showed me a chair. He sat down behind his desk and looked very comfortable, as though he had been teaching a long time.

"May I ask you some questions?" I said, still not quite at ease.

"Sure," he answered, smiling, and reaching across the desk to knock out his pipe on a big glass ash try, "let's get started."

I took out a long sheet of paper with my questions on it. "If any of these are too personal," I said, "just let me know." He moved his ash try over so I'd have a place to write and then leaned back in his chair looking more relaxed than I would ever be. I began my questions:

"Mr. Cowley, in what universities besides Michigan have you taught as a visiting lecturer?"

Answer: "Last year I spent a quarter at Stanford. I have also taught at Washington, Bennington and at summer conferences at Kansas, Connecticut and Utah, besides lecturing at colleges pretty much all over, from Puget Sound to Casco Bay."

Q: "Why?"

A: "First of all there must be some financial consideration, since writers must eat and support their families like everybody else, but aside from this economic factor I do it because I am full of curiosity about younger writers and I always hope I'll run into somebody good."

Q: "Have you ever found any good young writers in your teaching?"

A: "Oh, yes. Some of them are not yet well-known but will be with luck. Some names I'm not at liberty to reveal and others I can't remember. I'm very bad on remembering names, but there is Julia Siebel, author of *The Narrow Covering,* published last year by Harcourt Brace. She was one of my students before she had published anything. And just this last year I had a fine writer at Stanford, Tilly Olson. I think we'll hear from her. You know it is quite stimulating, quite a pleasure to discover somebody new who is full of promise. I wish there were more."

Q: "Why aren't there more?"

A: "I think there are a good many, but largely on a graduate school level. Generally the teaching of language skills in this country has been downgraded. You can't teach a man to write, but it can be learned if he's been taught the fundamentals. When I get a boy in college today I feel as though I were building a house on sand. Very few of them have the bedrock of how to write English. High schools have abdicated the job of teaching writing fundamentals. For instance, I doubt if there is a high school in the country today as good as, say, Oak Park was when Hemingway went there before World War I. The teaching of language skills has declined in our high schools in all phases, foreign languages, rhetoric, literature and classical languages, as well as oral and written English.

"Back in 1400 a boy first learned his trivium, rhetoric, grammar and logic. That's where the word trivial comes from. The trivium was basic grammar school stuff. It was so elementary it was "trivial." Nowadays a student doesn't know much about these "trivial" things even on graduating from high school. Everything in teaching has been deferred. We now have remedial freshman English courses to teach elementary reading, and we have graduate schools for what used to be undergraduate college training. It has got to be so bad in California, for example, that a teacher scolds parents for letting their child read beyond the group level. It interferes with the youngster's 'group adaptation,' which they feel is more important than picking up any knowledge."

Q: "As a Harvard graduate how would you compare Ivy League schools with the big state universities in this respect of undergraduate training for young writers?"

A: "Generally I would say the Ivy schools have one big advantage in that their students must take entrance exams, whereas the Big-Ten type state Universities have admission by certification. Admission by examination raises the level of knowledge of your freshman class so the Ivy League schools are starting with a higher lowest common denominator. The schools that admit by certification cannot insure any standard since the high schools they certify vary widely in their quality of preparation. Michigan is making a determined effort with its English honors program to take care of its exceptional undergraduate students, but most of the young writers one meets at Michigan and at Iowa are on the graduate level. As for teachers, Michigan had Robert Frost in the early '20s and he stirred up a great deal of student enthusiasm in writing. They also had W. H. Auden, then Katherine Ann Porter a couple of years ago. Last semester they had J. F. Powers. We all do what we can to stimulate new writing, but a student will invariably learn more from other students than from his teacher, so this brings us right back to the quality of the group."

Q: "Would you rate the best schools for writing?"

A: "I would guess that there are more undergraduate writers turned out at Harvard than any other school. I'd rate Princeton second and Stanford third. Then Kenyon, principally because of the good people attracted there to study with John Crowe Ransom. If you include the graduate school level, then Iowa, Michigan and Cornell come into the picture. Iowa is academically the most liberal. I believe they'll count a novel as a master's thesis. This sort of program is most attractive to fiction writers, who are not necessarily English scholars. At Stanford they made tests and found that the grades of their best fiction writers are very irregular. Poets and critics, on the other hand, are usually 'A' students. Many college writers complain that the teachers are too often poets and critics and not fiction writers. This is probably true because good scholarship is a prerequisite to college-level teaching and also because most poets have to teach to eat. There are only three poets who support themselves entirely on poetry earnings. One of them is Oscar Hammerstein II, whom you may not think of as a poet."

Q: "How do you feel about teaching writing in college?"

A: "To begin with you can't teach writing. It's practically impossible to teach anyone to write. It can be learned, however, and a good college writing program should speed up the process of learning. At the present time when all sorts of apprenticeships are being lengthened out and being taken over by colleges, they seem a logical place to learn about writing. Nothing is quite as good as the 1850 apprenticeship in a print shop, however. Those writers who began that way actually handled type and got a feel for words by handling them with their fingers. They didn't waste words and they knew how to use them. Writers like Ben Franklin, Mark Twain, Bret Harte and William Dean Howells all worked in print shops and all were brilliant stylists. Walt Whitman was the lone exception, but he was also a newspaper editor trying to fill columns. By 1890 nearly all the young writers except Jack London served their apprenticeships as newspaper reporters. These men didn't waste words either, but the printers came out better stylists than the reporters. Frank Norris and Theodore Dreiser were not good stylists. Stephen Crane was the exception, but generally setting up words in type gave a stricter feeling for words than the other newspaper jobs.

"Now you can't get these jobs. Very little type is handset any more and there are unions and better pay and no such turnover. You can't just walk up to a newspaper as Stephen Crane did and expect to get a job at ten dollars a week, then quit in three months and have some other ambitious young writer move in to replace you at the same starvation wages.

"After the Newspaper Guild made reporting a well-paid lifetime profession instead of a stopgap job, the training ground for young writers was book reviewing and magazine writing staff jobs. These avenues are closing up now, as there are fewer magazines. Now a young writer is more likely to stay in college or even go on to teaching."

Q: "Mr. Cowley, how many of your 'lost generation' contemporaries were college men and how does this compare percentagewise with today's young writers?"

A: "In the '20s Hemingway and Hart Crane were not college men, and Faulkner had only a semester or so. There were many others with only high school training, although the majority of us were college men. Of the post World War II writers I believe all but James Jones went to college. The level of formal education has gone up in the writing profession as it has in other kinds of work. This doesn't necessarily mean that the quality of writing has become higher. Remember that Hemingway had both the newspaper training and the advantage of high school fundamentals in English that would now be college level."

Q: "Why were so many word doctors interned in the Ambulance Service in World War I? What was it about your generation that turned out so many outstanding young writers?"

A: "On the ambulance service it was more a question of why we went into it than who came out. Most of us were able to sign up for six months, although a few stayed on for two years or more. It was adventure, a chance to see France, to get into the war, and the glamour of a foreign uniform. I keep finding new people who were in the ambulance service that I didn't know about—Hemingway, Dos Passos, Cummings, Nordhoff and Hall, Bromfield, Ted Weeks of the *Atlantic Monthly,* even Thornton Wilder's older brother.

"As to the question about our generation, I believe it was at least as much the times as the talent. The advertising catch phrase of the time was 'Accent On Youth,' and it really caught on. There has been no other time in our country when the young people so completely rejected the wisdom of age. They felt their seniors had made a mess of the world and they were taking over. The older people were inclined to think so too, and youth was served not just in writing but across the board. A young woman could become a department store buyer at 26, and a man could hold a seat on the stock exchange at 30. This sort of thing was unheard of before the '20s and it isn't common now. Publishers then were more anxious to publish young writers because of the amazing success of Scott Fitzgerald's *This Side of Paradise.* Nowadays a girl can get published if she's not more than 18 and is precociously wicked. If on top of this she photographs well, then she's got it made, but every year after 18 her chances decline." [Mr. Cowley's grin was wide on this answer.]

Q: "If college is currently the logical place for a would-be writer to serve his apprenticeship, then with the University of Michigan awarding $9,000 each spring in writing prizes, why don't we have more high school seniors enrolling at Michigan to take advantage of these prizes, the way an engineer might enroll at M.I.T. or Cal Tech?"

A: "I don't believe your analogy is accurate. Engineering, like law, medicine, etc., is a profession which can handle a steady flow of college graduates in well-defined categories. Writing is different in many ways. Numerically there are only 15,000 professional writers in the United States, and not more than 100 of them earn a living writing hard-cover books. Many high school graduates would not arbitrarily pick a college to study writing as a profession. As to the grants available to writers in colleges, I believe the best are the Stanford one-year fellowships. There are six of them with awards of $2,500 each. The Hopwood prizes at Michigan are also good, but less certain, as you must still compete to get them after you have enrolled." [The Hopwood prizes, set up in the will of playwright Avery Hopwood, provide awards up to $300 for freshman and undergraduates enrolled in Michigan and taking at least one writing course. Seniors and graduate students can win $1,500 for major awards in four categories: Fiction, Poetry, Drama and Essay. There are also smaller awards for summer school and, of course, winning a college literary prize will help attract a publisher's interest.]

Q: "Aside from literary prizes, what are a young writer's market chances today?"

A: "First of all, the important thing is getting published. You must write to be read. That is the point of putting words on paper instead of just dreaming them. Don't hide your work, but get it in print and before the public. How you do this is always the problem. I wouldn't be too proud about money at first. It is a good policy to get published regardless of pay. How else now are you going to become known?

"I suggest you try the quarterlies. Some of them pay fairly well, like the *Partisan, Kenyon,* and *Hudson* reviews. Some of them, like *Accent* and *Western Review* make at least token payments. Some of them pay nothing, but they are all good as far as getting your work out where somebody may read it.

"I know publishers read them looking for new writers, and the publishers' representatives who are out looking for new authors read a lot more of the little magazines besides those I have mentioned. Then there are the paperbacks like *New World Writing.* It is really a semi-annual magazine and well-read by publishers. They pay only two-and-one-half cents a word, but they have a distribution of 150,000. That is the largest distribution of any literary magazine."

Q: "What about the big magazines?"

A: "It was a real shocker to all of us when Crowell-Collier went out of the magazine business. The market for free-lance writing in the big magazines is shrinking, especially in fiction. They used to print 70% fiction and 30% articles, and now it is the other way around."

Q: "Why?"

A: "I don't know for sure, but it may be that the public's thirst for romance and entertaining stories is now being fed by TV and the comics. The all-story magazines which used to be huge sellers are now almost out of business. The big magazines are now principally specialty magazines of one sort or another—news, picture, household—and they don't publish much fiction. They are mostly staff-written."

Q: "With a magazine like *Colliers* folding, then how do the little magazines survive?"

A: "The little magazines will continue to come and go, depending on the enthusiasm of their editors and whether or not they can get backing. Very few of them exist on subscriptions or advertising alone. They are often subsidized by a university, in the case of a quarterly, or by one of the foundations, or by a private patron."

Q: "Mr. Cowley, you were an editor of two of the little expatriate magazines, *Broom* and *Secession,* in France and later an editor of the *New Republic.* How do you feel about young writers seeking editing jobs?"

A: "By all means! The whole business of student magazines and student papers is fine. Working as an editor means experience in preparing manuscripts for the printer and also a chance to write and be published. After the young writer is out of college it is best to start on a magazine staff somewhere and then look around. The best way to get a feel of your markets and learn to meet deadlines is to work on a magazine, especially now that there is so little opportunity to free-lance in magazine fiction. There is opportunity to free-lance in magazine non-fiction, but you'll need to know your markets before you do very well at it.

"As to my job on the *New Republic,* I found it a very fine job for five or six years, editing, writing, rewriting, copy reading, proof reading, and all the rest. It gave me a degree of independence you don't often get on a magazine staff, but I stayed too long and went kind of dead on it. I should have left after five or six years while I was still fresh. This is worth remembering. I believe editors often do stay too long in the same place."

Q: "Is there anything else you'd like to add, Mr. Cowley?"

A: (looking at his watch) "No, except that I'm late and I have to pick up my wife. Writers have to live, you know. We're a lot like everybody else."

It was four o'clock. He closed his office door behind him and we walked down the long hall, through the stone arch and down the steps and out across the campus, the visiting lecturer and the would-be writer, teacher and pupil walking lock-step, and I hoped that a little bit of what he knew would rub off on me during his semester at Michigan.

An Interview with Malcolm Cowley

L. L. Graelle/1964

From *Dalhousie Review* (Autumn 1964), 290–98. Reprinted by permission of the *Dalhousie Review.*

The interview was to take place in the quiet oak-panelled bar of the Harvard Club in midtown Manhattan. The atmosphere was that of an earlier period, perhaps Mr. Cowley's 1920s, and seemingly as a reminder of that fact, all the electrical outlets were DC, and we could not plug in our recorder. As a result we had to move to an upstairs smoking room where we finally found an AC outlet next to another instrument of this decade—the air conditioner.

Graelle: Do you think the practice of criticism is opposed to the literary impulse?

Cowley: No, except at one point. To specify, every writer is partly critic and partly creative writer. I hate the word "creative" but there's nothing else to use—unless we say "combinatory," on the principle that every new thing in the arts is a combination of familiar elements. From another point of view, every writer is partly speaker and partly audience. The inner audience is the critical side of him, and writing or reading too much criticism at a given moment may strengthen the audience to such a degree that it shouts down the speaker before he can open his mouth. The inner speaker, the silent voice, is the creative or combinatory side of his talent. When I work with beginning writers, I try to tell them to write first and revise later. Sometimes I also tell them that, if they want to be novelists, they should defer taking courses that involve the close and critical reading of contemporary masterpieces.

Graelle: So you think an overly critical faculty can harm a new writer.

Cowley: Obviously the ideal writer would have a maximum of critical ability, and a maximum of creative ability. I'm merely referring to the possibility that at some early stage in a writer's career, the critical side might develop too fast and might override the other side.

Graelle: You have said—"instead of dealing critically with the critical critics of criticism, I have preferred to be a critic of poems and novels, or at most a literary historian. . . ."

Cowley: I will stand on that point. I should think that the criticism of criticism of criticism becomes a reflexive activity carried on in a small closed room.

Graelle: Does this imply a condemnation of the academic critics?

Cowley: No, the academic critic is very good in his place and is sometimes brilliant or illuminating. But sometimes he forgets what the problems of a professional writer are. I'm especially disturbed by this idea that the intentions of a writer should never be taken into account, because that is practically a "free pass" for the critic to go anywhere he wants to go and sometimes very far from the work itself.

Graelle: You have also castigated the New Critics in a recent article—but don't they do exactly what you advocate—criticize the poems and novels themselves, directly?

Cowley: I didn't castigate all the New Critics. I think some of them have done extremely interesting work. But some of them have tried to erect criticism into an autonomous activity, of which works of art are merely the "field" . . . and when they read a work it's like an official in Washington going out into the "field" which he rather despises. In some of the critics one observes a tendency to treat the author as if he were a patient stretched out on a couch, and the critic a psychoanalyst.

Graelle: Do you think that this is a mistaken application of scientism?

Cowley: Scientism in this case is a developed interest in Freud and Jung, especially Jung . . . and once again I'm not attacking Freud or Jung. I'm just attacking the misuse of their work.

Graelle: Do you think that a lot of good critical ideas get lost in terminology, in the gobbledygook style of expression? Because so many critics nowadays get carried away with their pet terminologies?

Cowley: No, because ideas have to be expressed in words, and if the words are essentially meaningless, it means that the ideas themselves are also meaningless. I should think, for example, that a good deal of the recent criticism of Faulkner has been essentially meaningless because it has gone up into the air as if in a non-dirigible free-floating balloon.

Graelle: At the time—in the '20s—did you find that knowing writers personally—Hemingway, Fitzgerald, Pound, Hart, Crane—had any influence or effect on your writing criticism of their works?

Cowley: Essentially it must have had an influence, because into criticism goes everything you know about the author, but some of the best critical writing I have done has been about Faulkner, whom I didn't meet until after the essays were written. But it goes into your work, everything goes into your work . . . but knowing an author is not at all essential.

Graelle: Yes, your work on Faulker, your introduction to *The Portable Faulkner,* did much to bring Faulkner into prominence after a decline of his popularity and of course critics began to re-evaluate his merit.

Cowley: Well, that happened because *The Portable* was published at the right time. There was a situation with Faulkner that hadn't existed with any other author. There were a great many novelists and critics who deeply appreciated Faulkner, but the public at large had been told that he was only a master of Southern gothic horrors and "a Sax Rohmer for the sophisticated," as Granville Hicks called him at that time. When *The Portable* was published it gave the people who admired Faulkner a chance to review a selection of his work and to make their own statements too, so that *The Portable* was a key that unlocked a great deal of Faulkner criticism. It was an event in Faulkner's literary career because at the time I did *The Portable* his work was completely out of print.

Graelle: Do you think that sort of reprint and paperback publishing influences the literary situation to a great extent?

Cowley: Much more than when I wrote a book called *The Literary Situation.* The new factor that *The Literary Situation* was written too soon for me to consider is the so-called quality paperbacks—the more expensive paperbacks sold in bookstores instead of on the newsstand. These have been the means of keeping in print almost any book for which there is a sale of, let us say, a thousand copies a year. And that means that a great many books are always in print and therefore *alive* at present that wouldn't have been in print before. It's a great comfort to an author to have his books continue selling through the years.

Graelle: To get back to your contact with the authors of the '20s, did your association with them give you any insights into the creative process?

Cowley: Perhaps I got an insight through having lived through many of the same experiences, which meant that I would judge more readily the values that the author was trying to enforce in his work. For example, I was born the year before Hemingway and was also the son of a doctor. Where he had gone to Michigan in the summer, I went to central Pennsylvania and regarded that wild countryside as my real home. And then we both went to Paris in the same year, and although at that time I did not know Hemingway intimately, it seemed to me that the people he put into his stories, the language he used, everything was familiar to me and part of my own background.

Graelle: How do you think the writers today match up to those of the '20s?

Cowley: I think there is a very interesting group of writers today . . . very interesting. And I think a new situation has come to the fore . . . a new generation is moving into influence . . . literature is strikingly different from what it was in the hands of the generation of the 1920s [elipses in original]. I would say we're going to see a very lively period for the next few years. Saul Bellow, for example, is bringing out an important novel called *Herzog* this fall. John Cheever is an admirable writer who's been critically neglected for years and years because his stories were published in the *New Yorker.* The critics have a slight mistrust of people who write stories for the *New Yorker.* The fact that these were very different from the usual *New Yorker* stories didn't dawn upon them until Cheever published *The Wapshot Chronicle* and *The Wapshot Scandal.*

Graelle: Yes, and with writers like Ken Kesey, J. P. Donleavy, William Burroughs, Thomas Berger, along with a great many others, there seems to be a literary boom, if you can call it that, in the last few years.

Cowley: Oh, yes. Partly owing to the immense growth in college attendance. After all, although not every college student is a reader, a great many of them are, so that the reading and the writing population have both increased vastly in number in the last few years.

Graelle: Do you think literary taste has gone up as well?

Cowley: It has become more sophisticated. Whether it's better or not is always the question, but readers have more knowledge, more points of reference. Of course, when you run into a man who has read a great many authors, you have to stop and think that there are a great many others he hasn't read. There's a limit to the amount of reading that anyone can do, and as a new author is admitted into the canon of those who have to be read, then some older author is quietly evicted.

Graelle: A few years back you wrote about and described three myths or mythologies in the American experience: the frontier or country myth of man against nature; the myths that arose during the great industrialization and urbanization of the U.S.—man against society; and lastly, man no longer coping with the frontier or with defining society, but with himself. The last, you said, was still undefined and in the making. Do you think it has defined itself more clearly since then?

Cowley: The three are not so much, in that sense, mythologies as three emotional backgrounds for everybody, three conflicts with which all American literature has some sort of connection. The last *has* defined itself more clearly. A good deal more clearly. The present conflict treated in fiction is also that of the individual, against some faceless bureaucracy, as in *Catch-22,* or of the inner struggles of a man in search of his own identity, as in *The Adventures of Augie March;* or of a man faced by some psychological difficulty or moral scruple—and I'm thinking here of the adolescent in *The Catcher in the Rye.* These are very different themes from man against nature and man against society of the older novels.

Graelle: What do you think of the type of hero who is not the anti-hero found in *Augie March,* in *Catch-22* and in *The Catcher in the Rye,* but a hero with a great knowledge of the bureaucracy, great knowledge of the society he lives in and its complexities, but not the sophisticated hero of old—because he does *not accept* the society and, let us say, function within it but does use it and uses his knowledge to use it, but rejects its principles. I am thinking of the hero of Donleavy's book *The Ginger Man,* of Kesey's book *One Flew Over the Cuckoo's Nest,* of Ellison's hero in *Invisible Man.*

Cowley: Yes, there is a different type of hero in all those books.

Augie March is more in search of an identity, and the Ginger Man already has an identity. He's more in rebellion. That's more his problem and seems to bother all the current novelists—of how to create or assert an identity for oneself against all the social pressures on the individual. The great change from the 1930s is that nobody any longer believes in his duty or ability in any manner whatever to reshape or alter conditions. Heroes like these accept conditions, and they use what the French used to call Système D during the First World War. "D" stood for *dé brouillard,* that is, being able to get yourself out of it . . . get yourself out of trouble . . . or how to "wangle," which is the term the English used. And that can be applied to the Ginger Man.

Graelle: Do you think this is a negative type of morality?

Cowley: That's a very hard question because you'd have to argue what "negative" is and what "morality" is. Do you mean antimorality, amorality, immorality, or a new morality growing up against the old one?

Graelle: Well, in Hemingway, for instance, the hero—although at odds with society, and living according to his own standards—is much more divorced from society than most modern heroes who are also at odds with it.

Cowley: It's true that some things have changed. There is more of an individual rebellion against society at the present time in novels . . . or not so much rebellion. Couldn't we sometimes, although it sounds less appealing, just call it complaint or whining against society? It used to be for a while that everything was mother's fault; that was the theme of hundreds and hundreds of novels. Now it's all society's fault, the establishment's fault, the fault of "squares" or the fault of "the way things are." And sometimes it's a great relief to read again the exploits of a Hemingway hero, who, when something goes wrong, says, "It was my fault."

Graelle: And yet in some ways Hemingway maintains an innocence that is absent from many of the contemporary novels we were discussing.

Cowley: Do you know, anything written twenty years ago seems innocent. It doesn't matter what the age is. To the 1930s, the 1920s seemed innocent. To the 1950s, the 1930s seemed innocent. And very soon the 1950s are going to seem innocent. I can already sense new moods growing up. I'm not sure that the negativism of the last ten or fifteen years isn't going to give way to new illusions pretty soon. A sign of that is the growing interest in the 1930s at present. Another sign, of course, is the number of beats and beards and sandals who go off to work for the cause of racial integration.

Graelle: In another of your books you wrote about the revolt against the genteel tradition in American literature during the early part of the century. We have come a long way since then with Henry Miller, William Burroughs and the like, and almost anything goes. Now, this certainly is a loss of innocence. Do you think this is a good trend?

Cowley: Of course, my own conservative instincts would say no, especially to the use of a great stream of foul language because here were all these words which had an awful power because there were places where they couldn't be used. When an author finally first said "damn" in print or first said "hell," "damn" and "hell" had power. But now there is not a single word in the language that has any of the awful and mysterious power that the four-letter words used to have. The result is that certain resources of language are being lost. When an author says, "blank, blank, blank, blank, blank," filling in the blanks with four-letter words in succession, then those words become no longer awful in their power but simply boring.

Extending this from language to acts, I suspect that the lack of sexual inhibitions in fiction has led to some terribly boring novels. When you think that Samuel Richardson could write a seven-volume novel about a seduction! Today seductions have become so commonplace in novels that authors can scarcely use them to fill a paragraph. That's a whole subject resource of novelists that has gone out the window, and others are going with it, so I'm not sure that the greater liberty is always an advantage.

I was reading today a review in the *New Statesman* about a volume of erotic poetry. The reviewer pointed out that actually the erotic poetry of the Victorian period, using respectable language, was more interesting, because it was more titillating, than the out-right bawdy poetry collected in this volume.

Graelle: But isn't this progressing familiarity with words inevitable because of the super-sophistication in the U.S. today?

Cowley: I don't know whether anything is inevitable any longer.

All I know is that our super-sophistication will seem like innocence in 1980, by the same rule that I mentioned before. They will say, "The 1960s, when people *innocently* believed that sex would solve everything." Now things were much worse in the Victorian era. I couldn't have lived then. But actually the existence of inhibitions makes it easier for writers to produce strong effects: literature doesn't flourish best in a sexual Utopia or any other kind of Utopia. The very curious thing to me is that almost every ethnic group produces its first great work when it is rising out of an under-privileged into a privileged position. There has to be that feeling of "We are oppressed. I am speaking for all my people; we are going to strike back at the oppressors." If I wanted a recipe for making an author a genius at the present time, I would suggest a black skin.

Graelle: Would you then predict that Negro literature will be the dominant literature of the next few years?

Cowley: I don't know, but I do know that there is a wonderful opportunity at this moment for Negro writers because of the emotional pressure under which they work.

Graelle: In an affluent society like the U.S., what type of literature will we end up with when all oppressed groups have been eliminated?

Cowley: I don't think we shall ever have an absence of oppressed groups. I think the way society is constituted there will always be injustice against some group.

Graelle: I'm thinking of the evolution of so large a middle class of so powerful a body of similar beings that almost any minority would be ignored.

Cowley: Yes, it's hard to visualize that situation imaginatively. What worries me is the urbanization of culture. What worries me is that literature in the past was usually produced by people who had some sort of feeling for the soil out of which things came. The generation of the 1920s was almost the last in which the authors, most of them, had a fairly close connection with the soil, even ones that you don't think of as having that connection. Allen Tate . . . Hemingway . . . Faulkner, who prided himself on being a farmer . . . Thomas Wolfe from the North Carolina mountains—they could all talk crops or they knew something about them. Many of them were gardeners or at least they knew how to get along in the countryside.

Now this has changed. The new literature is an urban literature, and I wonder if something hasn't gone out of writing with the change of emphasis from vegetables to psychosis.

Graelle: Do you think, aside from the urbanization of literature, that there is any unifying factor, any thematic preoccupation that writers today share?

Cowley: What there is for better or worse is a search for identity, a search for a self that can be asserted against social pressures. That's what's going on at the present time. In some writers: almost gaily—as for example in *The Ginger Man* or in Saul Bellow. In some cases angrily, in some cases rather whiningly—"Poor me, I can't find my own nature, won't you please pity me"—and out comes a novel. Outside of that—sex plays a great part in today's fiction. One could say it always did, but I mean that in the number of pages devoted to it. The search for the perfect orgasm has become a theme used more frequently than the search for the perfect heroine was used in Victorian times.

Graelle: Does that show the transitory state of our lives today—limiting our range of endeavour to the single orgasm as opposed to wife, a lifelong companion?

Cowley: Well, you could say the transitory state of humanity on this earth.

Graelle: True, but it's the degree of the state of transitoriness. I don't know if it's nostalgia without any reality behind it—but one can imagine a less hectic time, a time when goals were larger than the next orgasm.

Cowley: Everyone over fifty looks back to childhood when the days were much longer. So that produces a backward turn. Of course, I've got to the stage where I think the United States was a much nicer place to live in when I was a boy than it is now; I drive on super-highways but I hate super-highways. I think the whole tendency is to make it easier and easier to drive by car from one parking lot to another parking lot without seeing anything in between. As a matter of fact, anyone who wants to live again in an earlier American age has only to visit some farming sections of English Canada. Prince Edward Island, where I spent some time, seemed almost exactly like central Pennsylvania in 1910—where I spent my boyhood. There you find the feeling of space and freedom, the lack of "No Trespass" signs, the greater self-reliance—but also the uglier, less comfortable houses, the briefer schooling, and the abundant but monotonous food, with everything fried or baked. When I was in Prince Edward Island they still had schooners tied up at the docks in all the little fishing villages. I really loved the island, but was driven away by indigestion.

Graelle: In spite of our super-highways, it seems to me that literature in the U.S. is certainly more vital than literature in England, for instance, where their novelists seem to be dealing in social protest—a theme exhausted here in the '30s.

Cowley: I think it's too soon to pass a judgment on that. Literature here is lively at the present time. In England you do get a resurgence of the social novels of the 1930s. Much, much more than here. Perhaps we'll get that here, too. Many Negro novelists of today are writing novels much like the proletarian novels of the 1930s.

Graelle: Do you feel that there are certain themes which are basic to the American experience even though a body of writing in a given period might ignore or evade them?

Cowley: I don't know. That is hard to say. One thing that I can say is that the U.S. has produced very few good social novels, in the course of our whole literature. That is to say novels of social observation, recording novels. And not only have we produced fewer of these and more authors of romances, as Hawthorne made that distinction, but when a social novelist appears in this country—even when he's a good one like James Gould Cozzens—he is likely to be widely condemned by critics who are more in favour of the intense and imaginative works.

Graelle: Yes, that's true, and even a social novelist like Dos Passos uses an expressionistic and imaginative style.

Cowley: Well, Dos Passos is not exactly the type of novelist I was thinking of. He has been a novelist of social protest more than a novelist of social manners, more than a recording novelist—or as it's sometimes called, an institutional novelist because so many of them study institutions, like foundations, colleges, churches, the legal profession, and so on. There aren't many novelists of this sort in the U.S., and generally speaking, they're not as good or serious about their work as the imaginative romancers. When they are good, and serious about their work, like Cozzens, for example, they're likely to be widely condemned by critics, who cling more to the Hawthorne tradition in the novel than to the Trollope tradition.

Graelle: Could that be perhaps because social mores aren't very stable in America and change is such a great factor that it is bound to be confusing and lead, as you have pointed out, to a search for identity?

Cowley: That may be. Yes, I would think because of that it would be harder to write *any* type of novel, not only a social novel, in the U.S. than in England.

Thirty Years Later:
Memories of the First American
Writers' Congress

Daniel Aaron, Malcolm Cowley, Kenneth Burke, Granville
Hicks, and William Phillips/1966

From *The American Scholar* 35 (Summer 1966), 495–516.
Reprinted by permission of the publishers.

The First American Writers' Congress met in 1935. In the
fall of 1965 Malcolm Cowley and Kenneth Burke proposed to the editor of *The American Scholar* that some of
the participants in the 1935 meeting be invited to gather
for a tape-recorded discussion of the congress.

Mr. Cowley and Mr. Burke believed that it would be
useful to have on record the story of the Congress, and
interesting to find out how perspectives had changed
during thirty years.

Such a meeting was held on December 8, 1965, and
the transcript of the discussion follows. Mr. Burke, Mr.
Cowley, Mr. Granville Hicks and Mr. William Phillips were
the participants, and Mr. Daniel Aaron acted as moder-
ator. Only one of those who had agreed to participate,
Miss Muriel Rukeyser, was, because of illness, unable to
attend.

Mr. Cowley: I will start by reading from the introduction to a book
called American Writers' Congress, edited by Henry Hart and published by International Publishers in 1935, a few months after the
Congress had taken place. "From 1930 on," Mr. Hart says, "more
and more American writers—like their fellow-craftsmen in other
countries—began to take sides in the world struggle between barba-
rism (deliberately cultivated by a handful of property owners) and the
living interests of the mass of mankind. . . . In various fields, in
various ways, American writers had been aligning themselves with

the forces of progress against the prevailing dangers of war, fascism and the extinction of culture. It soon became clear that the writer, like other members of the American community, must organize in his own defense. In January, 1935, a group of writers issued the following call."

Before reading some passages from the call, I should like to comment on that impersonal phrase "it soon became clear." Clear to whom? Obviously, it became clear to the Communist party of the United States, because the writers who issued the call were brought together by the party and its functionaries in the cultural field, notably Alexander Trachtenberg, the head of the party-affiliated publishing house, International Publishers. Incidentially, I attended some of the meetings that preceded the issuance of the call in January, 1935, and I remember that my self-imposed task was to persuade others at the meetings to make their pronouncements in English. It was a strange problem to face with a group of writers, but they all wanted to speak in international Communist jargon. I tried, but with a notable lack of success, to change the jargon into English. Anyhow, the half-de-jargonized call began as follows:

> The capitalist system crumbles so rapidly before our eyes that, whereas ten years ago scarcely more than a handful of writers were sufficiently far-sighted and courageous to take a stand for proletarian revolution, today hundreds of poets, novelists, dramatists, critics and short story writers recognize the necessity of personally helping to accelerate the destruction of capitalism and the establishment of a workers' government . . . .
> Many revolutionary writers live virtually in isolation, lacking opportunities to discuss vital problems with their fellows. Others are so absorbed in the revolutionary cause that they have few opportunities for thorough examination and analysis. Never have the writers of the nation come together for fundamental discussion.
> We propose, therefore, that a Congress of American revolutionary writers be held in New York City on April 26, 27, and 28, 1935; that to this Congress shall be invited all writers who have achieved some standing in their respective fields; who have clearly indicated their sympathy with the revolutionary cause; who do not need to be convinced of the decay of capitalism, of the inevitability of revolution. Subsequently, we will seek to influence and win to our side those writers not yet so convinced.

More comments on this reading of part of the call. "Writers who have achieved some standing" meant that they were leaving out the kids. The kids had played the largest part up until that time in the John Reed Clubs and other organizations of left-wing writers. Now the party had decided that the kids could be pushed to one side, and that the writers of "some" standing would be invited. These writers "of some standing" included two classes—those who were, perhaps, wavering in their sympathy. But others who weren't wavering, who had taken a stand against Russia or Stalin, or against the party, were not invited. The party could invite the so-called innocents, but they couldn't invite, for example, Max Eastman or Sidney Hooks or James Rorty or a number of other people in the same situation.

Nevertheless, two hundred and sixteen writers got together and attended, or sat on the platform at, [the] mass meeting in Mecca Temple (later the New York Community Theatre, I think). Now, there were four thousand people in the audience, and my impression is that they all paid admissions, and that these admissions went a considerable way toward paying the expenses of the Congress.

Mr. Hicks: I think that's true, as far as I know. I assumed at the time that these four thousand people were passionately devoted to literature. Since then I've become convinced that the party simply loaded the meeting. It told various units that they had to turn out for this particular meeting, that they had to sell tickets for it, and they did. I think it was certainly a party-packed meeting, but that didn't occur to me at the time.

Mr. Aaron: Granville, did you note how many of the original members of the John Reed Clubs were invited here, or was there a policy set by the party to exclude some of the more intransigent (and perhaps less) writers of less standing at this meeting?

Mr. Cowley: I don't know where the policy came from, but the—

Mr. Hicks: We have a witness here. Were you invited as a delegate to the Congress, Phillips?

Mr. Phillips: Yes.

Mr. Aaron: Did you go?

Mr. Phillips: Yes.

Mr. Aaron: Now, the Congress we're talking about is the one that met at the New School. Is that right?

Mr. Phillips: Yes.

Mr. Aaron: The first one, the one in 1935. The one that opened with a meeting in Mecca Temple?

Mr. Phillips: That's right. Excuse me, can I interrupt for a moment? Does the question directed to me assume that I was in some kind of opposition? Is that the idea?

Mr. Aaron: No.

Mr. Cowley: No, you were in.

Mr. Aaron: You were a member of the New York John Reed Club, weren't you?

Mr. Cowley: No, it's strictly a question of, you were younger. You see, they were playing a different tune this time. The original popularity of proletarian literature had been among the kids, that is, those roughly from the lower twenties to the lower thirties. And then suddenly the party decided it was going to shift to established writers. Now, a lot of the kids were dumped at that time, which was—

Mr. Aaron: I see.

Mr. Cowley: To my mind, it was one of the origins of the great schism in the literary movement later on.

Mr. Burke: Can I offer just a tentative suggestion at that point? You spoke of taking a stand for or against the party. You say "the party simply loaded the meeting," and that those who were against the party were not invited. Somewhere along that line tonight I'd like us to discuss a related question. Must there always be a goat? Is there any kind of political structure that's not based on the principle of a goat somewhere? Is that a reasonable question?

Mr. Hicks: Yes, but I do think it is rather important to establish the fact that the Communist party did initiate this Congress, and quite openly initiated it. I don't think anybody who came ever had any doubts about that. And the party initiated it very carefully. The call stated that non-Communists were welcome, as they certainly were, but the party was taking the initiative and, as Malcolm has suggested, anybody who opposed the party as such was not welcome.

Mr. Cowley: In other words, Max Eastman and Sidney Hook. Without the least question this Congress was organized or initiated by the Communist party. Of course, the impressive thing is that the Communist party at that time was able to organize a Congress that would be attended by a large number of American Writers and approved more or less or acquiesced in by a still larger number.

Mr. Hicks: This is important. What is also important is that from my point of view as one who was about to become a member of the party, this was a step ahead for the party. That is, since I'd been a kind of fellow traveler from 1931 on, I'd been very unhappy because the party was not doing very much to bring toward itself the writers who were sympathetic in their general ideals. And I felt that for the party to organize a Congress to which nonparty members were invited, and, indeed, pretty much allowed to say what they wanted to say—I thought that was a great step ahead.

Mr. Aaron: Granville, would you say that the decision on the part of the party to call the Congress was clearly a result of the new United Front policy, that it couldn't have occurred before this, if there hadn't been this historical event?

Mr. Hicks: Are you sure of the chronology of this? Wasn't the Congress of the International after the call for the Congress?

Mr. Cowley: Dimitrov called for the People's Front on August 2, 1935, which was some months after the Congress. But the premonitory rumblings of the People's Front were already spreading over the world. They were spreading a little less, a little belatedly, let us say, in the United States, where Trachtenberg hadn't quite caught on to the system yet. But nevertheless, they were reaching here, too.

Mr. Hicks: That's absolutely true. I remember talking to Clarence Hathaway, the editor of the *Daily Worker,* in February, I think. And he gave me very clear indications that the line was about to make a substantial change.

Mr. Burke: Well, still holding to that point I started with, about the goat: Doesn't the dialectic of the United Front, Popular Front, all those phrases, really get centered in the fact that we had Hitler in common as an enemy? And wasn't it in '33 that this trend began to come clear? This seems to me tremendously important, the opponent as a unifying force. And confusions since then reflect precisely the fact that we now don't have a goat of that sort in common.

Mr. Cowley: Oh, but you miss something in the Hitler chronology. In 1933 the orthodox Communist view was the dialectic, that is, thesis contends with antithesis and the result is a synthesis. The Communist International judged that in the German situation, Communism was the thesis, Fascism was the antithesis, and Communism again would be the inevitable synthesis. The sooner Facism took over, the sooner it would fall, and the sooner would come the establishment of the Communist world state. That belief survived

until the summer of 1934, two or three months after Hitler's Blood
Purge. I know, because I talked with Willi Münzenberg when he was
in New York that summer as a representative of the Comintern; he
was sure that Hitler would be overthrown within a few months. But
gradually the realists in the Comintern began to see that the dialectic
wasn't working out this time, that Communism as a thesis was simply
getting licked, and that the synthesis was going to be Fascist unless
they took some new measures. The new ones were strikingly non-
Marxian, a fact that introduces a strange element into the second half
of the 1930's. What they decided to do in 1935 was to let sleeping
dialectics lie. They would pave over the differences between the
liberals and the Communists in order to create a large enough United
Front, which would then be called the People's Front, to prevent the
victory of Fascism. In other words, to anticipate a later episode of the
Congress, the only forward-looking talk in the whole series of
speeches given at the New School was Kenneth Burke's speech on
"the workers" and "the people."

   Mr. Phillips: Now I think Malcolm Cowley makes a very good
point, that if you think of the Popular Front policy as Kenneth Burke,
I think, was suggesting, as a rapprochement with reality on the part of
the Communist party, certainly it is true that it was a rectification of a
terrible error made earlier. I believe a good case could be made for
the view that the Communist party had some responsibility for the
failure to stop Hitler because it failed to make a united front with the
Socialist party in Germany. But how valid and how meaningful this
new Popular Front policy was, is, I think, a large and separate
question of its own. But there is, of course, an interesting contradiction and that contradiction is one of the things that puts us, I suppose,
where we are, and has us discussing this question. The Communist
party seemed to be broadening out and, as I suggested earlier, trying
to come closer to a more realistic position—I think the word "realistic" was used in the connection. In other words, it realized that in
order to fight Fascism it would have to make broader alliances than
with just fellow travelers: it did try to work with writers and intellectuals. And yet the Communist party, as was suggested here earlier,
kept insisting that only people who supported the Communist party
could be present at these meetings.

   Mr. Aaron: I'd like to ask a question at this point. Mr. Cowley has pointed out that certain writers who had already criticized the party, were not invited: Max Eastman, Sidney Hook and others. And yet this was an attempt, after all, to bring together a common front. What about the Socialist party? Were they represented? Was any member of the Socialist party considered as a sponsor?

Mr. Phillips: Well, you wrote the history; you should remember the facts better than any of us, Aaron.

Mr. Aaron: Well, I didn't think so, but maybe Mr. Hicks would have something to say on this.

Mr. Hicks: No, they weren't considered at all.

Mr. Aaron: Yes.

Mr. Cowley: Of course, in a writers' congress at that time, that wasn't terribly important, because there weren't very many Socialist writers, except very old men. So you could get together quite a large writers' congress without having any Socialist party representatives.

Mr. Hicks: I think I must repeat myself. We have to understand that the party was just beginning to adopt the new line that led to the people's fronts and there was great uncertainty as to what could be done and what couldn't.

Mr. Aaron: I want to go back to a point that Kenneth Burke raised, this question of the goat. The fact is that of these more than two hundred and twelve writers who came—

Mr. Cowley: Two hundred and sixteen.

Mr. Aaron: Two hundred and sixteen writers. Most of them were not privy to the decisions of the Community party, knew very little really about the Communist party, but were brought together simply because of their common opposition to Hitler, Fascism, and by the general feeling that somehow the Soviet Union represented the forces of progress. But as a group they weren't particularly ideological-minded, were they?

Mr. Burke: No, they weren't but—

Mr. Cowley (taking it away from Mr. Burke): One feature of the late 1930's was the fact that the ideological level was quite low. It was low for many reasons, but one of those reasons was perfectly respectable. That was the feeling of a present danger, represented by Hitler. In the face of that danger, people were willing not to pursue their ideas to the last point. They would glide over, smooth over, ideological differences if they could get cooperation in action.

Mr. Burke: What I'm trying to get at here, all the way through this thing—whether we have ideology or not, is it not a terrifying fact that you can never get people together except when they have a goat in common? That's the terrifying thing that I begin to see as the damnation of the human race. That's how they have to operate; they get congregation by segregation. You might put that as your formula for this whole scheme. Is it true or is it not, if you can safely—

Mr. Hicks: Of course it's true. H. G. Wells sixty years ago said we could never unite unless there was an invasion from Mars.

Mr. Burke: That's true.

Mr. Phillips: By the goat you mean Hitler—Fascism.

Mr. Burke: At that time.

Mr. Cowley: To take a word away from Kenneth, I think the word "goat" is wrong here because he's thinking of scapegoat. The word is "enemy."

Mr. Burke: I was thinking of tragedy, the Goat Song.

Mr. Cowley: It has proved very difficult to bring people together except against an enemy.

Mr. Phillips: Well, maybe it isn't necessary if there's no enemy. In other words, don't we have a tautology here? If there's no problem, if there isn't something to fight against, then we don't have to bring people together. The enemy or the goat, whatever term you want to use, can be either capitalism or fascism, or—segregation. In other words, if you didn't have segregation, you needn't have a civil rights movement. I'm wondering whether we've got anything more than a political tautology here.

Mr. Burke: The point I'm suggesting, or at least my fear is, that you cannot run a world otherwise. For people do have to get together, they do have to cooperate; and (Granville is backing me on this point) they get together by having an enemy in common. This is to me a tremendously important thing because there is talk of having moved on. All right, we might have moved on, in relation to certain questions of ideology. But as for having moved on from the stand-point of the way to confront the world, are we just going to do these same things all over again, in some other form?

Mr. Cowley: The answer to your question, have we moved on, is no. The answer to your question, are we going to have to confront the world in the same way against an enemy, is yes. I think this is a fundamental human pattern. So the reason I interrupted here was to get us back to the Congress itself, because we have here four people who actually took part in that Congress. To ask one question of one of them, Granville, do you remember those meetings at which the Congress was organized?

Mr. Hicks: No, I attended very few of them because I was living in Troy, upstate. I did go to a couple maybe during the course of the spring, but I didn't go to anywhere near as many as you did.

Mr. Phillips: I remember a couple of those meetings. I went to a couple of them.

Mr. Aaron: Can you describe some of these meetings, can you recall anything that took place?

Mr. Phillips: Well, actually the thing that I recall most vividly is something funny. There was, as we all agree, a shift of the Popular Front line. (I notice we are falling back into the language of the thirties—I haven't used the word "line" in years.) Anyway, whenever there was a shift of position, adapting to the new position naturally was not too easy. Some people were addicted to old positions and some went too far, and some didn't go far enough, and so on. I remember at one meeting Trachtenberg, who was officiating, was asked whether people who were opposed to the Communist party should or should not be invited. And Trachtenberg kept saying, "Well, on the one hand there are these reasons for not inviting them; on the other hand, there are these reasons for inviting them." And he went back and forth, on the one hand, on the other hand. And at one point, I remember, Joshua Kunitz yelled out, "Trachtenberg, we know on the one hand, on the other hand; what we want to know is which hand."

Mr. Aaron: I notice that so far we've been talking about all the political considerations for calling this meeting, but were there any literary reasons? Was there much discussion about what value organizing a league would have for writers themselves, encouraging their writing, widening their audience, directing them, the kind of thing that you talked about, Malcolm, in *Exile's Return,* the advantages that would come to a writer who affiliated himself with the Left, not for political reasons but for literary reasons.

Mr. Phillips: My recollection is, it was considered square to discuss these questions.

Mr. Cowley: There were a great many arguments going on at the time about proletarian literature, for example, and the people who were interested in the arguments were also interested in the opportunity of discussing them at a Congress. And they did discuss them, as a matter of fact.

Mr. Aaron: Who appointed Trachtenberg to this particular position and in what ways was he qualified to be the general impresario?

Mr. Phillips: That's a very tricky question.

Mr. Hicks: I don't know the exact answer. This was a self-appointed committee. The second part of the question is very easy to answer and that is that Trachtenberg was the cultural head of the Communist party in this country at that time. He was responsible for this sort of thing. And I don't think many of us were innocent enough not to realize that.

Mr. Phillips: In other words, he was the head *ex officio*.

Mr. Hicks: Yes.

Mr. Phillips: Well, when I said tricky, I meant that's something you could never establish.

Mr. Hicks: No.

Mr. Phillips: Something that some of us sensed.

Mr. Cowley: It is a rather difficult thing to express, but when we're discussing these matters we always tend to follow the old, old policy of cheapening them. Our emotions at that time were not cheap; they were deeply felt. Some of them were quite personal. There were at that time a great number of breakdowns among writers, actual psychological breakdowns. The 1920's had been like a long party, and it was getting to be four o'clock in the morning. It was getting to be the hour when a man went up to another man and said, "I've always thought you were a son of a bitch. Did I ever tell you that?" Or went up to his wife and said, "We've been living a lie, it's time for us to break up." So these people with psychological problems were looking for some cure outside themselves, which they found in the idea of uniting themselves with the mass or the group, and being not leader, but just one in the ranks of the great army that was marching toward a new dawn. If they could forget themselves, they could solve their psychological problems. So there was a great deal of almost religious feeling going on at the same time among people you would never suspect of having it, and who tried to hide their religious feeling in talk of the Marxian dialectic, *et cetera, et cetera*. The feeling was there.

Mr. Burke: I got into that tangle, too. I remember, when the Leftists first began to move onto the scene, I began to fear that they were dishonoring Shakespeare. For a couple of years there, I took all sorts of notes for articles in defense of Shakespeare. Then all of a sudden I made the discovery: Look, this fellow has taken care of himself for a long time, and probably will continue to survive without help. That did get me off that particular hook, at least. From that time on, at least that much of my puzzle was resolved.

Mr. Phillips: I'd like to pick up what Malcolm Cowley just said. I think it's absolutely true that the only way to look at this period, and we've all written this and said this in one way or another, is that it was a peculiar mixture of truth and nonsense, of cynicism and idealism, of clarity and confusion, and so on. If we don't see it as being a combination of these polarities, I think we are too frivolous and too negative about our own past, about something that did have some meaning, and some reality. But at the same time I think we have to recognize some of the nonsense in it. I remember one incident, Kenneth Burke, when you and I, and a lot of other people, were marching in a May Day parade. I've told this story many times and I think it illustrates a lot of things. I remember your joining in the shout, "We write for the working class." And I remember wondering whether Kenneth Burke really thought he wrote for the working class. How many workers read Kenneth Burke?

Mr. Burke: I do not remember the incident, but I couldn't deny that it is possible. Few can subscribe to all the slogans printed or shouted in a parade, but I probably joined in the shouting.

Mr. Phillips: I've thought of the story many times when I give graduate courses in criticism, and assign something by Kenneth Burke. Some of my graduate students have a little difficulty understanding you, and I have to explain the text to them.

Mr. Burke: That was the basis of my talk at the first Writers' Congress. That's precisely what they got after me for: I said I couldn't write for the working class. That was the irony of the case. You remember it, I've forgotten it, but I'll take your word for it. I'm sure I paraded, I know once—

Mr. Phillips: Can I have one more minute here? I think the reason that it's meaningful perhaps to talk about this, unless we just want to sit around and reminisce, is that some of the problems we faced, and I think probably fell on our faces in an attempt to face, and many of the mistakes we made, are now plaguing some of the younger people. We have a new mood now—we're all aware of it— among the students and all over the campuses. They're facing some of the same problems we faced, and the same contradiction— enormous idealism, really marvelous, marvelous idealism that you cannot but help admire and respect, plus a certain amount of confusion and a certain amount of foolishness. They're moving in directions they're not completely aware of, and of course they don't want to listen. The one thing students keep repeating is that the people who had anything to do with the thirties, the Old Left, as they call it, have nothing to say to them. I think it would be sad if nobody learned from our mistakes.

Mr. Hicks: You're quite right, but I'd like to go back just a little way. We've talked so far, I think, as if the Writers' Congress in 1935 was the beginning of something, but it really wasn't. There had been a leftward movement of the writers from 1930–1931 on, and a kind of climax had been reached with the statement for Foster and Ford in the election of 1932. As somebody who signed that statement, and who was very much involved with Communism throughout this whole period, I would like to point out that in 1932, all the writers could do was to sign a political manifesto. Why I felt the Writers' Congress was important was that it asked writers to do something *as writers,* and that seemed to me to be a definite step ahead.

Mr. Aaron: Coming back to what you said, Mr. Phillips, don't you feel that the young intellectuals, those who came to the first Congress, and those who affiliated with the League of American Writers afterward, differed from the young radicals of today in that they did feel that there was a focus to their radicalism? It was centered, after all, on two or three important positions or concepts, whereas today there doesn't seem to be this focus. And this is one of the reasons why today's radicals have a difficult time identifying with the period of the thirties.

Mr. Burke: Isn't the lack of focus due precisely to the lack of an enemy in common? Isn't it always this same situation? Is there anything else to it? If we had a clear enemy in common today, wouldn't you get exactly the same kind of focus?

Mr. Phillips: Well, some of these students on the New Left, or most of them, I think, do have a general or a vague sense, don't you think, of an enemy. That is, they're against something called the Establishment, they're against something called the System, they're against something—

Mr. Burke: Let's—

Mr. Phillips: Let's translate System into capitalism, translate Establishment into existing society and its values, and this is more or less what Marxists and radicals generally were always against. However, there are some very important differences.

Mr. Cowley: The great difference to me is the Communist party, which is playing a very small role at the present time. And about that I've thought at times—all I can say is I've thought—and it seems to me now at times that if it hadn't been for the Communist party there might have been a revolution in 1932–33. I'm not sure that the Communist party didn't play as large a part as Roosevelt in preventing a revolutionary movement during the early 1930's when the country was actually in a revolutionary situation. And, for the established order, I think that this quasi anarchy that reigns at the present time, with nobody knowing what he wants, is perhaps more dangerous than a Communist party that actually did not want a revolution in the United States, no matter how much they talked about it.

Mr. Phillips: I think you're right, but I think there are a number of interesting and perhaps meaningful ironies and contradictions here. Look, weren't we all in this kind of dilemma in the thirties? In one way or another, and in varying degrees, we felt that the Communist party was a bad influence, organizationally and ideologically. At the same time it seemed to us to be the only party capable of doing anything, the only party capable of providing some kind of central force around which to organize. And we were all caught at various times, and in varying degrees, in this contradiction. The questions seemed to be: to what extent would it be desirable to cooperate and suppress some of our critical feelings, some of our critical sense, in the name of some large cause? Now today, I think, Malcolm Cowley's right. There is no Communist party in that same organizational sense, although I think it's interesting to note that it's there as a historical presence. And one of the things that the New Left feels separates it from what it calls the Old Left is the question of Communism. They feel that the Old Left might be characterized basically as a movement that got burned by the Communist party. And they don't want to get burned. In other words, they feel that there's no point in their carrying on the intellectual or the ideological criticism of the Communist party that dominated the thirties. They feel that they face a new world and a different world. This I personally find a little confusing. I don't now what the answer is. I think perhaps the situation is so complex, and so mysterious and so contradictory, that it may be difficult to get an answer, because the world is different today in very many ways. One important way is the presence of the atomic bomb. The change in outlook of the Soviet Union is another important thing, and the emergence of China is a third. It's a very complicated and difficult and new world, and what the more conscious students are trying to do—and partly succeeding and partly failing—is to move into this new world without ideological preconceptions. But without having ideological preconceptions, at the same time they have an enormous ideological innocence which makes us feel terribly sophisticated compared to them. And yet they're willing to face this world in a way that I'm not sure we're able to do. I've said that so fast it isn't exactly what I mean, but—I should stop.

Mr. Cowley: What about the tremendous failure of the intellectuals in the twentieth century? As late as the nineteenth century, as late as Marx, Darwin and Freud, you would run up against an occasional intellectual who was able to give a form to the entire world. Today there is nobody like that; there is nobody who has worked on the economics of today and the society of today in the way that Marx worked on the society of, let us say, 1850. He has been passed. You cannot apply Marxism, without enormous modifications that destroy it, to the situation today. And yet there is no single thinker in the twentieth century who has acquired the stature of Marx or Darwin or Freud.

Mr. Hicks: I think that's the fault of the twentieth century, not of the thinkers. It's all grown too big, too complicated; nobody can, no one person can begin to take it all in. I think that's the fault of the times we live in.

Mr. Burke: I wonder whether we might have a form in a certain sense, at least as educators. Can't we have a form in the sense that we can try to train people in the kind of temptations to which we are naturally prone, like this damn business of always blaming it on the other fellow, and so on? And there's the fact that we confront somehow or other the needs of a world order, whether we want it or not, because technology is forcing that kind of conclusion upon us. Isn't that a form? And a fact? I think that the avoidance of revolutions in a society like ours is "wholesome" in the sense that a highly complex industrial state can't stand anything but a palace revolution. You get your revolutions, ironically enough, in places unlike those prophesied by Marx, places with economic systems that you can't destroy by cutting a spinal column. Each section can survive locally, without need of a center. It was the kind of situation that existed in Russia before the high development of industry—and you can see it in many parts of Asia.

Mr. Hicks: I'd like to come back to something that Phillips was saying a little while ago. Certainly we did, all of us who grew near the Communist party, realize that it was extremely fallible and dangerous, but I at least, in that particular situation, didn't doubt that it was the best thing that we had, and I was willing to make some compromises. Well, isn't this exactly what the writer has to do in any kind of political activity? I mean, whether you support a Republican or a Democrat or a Progressive or whatnot, you don't commit yourself one hundred percent; you have your reservations. I don't think this is peculiar to the supporters of the Communist party.

Mr. Phillips: I think, Granville, what you're saying is theoretically true, but I wonder if the question of degree here is not important. You are referring to the means-end question, which usually involves compromise. But I think if you support the Democratic party or the Republican party, don't you do it in a very loose way? You don't do it with your whole being, you don't do it with all your feelings, with your whole theoretical self, with your whole mind, as it were. It doesn't exclude all kinds of other ideas, beliefs, doubts. Too much of us got absorbed, we might say, in this kind of compromise. In the case of a partial compromise, obviously what you're saying would be true.

Mr. Hicks: Yes, but that is a matter of degree and I think a great deal depends upon how urgent the individual feels the situation is at a particular time. In the thirties I thought the situation was terribly urgent, and therefore I was willing to commit myself to the rather desperate measures of which, even then, I didn't really approve. I think that some of our younger radicals today would say exactly the same thing. This is a very desperate situation and we must take any action that is available to us under the circumstances, even though we know it's not the ideal one.

Mr. Aaron: In 1932, when fifty-two intellectuals signed the open letter for the Foster and Ford candidacy, the United States was in a very desperate situation; this was really the low point, 1932 and 1933. By 1935 the New Deal had already gotten started; there was considerable hope in the country; it was in a much more positive and dynamic mood at this time than it had been two or three years before. Do you suppose that if the Congress of American Writers had been called, say, a couple of years earlier, it would have attracted as many people? And I also want to know what the attitude toward the New Deal was at the time when the Congress was called. Was it possible to call this Congress and bring as many people to it because it seemed now as if the Left movement was beginning, not necessarily to affiliate, but to support, in some measure, some of the New Deal proposals?

Mr. Cowley: No, you're getting off the sequence of events. There was a considerable lag then in the intellectual ranks. The New Deal was still formally regarded as fascist, formally, although there were signs of reconciliation, a few signs, but the party line was still that the New Deal promoted not only a fascist organization of society but something approaching fascism in the arts. It was the time when painters like Grant Wood and Tom Benton and poets like Paul Engle were being attacked as representatives of artistic chauvinism. The reasons that a writers' congress could be called in 1935 and not in 1932 were, first, that the Communist party was no longer making its appeal purely to revolutionaries—they were beginning to attract other people, for example Granville Hicks—and second, reverting to the intellectual lag, that writers in 1935 were only beginning in large numbers to catch on to the situation in 1932. They were still living or feeling in the crisis of 1932, and they didn't think that the New Deal had ended it.

Mr. Hicks: Nevertheless, I doubt if you will find in this report on the American Writers' Congress one single attack on the New Deal. I think the party had reached the point of being neutral on the New Deal but dead against Fascism. And it was exactly on these grounds that the Congress stood.

Mr. Phillips: I want to get back to what you were saying before, Granville Hicks. You were saying that the situation was so desperate that it justified the waiving, as it were, of our critical sense. I think you're absolutely right if what you're saying means that many of us at various times felt that way. But, if you look back retroactively, look at this as history, then I think the natural questions arise. Let me put the whole question in a very extreme way. I think Malcolm Cowley touched indirectly on what I want to say when he said that had it not been for the Communist party, there might have been stronger and more effective political activity. If the activities of the Communist party had corresponded to the political needs of the time; if the Communist party in organizing the League of American Writers had permitted what seems to me essential, some kind of dissent (after all, everybody is screaming now about the right to dissent, that people have a right to disagree on Vietnam, and there should have been at least that much right to dissent from the organizational or intellectual views of the Communist party); if the Communist party had been a genuinely democratic and revolutionary party, then obviously the whole course of history would have been different. I think most intellectuals would still be supporting the Communist party.

Mr. Hicks: That's an awfully big "if." Let me go back a little. What I've said again and again, speaking of myself and other ex-Communists, is that our intentions were of the best but that we made mistakes of judgment. I've said it to myself another way. Sometimes I look back on that period and I just can't imagine how I could have been damn fool enough to support the Communist party. In other moods, I look back on that period and it seems to me that that was exactly the thing that I had to do in that particular time.

Mr. Phillips: I think this is what we're faced with: that both statements are true. Really, both are equally true and that's why the whole question is so difficult.

Mr. Burke: I don't think that at that stage anyone would have been a damn fool in supporting the Communist party. For instance, the party took the proper policy with regard to Spain; and if only Roosevelt had carried that through, I think we'd have a different world today. As for an attachment to the party, in a way, in an ambiguous way, I was attached to it. Emerging from a sense of complete isolation into a sense of participation in a movement, that was tremendous. So when I took a beating at the Congress, I felt hopelessly rejected. That's what the whole thing meant to me.

Mr. Cowley: There were certain enormous ideas working through the 1930's, and one was the idea of comradeship, that you were no longer alone, isolated, helpless, but if you took the side of the working class you were one of a large body of people marching toward something. I have found that idea expressed in one poem after another, including a poem of Kenneth's in here—you know, your little poem "Plea of the People"—in one work after another, and sometimes with enormous feeling, as you would find it in early plays by Odets, for example. That was almost the master feeling. The other feeling was the value of human dignity, which you would get in such disparate works as James Agee's *Let Us Now Praise Famous Men* and Malraux's *Man's Fate*. In one work after another, you would see this feeling that each individual person had a right to dignity. And these ideas all worked together to a synthesis which the Communist party had taken advantage of. There was an enormous prestige at that time for people who belonged to the party. They were listened to as if they had received advice straight from God; as if they weren't quite inspired prophets, but had been at meetings where the word was passed down from Mount Sinai, and as if they were making sacrifices that other people were not making. So they had a sort of mana that surrounded them and destroyed many of them in the end.

Mr. Aaron: I'd like to pursue this observation a little further. You say that there was a certain satisfaction, a great satisfaction, in feeling that one was affiliated with a progressive force, the working class, of feeling that one belonged in the vanguard of contemporary life. But what about the feeling of associating with writers, the sense of solidarity that you had as a writer affiliating with other writers? It seems to me that there's nothing quite like this since then. To some extent perhaps in the past, from time to time, there were groups of writers who would join together opposing some policies or supporting other policies, but one of the differences I think between literary organizations in the thirties and those of today is that group actions or writers today seem always a bit artificial, a bit self-conscious, when a half a dozen writers will get together and protest a Presidential policy or oppose some action that the Soviet Union is taking. Just recently, I remember, a number of writers protested to the Soviet Union against the imprisonment of two Soviet writers. But that sort of thing was done more easily in the thirties. There must have been enormous satisfaction that writers took at this time in cooperating with one another and feeling somehow that they were important, that they were making some impression on a society that hitherto hadn't paid very much attention to them. Maybe one of the differences now is that writers today, because of their general prestige, because they are accepted in the sense that they weren't at that time, make a comparable action seem more self-conscious.

Mr. Hicks: Dan, let's not be romantic about this. Writers were at each other's throats in the thirties the same as they are today. Am I right? No, this is not true, Dan. There was definitely the feeling about having an impact on society at large, but there was no more feeling of solidarity among left-wing writers than there would be in any other group of writers.

Mr. Phillips: There was also the feeling that there was an awful lot of nonsense going on. This is one of the things that I have never been able to reconcile. George Orwell once said: "There's a certain kind of nonsense that only intellectuals can invent, that the ordinary person could never think of." There's always this enormous contradiction: writers, intellectuals, are supposed to be smarter than other people. And yet when they get together, at meetings and conferences, you hear an awful lot of nonsense.

Mr. Aaron: But then as you read the reports (now, I'm speaking as a complete outsider), as you read the reports in the first publication of the American Writer's Congress you do have a sense that in supporting the Soviet Union, in making declarations in support of the Loyalist cause in Spain, the writers felt a unanimity. Maybe there were personal quarrels between writers, but there was a sense of—

Mr. Phillips: I think that's true.

Mr. Aaron: —of excitement and exhilaration, that numbers of people were getting together and voicing a common protest against certain acts.

Mr. Hicks: This was not on literary grounds, Dan.

Mr. Aaron: No. I know that.

Mr. Hicks: To support Spain and this and that—

Mr. Cowley: You might have noted, Aaron, because you looked into my correspondence at the Newberry Library, how many letters I got from how many people, many of whom I didn't know at all, but they were all writing in because I was an editor of a paper that took the progressive stand. And even while they were getting involved in worse and worse quarrels, there was at the same time a feeling, even within the quarrels, that everybody was marching together toward one goal—against, as Kenneth pointed out, the enemy, the enemy being Fascism and Hitler, and the aim of the Communists being to show that Hitler was only an expression of capitalism.

Mr. Aaron: Let's go back to that 1935 Congress. Was there bitterness, was there a good deal of ferocious self-criticism, even at that point, at these meetings? Of course this doesn't come out in the reports of the Congress, but you people were there. Did you notice even at the time that there was a good deal of backbiting? I know that there was in some instances. In your lecture, Kenneth—

Mr. Burke: Yeah, well, that's a rather long story. Perhaps I'd be hogging too much of the time in going back over that.

Mr. Aaron: No, that's an important—

Mr. Cowley: No, no, I think that your paper was, or seems in retrospect, a focal point of the Congress, because you were pointing toward the future and most of the Congress was pointing toward the past.

Mr. Burke: I'll try to get it down to a few rudiments. But I think the incident does have a certain literary quality, or sociological quality. It's a time when I was fighting on many fronts, some purely personal. As Malcolm said earlier, that was a time when you were fighting on many fronts. When I wrote my piece for the Congress, I didn't know how things stood. I had a friend whom I took to be a member of the party (I didn't know, but I assumed that he was). I showed him the article before I read it at the Congress. I asked him to tell me what he thought of it, for I didn't want to do anything that in any way would be considered wrong. I had a terrific desire to belong; as they put it later in the mass media, you know, "togetherness." My friend looked at it, and told me that he didn't see anything wrong with it. So I felt reassured. But after I had been reading for a while, and was nearly finished, the Chairman, John Howard Lawson, announced that my time was up. I still had about two pages to go. Holding up the two unread pages, I asked for a bit more time. The audience applauded—which was taken to mean that I should be allowed to finish, although it could have been interpreted less favorably. In any case, I was allowed to read the two pages—and the audience gave me a nice hand. Since I was greatly afraid of audiences, I sat down feeling wonderful. Then a couple more talks followed. I remember Waldo Frank coming over and sitting down beside me. He started telling me about some similar article that he had written. I wasn't interested in Waldo's article; I wanted to bask in my own self-satisfaction. When Waldo had left and the other talks were over, then the boys got going. Oof! The point was this: As regards the question of the workers, the proletariat, I had admitted that I was a petit bourgeois, and could speak only as a petit bourgeois. But Joe Freeman gets up, throbbing like a locomotive, and shouts, "We have a snob among us!" I was a snob, in conceding that I was a petit bourgeois and would have to speak like one. Then Mike Gold followed, and put the steamroller on me. Then a German émigré, Friedrich Wolf, attacked my proposal to address the "people" rather than the "workers." He pointed out the similarity between this usage and Hitler's harangues to the *Volk*. And so on, and so on— until I was slain, slaughtered. The whole situation was reversed now. I felt wretched. I remember, when leaving the hall, I was walking behind two girls. One said to the other, as though discussing a criminal, "Yet he *seemed* so honest!"

I was tired out. I went home and tried to get to sleep. (There had been a late party the night before, after the meeting in the big hall uptown.) I lay down and began to doze off. But of a sudden, just as I was about to fall asleep, I'd hear "Burke!"—and I'd awake with a start. Then I'd doze off again, and suddenly again: "Burke!" My name had become a kind of charge against me—a dirty word. After this jolt had happened several times, another symptom took over. Of a sudden I experienced a fantasy, a feeling that excrement was dripping from my tongue. Some years before, in an early story, I had used this image in connection with an imaginary character—and now it was happening to me almost literally. I felt absolutely lost.

Later in the day, I ran across Harold Rosenberg. He took me down to some group that was a splinter of a splinter of a splinter—and that episode helped me get things back into proportion. Those fellows thought that the incident that I had taken so seriously was funny. "So they put the screws on you!" They laughed. That helped.

But I should add one more detail. The next day there were some meetings of special groups: playwrights, novelists, poets, et cetera. I attended one chaired by the friend to whom I had originally shown my paper before I read it at the general meeting. When someone indicated that he wanted to speak, my friend would acknowledge him: "Comrade So-and-So." Then someone else—again he was recognized by the chair as "Comrade." Then I put up my hand, rather timidly, to indicate that I had something to say. My friend said: "Com—er—Mr. Burke." No *tovarich,* just *gospodin* Burke. It's amusing to think back on such things now—but I was greatly scared at the time.

Mr. Phillips: I don't think I was at that session. What specifically were they against?

Mr. Cowley: Let me read at this point. Burke had written:

> The question arises: Is the symbol of the worker accurately attuned to us, as so conditioned by the reactionary forces in control of our main educational channels?
>
> I tentatively suggest that it is not. By this I do not mean that a proletarian emphasis should be dropped from revolutionary books. The rigors of the worker must certainly continue to form a major part of revolutionary symbolism, if only for the reason that here the worst features of capitalist exploitation are concentrated. But the basic symbol, it seems to me, should be focused somewhat differently. Fortunately, I'm not forced to advocate any great chance—though I do think that the shift I propose, while minor in itself, leads in the end to quite different emphases on our modes of propaganda. The symbol I should plead for, as more basic, more of an ideal incentive, than that of worker, is that of "the people."

This comes from *American Writers' Congress,* page 89.

Mr. Phillips: What was so unorthodox about that?

Mr. Cowley: This was what Joe Freeman, and Allen Porter, and Friedrich Wolf and others jumped down Kenneth's throat for, and left him feeling that he was dripping excrement from his tongue. And merely because he had suggested what was actually going to be done by the Congress of the Comintern on August 2 of that same year.

Mr. Burke: Between the time of the Congress and the time when the book came out, they had a chance to change history, all right.

Mr. Cowley: They'd already decided to change "the workers" to "the people."

Mr. Burke: Before the report of the Congress the party line had changed—so the strongest details of the slaughter are simply omitted.

Mr. Cowley: Burke's paper was almost the only one delivered at the Congress that can be read today, not historically, but with interest in what he had to say. It was a paper on revolutionary symbolism.

Mr. Aaron: And yet, I think it's only fair to say that this line that Kenneth Burke took did not stop in 1935, and you can find articles and reviews in the *New Masses* when Granville was editing it in which similar ideas were expressed, where proletarian literature was criticized for failing to take into consideration many of the ideas that you suggested. James Agee would be one and there were a number of other critics and writers who pointed out that it might be a good thing for proletarian writers to look at bourgeois literature and to take certain hints from bourgeois literature in appealing to the broad masses of the American people.

Mr. Hicks: I never edited the *New Masses*.

Mr. Aaron: Well, you were a literary editor of the *New Masses*.

Mr. Hicks: For a while, yes.

Mr. Aaron: Yes. But while you were a literary editor of the *New Masses* such articles did appear. This is my point.

Mr. Cowley: I want to read some more about this. This is funny. This is a novel by James T. Farrell called *Yet Other Waters*. Jim Farrell, who believes in truth in fiction, set down his memories of the Writers' Congress as accurately as he could set them, and accurately enough so that I recognized everybody he mentioned. Here comes the Burke episode.

John Keefe, a chunky little man, with a esoteric critical reputation, was monotonously reading his paper in which he suggested that the slogan "a people's literature" would be more attractive than the words "proletarian literature." But his reasoning was involved and obscure, and Bernard [that means Jim Farrell], along with many others in the audience, became restless. He thought Keefe was totally wrong in trying to approach the problems of literature in terms of slogans even though his was more liberal than the one prevailing.

When Keefe finished and was vigorously applauded, Jake [that's Joe Freeman] rushed up on the stage. Howard Mather [that's Granville Hicks] gave him the floor, and Bernard was surprised when Jake spoke with such vehemence. Why should Keefe's paper rouse Jake in this way? Pounding the rostrum, Jake stigmatized Keefe's slogan as dangerously and subtly reactionary. It could be used as a justification of the Kuomintang in China, he shouted. And, in even greater anger, he declared that a reactionary Social-Fascist government in Mexico had used Keefe's slogan of "the people" and "a people's literature" to fool the workers. Banging his fist on the rostrum again, he cited the pre-revolutionary history of Russia as a further refutation. For, Jake shouted, the Narodniki, the intellectuals, had gone to the people with a nonclass slogan, and, after having played a progressive role, had then proved completely reactionary. Jake next mentioned Senator Huey Long, and, gesturing extravangantly, he asked:

"Is it or is it not true that Huey Long could use this slogan of—the people?"

That is page 123 of Farrell's novel called *Yet Other Waters.*

Mr. Burke: I'd like to add, finish one final point about all this. The next day, as I walked down the hall, I saw Joe Freeman coming. And I started to cringe away. I felt embarrassed at such a meeting. But Joe came up and smiled and shook hands with me, and said, "Well, I'm sorry, old man." It was all over! And when the list of members for the Council of the League of American Writers was proposed for adoption by the Congress (and of course adopted) my name was among them.

I have one further little story. I want to tell that, and then I'll shut up. Some friends of mine had an aquarium, with a frog in it. He was a big frog, but there was a cover on it so that he couldn't get out. Then somebody gave them a little frog, and they put the little frog in the same aquarium. And the two frogs would sit there side by side. One day my friends looked in—and by God they couldn't find the little frog. The top was on, but where was the little frog. They looked all around, no little frog. All of a sudden they spotted him. There were his feet sticking out of the big frog's mouth. So they pulled him out; and since he hadn't started to get digested yet, he was all right. All they could do with him was put him down in the aquarium again. And they did. The next time they looked in, these two fellows were sitting side-by-side. All was forgiven. I often think of that story when I think about politicians.

Mr. Cowley: So Joe Freeman was the big frog and you were the little frog, and you finished up sitting side-by-side.

Mr. Aaron: Where you presiding, Granville, at that?

Mr. Hicks: Apparently. I didn't remember that.

Mr. Cowley: Granville remembered another occasion, but that was the Second Writers' Congress, on which the critics' commission got together. That was a nice story in your book, Granville.

Mr. Hicks: Well, that was a very sad episode for me. Anyway, Phillips and Rahv and the *Partisan Review* had removed themselves from the party auspices. And they were joined by Dwight Macdonald and Mary McCarthy. Am I right?

Mr. Aaron: Among others.

Mr. Hicks: They picked out the session on criticism in the second Congress over which I was presiding to make a kind of demonstration. And they made it. Well, the one smart thing I said, as far as I can remember, is when Joe Freeman spoke up and said, well now, can we discuss criticism? I said, no, Joe, that's the one thing we cannot talk about. We never did talk about it.

Mr. Phillips: What did we talk about?

Mr. Hicks: The fact that the Communist party was dominating the Second Writers' Congress. It was the truth.

Mr. Phillips: Yeah. I had confused for a moment the two Congresses. This one was at the New School. At the second one I was a member of a small, dissident and noisy band—Macdonald, Mary McCarthy, Eleanor Clark, Fred Dupee, Rahv and myself.

Mr. Hicks: That's right, I had forgotten that. And, to my great amazement, F. O. Matthiessen lent you aid and comfort, which I was very unhappy about.

Mr. Phillips: I haven't read your book yet. Is this in your book?

Mr. Hicks: Yes.

Mr. Phillips: Well, this may amuse you, what I'm going to say. It may be interesting; it's the underside of the picture. This band of ours, this dissident band, was really pushed or propelled by Mary McCarthy and Dwight Macdonald. The rest of us thought that it was silly and a waste of time to go into this conference and be critical, and be steamrollered.

Mr. Hicks: No.

Mr. Phillips: Mary McCarthy and Dwight Macdonald felt it was immoral not to express our opposition to the way the meeting was run—that's why we spoke up at the session of which you were chairman.

Mr. Cowley: I want to get in at this point, lest I fail to get it in later, one story about me and the *Partisan Review.* Bill, did you ever know that I saved the *Partisan Review?* I saved it on two occasions, as a matter of fact, and the second I won't bother to mention, but the first was very funny. After that first Writers' Congress, the idea was to ditch and destroy all the magazines that had been issued by the various John Reed Clubs and to substitute for them a new quarterly that was to be gotten out by the League of American Writers. I wasn't much interested in the new quarterly because I was working for the *New Republic,* but I attended the meetings of the executive commit-tee at which plans for it were being laid—of course, they were never carried out. At one point Trachtenberg said, "We'll tell them to stop publishing the *Partisan Review.*" I was pretty indignant. "They've gotten out a good magazine," I said, "and they've done it themselves. Let them go ahead with it." After meeting with this opposition from the executive committee, Trachtenberg didn't carry out what seem to have been party orders to kill the *Partisan Review.*

Mr. Aaron: What year was that, Malcolm?

Mr. Cowley: Thirty-five, the summer.

Mr. Phillips: I'd forgotten this. I vaguely recall now hearing a story that sounded something like this, but I never knew it exactly as you're telling it now.

Mr. Aaron: I would like to know from William Phillips just exactly how the change from the old *Partisan Review* to the new *Partisan Review* took place. Can you explain this to us?

Mr. Phillips: You mean practically, financially, intellectually?

Mr. Aaron: Well, practically—

Mr. Phillips: What do you mean?

Mr. Aaron: Practically and intellectually. I'm not so concerned about the financial aspect, although that may be important.

Mr. Phillips: Well, when you say changed from one to the other, I don't know what you mean.

Mr. Cowley: From thirty-six to thirty-seven.

Mr. Aaron: The old *PR,* and the new *PR.*

Mr. Phillips: When you say, "How did it happen," you mean you want me just to recite events—

Mr. Aaron: Yes.

Mr. Phillips: I should say something else first. I've thought a lot about the period. And I used to have a pretty good memory; I had something close to total recall of these events. And I found myself, as the years went on, suppressing it. I must have been doing this for very good reasons, but I won't go into them.

Mr. Burke: No.

Mr. Aaron: His own experiences later—

Mr. Phillips: I found myself suppressing many of these things and not thinking about them. So I now have to recollect in a kind of stammering way. Well, we were, as you know, becoming more and more critical of the way the Communist party acted like an octopus, putting its hands on everything and trying to keep everything under control. And as we became more and more disaffected and more and more critical, we decided that we couldn't go on any more with the old *Partisan Review.* It is as simple as that. So we stopped publication.

Mr. Aaron: Now, when was this?

Mr. Phillips: This was in 1936. We thought of putting it out again as an independent magazine. But you will all recognize immediately what I'm saying. It's perhaps an historical cliché, although it is the opposite of what Cowley was saying, the other side of the coin. Aside from the fact that there were some practical difficulties (like not having any money), when one broke away from all these things one considered awful, one had a terrible sense of loneliness and paralysis. It was very hard to do anything. None of us was so sure of himself that he could just go out and act simply and directly. There was a period of about a year or two of drifting. In that period I met Fred Dupee, who succeeded you, Granville, I think, on the *New Masses* as literary editor. I noticed that Fred Dupee was also disaffected. And Fred Dupee asked me if I'd like to meet a friend of his—is this what you're asking?

Mr. Aaron: Yes.

Mr. Phillips: He thought his friend—who turned out to be Dwight Macdonald—would be interested in my views. I'd also talked to Fred about starting up *Partisan Review* again as an independent left-wing and anti-Communist organ. Anti-Communist means something else now. It's had so many meanings all these years that I hesitate to use the term.

Mr. Aaron: May I interrupt. When you say anti-Communist, would it be fair to say Trotskyist?

Mr. Phillips: No. I'll get into that in a minute. Well, I can answer that right now. We've called other people names, we've been called names, you know. The so-called historical record has been muddied up a little bit with some of these names. We were never real Trotskyites. I would say that we were vaguely sympathetic to the Trotskyites because Trotsky had been critical of the Communist party in a constructive way. His criticism was made in the name of freedom and democracy, and this was what we ourselves were fumbling for.

Mr. Hicks: I certainly thought at the time that Macdonald and McCarthy were Trotskyites; I thought they were taking you other three into their net.

Mr. Phillips: No, Mary McCarthy was not very political at all. Dwight Macdonald became, I think, for a short period a Trotskyite, although he was really associated with one of the factions. But we actually were the ones who converted Macdonald. Macdonald was moving toward the Communist party when we met him. He came down to my house one day and we argued all day long, from morning to night. I had his back up against a wall. I remember my wife was yelling, "Leave him alone, leave him alone, leave him alone, let him breathe." This was on a Sunday and I remember we called it Bloody Sunday. He came in at nine o'clock and said that he felt sympathetic to the Communist party. He had worked on *Fortune,* and he was moving left. We said it would be a mistake to work with the Communist party. The argument went on all day long. At the end of the day Dwight Macdonald finally gave in. Then we became practical and decided to put out *Partisan Review* again, with the help of Macdonald's friend, George Morris, who was totally unpolitical. Then Mary McCarthy and Fred Dupee joined us. Mary McCarthy was not very political at that time, although she had moral convictions about politics.

Mr. Cowley: Mary's sentence to me at the Second Writers' Conference was, "We're just wreckers."

Mr. Phillips: We're just wreckers. Really, I don't remember that. She must have been boasting.

Mr. Cowley: And that, that applied to Mary but not to the others.

Mr. Phillips: Well, let me say this again about Mary. It could help to be objective about this. Mary is a good friend of mine, and I think highly of her. I think that she was very intelligent, she had proper instincts; she loved intellectual excitement, and the situation was exciting. She was really at her rhetorical and intellectual best when people were arguing and fighting. At that time there was a lot of ideological commotion and people were at each other. Anyway, Mary was engagée, although she was one of the least political of us. Dwight Macdonald was rapidly becoming politicalized. Fred, strangely, was not a very political man. He was just the literary editor of the *New Masses.* I think you agree with me, Granville?

Mr. Hicks: He had been on the waterfront, he was working in a waterfront union; and yet you're quite right, he was never very political.

Mr. Phillips: He wasn't very political, no. I mean, he was and still is a man of considerable sensibility, but not very political.

Mr. Aaron: One more question, why did you keep the name *Partisan Review?*

Mr. Phillips: I don't know whether I can answer that question honestly and objectively. I would answer it with a reconstruction, and perhaps, therefore, I shouldn't answer it. What I was going to say was that we felt we were going to continue the traditions of the magazine. We believed, as everyone believes, I think, that people, especially writers, in order to exist at all have to have a sense of their own continuity. I'm really trying to be objective when I say this. We felt at the time—and obviously let's say Granville Hicks did not feel the same way—that we were going to continue whatever was good in the magazine, which would include its radical tradition, without benefit of any supervision or direction by any political group or organization.

Mr. Hicks: I now think you were entirely right. Tell me one thing just for the record, how was *Partisan Review* financed in '35, '36?

Mr. Phillips: You mean the old *Partisan Review?*

Mr. Hicks: After the John Reed Club folded up, how did you keep going?

Mr. Phillips: Well, of course, a dollar went further then than it does now, so you didn't have to raise so much money. Nobody got paid very much. In other words, expenses were very low. You know how the initial money was raised.

Mr. Aaron: You mean, after the breakup of the John Reed Club?

Mr. Phillips: You're not talking about the initial money?

Mr. Hicks: No.

Mr. Phillips: Well, only a few issues came out around that time. We still ran, but not in the name of the John Reed Club, a couple of lectures, and a couple of dances. In other words, we continued some of the activities which we had been running before under the auspices of the John Reed Club. We had the best dance floor in New York—

Mr. Aaron: This was at Webster Hall.

Mr. Phillips: No, it was in a building downtown on Sixth Avenue near Eighth Street. And we had a few lectures for which we charged some admission—

Mr. Hicks: One of which I gave.

Mr. Phillips: That's right, one of which you gave. I'd forgotten that—

Mr. Hicks: And a woman fainted.

Mr. Phillips: Well, that's all, it was as simple as that.

Mr. Burke: I have taken a few notes here, on the present discussion. I think there are two kinds of considerations being dealt with. There are organizational problems, problems of how you ran a magazine, matters of that sort. And there's something that, for lack of a better word, I have thought of calling "formal" matters concerning human nature in general. When William Phillips was trying to explain a matter of organization, he brought up what seemed to me a tremendously formal, tragic or comic or satiric kind of issue that involves human nature in general. He said he found himself "suppressing" memories. In other words, here was a change of identity that went much deeper than the problems of running one of those particular machines in a particular way. And as I once wrote you, Dan, although I felt that you'd done a wonderful job of summing up the era on the top level, you didn't get into the question of personal quandaries. It wasn't your job. But this other field is involved—and I think that William Phillips touches on it when touching on questions of identity implicit in the suppressing of memories. So I was wondering what is the ultimate implication of all this. That is: What are the problems, the risks of automatism and so on, that we confront, as we go from one such situation to another? Insofar as we're all pedagogues of a sort, how might our concerns fit in with those of *The American Scholar?* When we talk of action, we do so as pedagogues. What, then, in sum, is our problem as pedagogues? Could it be the study of human temptations, the lore of human stupidity, including one's own? We come here this evening not in the attempt to get back at somebody, but because we're trying to understand things. And isn't that the best thing we've got to offer as regards the whole blamed business, isn't it? Okay, I—

Mr. Haydn: Mr. Chairman. What Mr. Burke just said is terribly interesting to me as the editor of the magazine. In what spirit have you come here? What have you felt as you talked? I've heard, I thought, some intimations of happy nostalgia, of affectionate amusement, of anger, of all sorts of emotions. Do you mind asking each member this question?

Mr. Aaron: I think that would be a very good way to end this discussion tonight. What do you think, Malcolm?

Mr. Cowley: I wanted to put on record about the 1935 Writers' Congress whatever we are able to put on record, while there was still time. For that reason I'd like to mention one thing we have missed up to now, namely, that nothing else but the radical movement, and specifically the Communist party, could have brought together such a large body of writers. Then I would like to say that the meeting served other purposes than were contemplated by its actual sponsors. For, when the writers were brought together, they were found to be interested in discussing not only the problems of the revolution that was then believed to be just around the corner, but also the problems presented by their various crafts, which were discussed in many of the papers. There had been one previous congress of writers, at the Chicago World's Fair—in 1891, wasn't it?

Mr. Aaron: 1893.

Mr. Cowley: Yes, 1893, and it was the only other congress of writers that had ever been held in this country. In a way, then, for the craft of writing, the 1935 Congress was a decisive event. I would also like to mention that there were various sequels to the Congress. One of them, to which I have already referred, seems to me quite interesting. From 1930 to 1935 the radical writers in America were mostly young writers; proletarian literature, so-called, was essentially a youth movement. In those years, too, whole congeries of writers appeared from impoverished backgrounds; I am thinking of William Saroyan, James T. Farrell, Otis Ferguson, Erskine Caldwell, Alfred Hayes, Robert Cantwell and many others. Those I have mentioned made names for themselves, but most of the new men who appeared in those years have been forgotten. Alfred Kazin for one has written about the period—

Mr. Aaron: He hasn't sunk.

Mr. Cowley: Until the 1930's, literature in this country had been first an upper-middle-class affair, then a middle-middle-class affair, then a lower-middle-class affair, but now for the first time we began to hear from whatever you want to call the impoverished classes, including the immigrants. The Armenians, the Russian Jews (not the German Jews, who had made an earlier appearance in literature, being more prosperous), and the Irish—not only the lace-curtain but the shanty Irish—one after another came forward during the 1930's, and their presence was very marked at the Congress. But most of them were among the youngsters, and the party had decided to shift over from the youngsters to the writers "of some standing" whose mere names would help along the revolutionary movement. The result of that decision became more and more marked during the four years between the First Writer's Congress and the Third, where almost all the delegates were persons "of some standing," and where they included many writers who had earned their standing through publishing in the cheapest sort of popular magazines. The effect on the younger writers was to alienate them from the Communist party. Some of them became Trotskyists, some became independent radicals, and some sheared off from the movement entirely. There was a new war between literary generations that started at this First American Writers' Congress.

Another result of the Congress was organizational; it was the founding of the League of American Writers. On that subject I have a number of memories. The League chose Waldo Frank as its president, and Waldo didn't do much work for it, so that the League by September of its first year was reduced to no dollars in the treasury, no organizational activity, and if it was going to survive at all, something had to be done. The League was kept alive by me, Isidor Schneider, Marjorie Fischer and Harold Rosenberg. We formed ourselves into a lecture committee.

First there was a great argument about whether or not to hold lectures. I attended that argument with a broken arm, coming down from Niantic, Connecticut. It was a broken arm on which I had a very complicated splint, rubber bands coming up above the shoulder to hold the bone in place, and extremely painful, and I was carrying a large suitcase. I stood in the corridor with no seat until a man gave me one. He had a seat next to the window, but looking at my broken arm, he made the other man move and gave me a seat on the aisle, so there would be room for the splint, and he talked to me. And who was he? He was a labor skate, an official of the Trainmen's Union, whom I had been taught from all good radical sources to despise. When we got into Grand Central Station, he carried my bag into the station and said he was going back on the 4:30 train, and if I would come back on that train too, he'd see that I got an aisle seat, and he'd take care of my bag at Niantic. So I left him and in the evening went to this meeting of the League, where we had a terrific argument about whether or not we were going to hold a lecture series. I won the argument finally, but as I went out of the terrible place where we were holding the meeting, there were double doors. I got to the first door, and two people went through ahead of me still arguing about whether the League should hold a lecture series, and slammed the door in my face. So I put down my suitcase, I opened the door, I held it open with my foot, I picked up the suitcase, I got through, and two other members of the League pushed ahead of me, opening the second door and closing it in my face. So I put down my suitcase and I pushed upon the door, held it open with my foot. I picked up the suitcase, and I got through. And I thought, My God when the revolution is won, is life going to be like this? But I had won my point and we did hold the lecture series. Meanwhile, the whole funds of the

League were held in a tin box on my desk. The lecture series was a success, not a grand success, but each time we held a lecture it proved very easy at that time to get speakers without paying them anything at all, while charging a quarter or thirty-five cents admission. A little more money would go into the tin box at each lecture, and by the end of the spring I had three hundred and fifty dollars in the box. That carried the League through the summer of 1936.

Mr. Haydn: Mr. Chairman, at the risk of seeming persistent, do you think Mr. Cowley was evading my question or simply answering it subtly?

Mr. Aaron: I think it's tangentially answered, but I think that we might go around now and see what other people have to say about their views and memories. What would you say, Granville?

Mr. Hicks: In 1950 or 1951 I was asked to give a talk at Bennington College about the thirties. The McCarthy era was beginning then, so I thought I would really try to tell these kids what it was like in the thirties, and I laid it on fairly hard. And after I had finished, several of the girls came up and said: "Weren't you lucky to have something to believe in, wasn't that wonderful, wasn't that a terribly exciting decade?: And I was unhappy about this, I was embarrassed, I'd oversold. But I think, now, on the whole, I was right and they were right. I mean, if you look back at it from a sufficient perspective, wrong as we were in many points, I do think it was a hell of an exciting decade.

Mr. Aaron: Was what?

Mr. Hicks: A hell of an exciting decade.

Mr. Cowley: Now what do you think of Auden's lines: "As the clever hopes expired/Of a low, dishonest decade," in that fine poem of his, "September 1, 1939"? It doesn't seem to me that our hopes were clever in the least. They seem to me rather innocent than clever. And the hopes expired, but with them, with those expired hopes, a sort of innocence and confidence went out of the world.

Mr. Hicks: Well, it looked bad from the point of view of 1950, but from the point of view of 1965, I think the thirties were a very exciting decade and a fairly productive decade.

Mr. Burke: Let's be frank. I think I inherited some feuds, and I think that if I had been slain, as maybe some of my enemies tried to slay me, I'd probably have been pretty vicious about it. But as it is, I thank God for my enemies. So far we here all have survived, and we can look back on that period with some equanimity. I inherited a feud with your magazine, friend Phillips, and I would like to end up by just reading a little quatrain which is off the record, and it goes like this, to do with your having given Sidney Hook the hatchetman job of reviewing a book of mine. But here is the quatrain:

Cockneys get their aitches wrong,
But if you would get yours true,
Then join the evergrowing throng
That puts an aitch in P()artisan Review.

Mr. Aaron: What about your reviews, William Phillips?

Mr. Cowley: "As the clever hopes expired of a low, dishonest decade."

Mr. Aaron: What would be your comment, Mr. Phillips? Is it a low, dishonest decade?

Mr. Phillips: No, it's not totally one. It's a half-honest decade. I really have mixed feelings. I think it's impossible to view this whole experience except with mixed feelings. Kenneth Burke seems to have unmixed feelings. Don't jog my memory because I'll tell everybody what happened with—

Mr. Burke: I think you're entirely right, I think you're entirely right, half-honest, half-assed.

Mr. Phillips: Exactly, half-honest, half-assed. As a matter of fact, this should be off the record, but you know, Kenneth, if I can call you Kenneth now, I must say this because I think this characterizes both the situation and our recollection of it. Memories that I've suppressed are being jogged now. You came up to the *PR* office after that review was written to complain about it and I said to you at the time that I'd like to see you write an answer to Sidney Hook's review—

Mr. Burke: I did write an answer, it's published in the—

Mr. Phillips: But you said before you wrote the answer you'd have to think about it, because you weren't sure but that the people on the *New Masses* and the Communist party might not like your doing that sort of thing.

Mr. Burke: I don't remember that, but you may be right. I couldn't deny it. It's very possible; I couldn't say that it isn't true.

Mr. Phillips: I'm reacting to your remark and I shouldn't.

Mr. Burke: I don't remember it, but it may be so. I will say that I did write an answer to it, and the answer was published in your own review. But from that time on, oof! What you boys did with my later works, by silence, plus Clem Greenberg's hatchetman job on my *Philosophy of Literary Form.* But that's off the record.

Mr. Aaron: Let's come back again now to William Phillips.

Mr. Phillips: Well, all of us suffered. We can probably match each other's sufferings. Now, as I was saying, I really have mixed feelings. First of all, I think I learned something. I think those of us who went through this period, in an active way, have a sense of history, of politics, of the relation of people to politics, of writers to politics, that people who did not go through this simply do not have. We may have done foolish things, we may have done naive things, we made a number of mistakes, but we're not so innocent, we're not so naive as—we're simply more sophisticated than—those people who never went through the experience that we did. I think there's no question about that. We can quickly, I notice, understand certain political things that other people don't understand.

As you remember, Eliot in *Tradition and the Individual Talent* says something about people who are always smarter than the past. He says, of course, they're smarter because what they know is the past. And it's very easy to be retrospectively smarter than ourselves or than each other. But I think that it would be shameful if we were to deny that past. I would like to stand by it, stand by its idealism and its stupidities. I did many, many foolish things. In fact, I was going to raise the question of how to write about this period earlier. I haven't read your [Hick's] book yet, but all of us have been at one time or another tempted or seduced, almost bribed into writing some kind of history or memoir of the past. I've always resisted, and one of the main reasons I've resisted is—I have written a little theoretically about it but never in the form of memoirs—is that I don't have the feeling that everything that happened to me was so important. Also I don't know how to write about my foolishness. Honestly, I haven't read your book, so I'm not being tactful here. But some of the other records I've read are full of self-inflation. If somebody was discussing how he reviewed a book, how his book was reviewed, or what someone said to him at a party—that becomes part of history. And I don't know just how to relate the little things that I was involved in to something big called history.

Another thing that occurs to me is that frankly I have mixed feelings about writers engaging in politics. On the one hand, of course, where else is this sort of free-lance, uncommitted or unfettered conscience or consciousness going to come from? Who else is going to scream about Vietnam now or Franco some years ago? On the other hand, writers are pretty stupid about politics, and that includes me, too. We're always making mistakes, we're joining the wrong movements or signing the wrong petitions, and making the wrong predictions. And there's a contradiction here which I cannot resolve. I don't know, maybe we just have to be both stupid and morally responsible—whatever that means.

I'm also very strongly conscious of the fact that we're living in a new period, and we simply must learn not to try to apply literally to the present what happened to us in the past. It won't work and nobody will listen to us. One thing the young people won't do is listen to us, whether we preach moderation to them, or our special brand of wisdom, or the need of ideology, or the need of abandoning ideology. First of all, they exist in their own situation and they simply cannot take over, as it were, our lessons and apply them to their situation. Besides, I feel some inhibitions when I talk to them because after all, how great were we? What problems did we really solve? Most of us gave up politics at some point, because it had become too much for us.

Mr. Cowley: Bill, what are you doing—now? You're teaching.

Mr. Phillips: Well, one of the things I'm doing is teaching, yes.

Mr. Cowley: Where?

Mr. Phillips: At Rutgers. And I'm editing *PR,* which is at Rutgers, and I'm writing—as Hiram Haydn very flatteringly thinks—not enough. Now the last—

Mr. Cowley: You have my feeling, Bill—to interrupt—that essentially the generation of the 1920's ruled the roost in American literature for about forty years, through a series, a concatenation of events. Now there is a new generation coming forward which is very very different. I say that mildly, but my feeling of this is as if a forest of pine trees were cut down and a new forest were growing up to take its place. Now I'm one of the last trees standing in the old forest, but I've seen this at last, at last. Owing to all these accidents, people kept discovering them up to 1950 or 1960. But now essentially a new generation is coming forward, the whole thing has changed, and a good deal of the new language I actually don't understand, and some of the rest of it I don't read.

Mr. Phillips: I think Malcolm is absolutely right. And before we talk, as I think we should, about some of the concrete qualities and views of the new generation, I'd like to make one observation I think might be suggestive about how intellectuals and writers function in relation to politics. In the thirties, I think we were acting on an implicit idea, the Marxian idea of the writer and the intellectual as the alienated man. And as the alienated man he naturally was outside of society. But having a little bit of class consciousness, he sided with the radical forces of society. That was his political role, in alliance with the working class and other active and strong social forces. Later the writer continued to give his opinions on politics, mainly because he was a celebrity, not because he was an alienated member of society, or because he was an ally of some progressive historical force, but because he'd written a television play or something. He was a celebrity, he was famous, and if he was famous, he was supposed to say something about what was going on, usually in protest to what was going on.

Today, I think we've got a different situation, and you will notice that the New Left doesn't feature established intellectuals and writers as such; it features people who want to do something, activists. They want to go to Mississippi or they want to demonstrate. Some things they're doing are wonderful, some foolish, but they are acting, not theorizing. They burn their draft cards, they march, they have sit-ins. They don't have their poets or their novelists issuing statements to the press. In this respect they've emancipated themselves from some of the Marxian assumptions taken for granted by most of the people who belonged to the League of American Writers.

Mr. Burke: I get about six petitions a week. They ask me to sign these damn things; I don't know where they come from.

Mr. Phillips: Not the New Left. No, not the young Left, they aren't circulating petitions for you to sign.

Mr. Hicks: Didn't Irving Howe's statement in last Sunday's *Times* [December 5, 1965] sound essentially the same?

Mr. Phillips: Irving Howe is not a member of the New Left. Both Howe and the New Left would agree on this. As a matter of fact, some students once said to me, "You're not"—I told this to Irving Howe—"You're not like Irving Howe, you listen to us. Irving Howe doesn't listen to us, he's always telling us what to think."

Mr. Haydn: Perhaps it's time to wind this up.

Mr. Burke: Can we agree on one thing? Thank God for the enemy.

Mr. Aaron: I think that the whole question of the Left in the 1930's and the Left today might be the subject of another meeting which *The American Scholar* could sponsor, and that would be a very interesting one indeed. I hope, Mr. Haydn, that you might be interested in it to sponsor us at another meeting.

Mr. Haydn: Don't think I won't call on you.

An Interview with Malcolm Cowley

Page Stegner and Robert Canzoneri/1967

From *Per/Se* (Winter 1967–68), 34–39. Copyright © 1967 by *Per/Se,* Inc. Reprinted by permission of Robin White. All rights reserved.

Mr. Cowley, in a conversation at Denison University in November of 1966, discusses the current situation in literature, including the advent of the NOT-writer.

Stegner: Mr. Cowley, in your book *The Literary Situation,* speaking about the early fifties, you remarked that while there was a great proliferation of talent around, there seemed to be no single writer of great influence who was providing a directing force for young writers, as Hemingway had in the twenties and thirties. I wonder if in the years since you made the statement you think that such a figure has appeared on the literary scene?

Cowley: Not in any general sense. But within one important group of novelists—the Jewish novelists—I think that Saul Bellow has been giving a sort of leadership and direction. Among other groups I don't notice it so much. I can't tell whether any one person has begun to offer himself as a model that others are imitating, or whether it is just a group movement all in one direction.

Stegner: This might be called the age of the Jewish novelist.

Cowley: Oh, yes. We've had the age of the Midwestern novelist, the age of the Southern novelist, and at present it is more or less the age of the Jewish novelist.

Stegner: Why is that? Can you say?

Cowley: I don't know, except you can think this way, that the disadvantaged are advantaged in literature, because they have more pressure behind their wish to say something. That's something you have seen in this country as one group after another came to literary maturity. You can find that pressure or feeling of certain social disadvantages in Scott Fitzgerald, for example. Whatever else he

92

does, he is always making a reaffirmation of Irish virtue. I should think that in time, perhaps not in the distant future, we'll hear a great deal more from Negro novelists, as, of course, we *are* beginning to hear from them.

As one group after another becomes established, it loses some of the drive that is offered by the fact of its being disadvantaged. The Irish novelists of today do not feel the least bit of inferiority that they have to overcome. They are part of the establishment, but they still have some feeling of being alienated that gives a good deal of drive to their writing. The Southerners certainly felt disadvantaged.

Stegner: So that it is not necessarily a racial syndrome; it can be regional as well.

Cowley: It can be racial or regional or class, or anything else. But this drive created by the necessity of affirmation not only of yourself but of your whole group, racial or regional, is a powerful thing in literature.

Stegner: How much do you think the critical establishment affects or directs public taste?

Cowley: It affects it a great deal, but in complicated ways. For example, if the public begins to feel that any single group is pushing too hard in one direction, it begins to revolt. The only rule I have had to go on in looking at literary fashions over the last years is: Anything that is in fashion will go out of fashion. In other words, it all comes out in the wash.

Stegner: We may get a Western tradition yet.

Cowley: We may get a Western tradition. It is extraordinary, though, that there has been no Midwestern writing of much interest for the last thirty years.

Canzoneri: Is that because it became so much a part of the establishment?

Cowley: No. No. Perhaps Midwestern life was too comfortable, self-satisfied, to produce introspective writers.

Canzoneri: One question we have wondered about (and it is in connection with the critical situation): If a new Faulkner arose today, an experimentalist such as Faulkner was, do you think he would likely be out of print in some fifteen years?

Cowley: That depends on just how much he affronts the customs and standards of the age in which he writes. Some people go along with an equable reputation not varying much from year to year, and others do it like an inexperienced skier coming down the slope, making great yaws to right and left and tumbling head over heels. It seems that the more a writer is overestimated one year the more he is underestimated the next.

Canzoneri: What do you think of the present critical establishment in terms of power, in terms of the justice of its judgment? Do you think it is any better than it was in the early '40s?

Cowley: Criticism is better than it was in the early '40s. There wasn't very much of a power establishment in criticism in the early '40s, and then in the '50s the New Critics were more interested, for the most part, in expounding established works than they were in discovering new ones. Now there is once again an effort to establish a new group of writers, establish its members at the top of things. And that may be good or it may be bad, depending on the writers.

Canzoneri: What kind of work do you think is likely to be overlooked now?

Cowley: Plainly the social novel. That is the novel of manners dealing with a large area of interest and composed in a sound, complicated form. That sort of novel has not been popular with critics in the United States for a long time, as witness the great weight of critical disapproval bearing down on James Gould Cozzens. Now, Cozzens has faults as a novelist, but he also has some extraordinary virtues. One of them is that he is the best technician we have at present, the master of architectonics in the novel. A Cozzens book when it's going good is about as soundly constructed as any novel you can find. But that sort of novel has seldom been written in the United States by good men, and when it is written it doesn't seem to be valued.

Canzoneri: This is a thing that should come out in the wash, though.

Cowley: It takes a very long time.

Stegner: John O'Hara has made a fortune . . .

Cowley: He has made a fortune, but not by the aid of the critics.

Canzoneri: You were talking about the Midwesterner maybe being too comfortable. I wonder about an evaluation, looking back, of writers who like yourself went to Europe and came back and went to Connecticut? Would you evaluate Connecticut as a place for the writer to mature?

Cowley: Well, it is just a place; it's not a school of writers. It has an extraordinary mixture of people—popular writers, movie writers, dramatists, good, bad, all sorts. It is essentially people who are living in the far suburbs, or in a country district, so that it's had no deep effect on literature. People come to Connecticut to live and it doesn't seem to affect their writing.

Canzoneri: People who are uprooted from their original region?

Cowley: People who are uprooted, but at the same time would like to get back into a rural setting again.

Canzoneri: So they find a rural setting which doesn't have the social roots but does have at least the environment?

Cowley: It has the environmental roots and it's near New York, because business brings them into New York. I originally chose the little town in Connecticut that we live in because it was the closest real country to New York . . . the closest place where you had trout streams without No Trespass signs.

Canzoneri: It didn't take you long to see No Trespass signs, did it?

Cowley: No, the No Trespass signs came in and the trout went out, but I'm still there.

Canzoneri: I wondered about another thing which in my mind is connected with this. Do you see any group—I think of the campus group now—which is similar to the older generation of Villagers you describe in *Exile's Return*—the bohemians and the radicals who believed that the world could be saved, and who adopted costumes—as opposed to the younger group coming in, who, because of experience and other things, didn't have this kind of attitude?

Cowley: The younger group was cynical about the world, the social world, and wanted to find its compensations in the world of art. Its members were willing to live a quite modest life in the real world meanwhile and dress in whatever clothes they could afford to buy. That was a real division in Greenwich Village at that time. The big division at the present time is of course between the beards and the non-beards. The beards write a certain kind of poetry and the cleanshaven people write another kind of poetry—the cleanshaven people whom what's his name, you know, in San Francisco?—Kenneth

Rexroth—has called the bow-tie conspiracy. And that division is so marked in poetry that there were, two or three years ago, two anthologies of the new poetry in the United States, and I don't think any single poet was in both volumes. One volume was free-swinging and the other was academic.

Canzoneri: But don't you now see a rising group of people—beards and non-beards—who are socially activated, who do have a kind of costume in a sense and seem to believe very much what the older Villagers did—only now they are on the campuses? What I'm wondering is, with the Viet Nam conflict, if we aren't likely to have another highly disillusioned bunch of young men coming back to these very same places for a kind of repeat of the Village on the campuses.

Cowley: In the first place they couldn't be disillusioned by the war in Viet Nam because they were never illusioned by it. During the first World War there was a mass of patriotic sentiment and oratory—Save the World for Democracy. People did really march off to the war with the feeling that they were saving the world, and then when they found out that they had won the war and the world hadn't been saved, they came back disillusioned. But I can't see anybody coming back from Viet Nam with that same sort of disillusionment. He might come back angry, very angry, but not disillusioned, because he didn't go off with illusions. I don't know about these protests. Everybody has remarked on the decline of the civil liberties movement on the campuses. Of course SNCC really is partly responsible for that, because the white people who have been going to Mississippi recently haven't received a great warm welcome from the Negroes there. Some of them have come back disillusioned. I suppose it is a good thing—for the Negroes to run their own affairs, but every other minority in this country that has learned to prosper has done so by making alliances, and the Negroes at present seem to be unwilling to make them even with the Mexicans in this country, or with the Puerto Ricans, or with the Jews, who have always helped the cause of civil liberties more than any other group. The Negroes keep saying, "We'll go it alone," but how can eleven percent of the population go it alone?

Canzoneri: There is a problem there.

Stegner: The role of the university as a patron of the artist seems more and more prevalent. More and more universities seem to be getting writers in residence, and so on. Would you comment on the effect this has on our current literary situation?

Cowley: Of course, that's a completely new development. The whole relationship of a university to writers is new since World War I and almost since World War II. Remember that at the time of World War I and during the '20s there was no course in American literature at any but a few colleges. I don't think Harvard had one. It may have had a doctoral seminar in Emerson, or something like that, but for the rest there was no course in American literature. Then that began to build up during the 1930s at various universities, and at the same time they began to offer more writing courses. Of course there had been writing courses at Harvard since the 1890s, but soon they began to spread across the country. Michigan was one of the first to have a good writing department. Then came the business of bringing in writers-in-residence; Robert Frost at Amherst was one of the first. But all of this has spread broadly now, so that among writers the idea of going to a university for a year, a week, or a lecture is becoming much more common than it was previously. In many cases the university tries to put the writer or the artist on such a limited schedule that he will have time for his own work, and in that case the universities actually become patrons of the arts, as they have been patrons of the drama, too. This is an interesting development. I don't think it is all to the good all the way around. I'm always a little bit afraid of Mandarinism growing up in this country; in fact, one can see signs of it already. Nevertheless, it has been a good thing as a whole. It has been good for the universities, too, I think. It has brought them in more immediate touch with the living arts.

Canzoneri: Is the writer in this country, by virtue of being also a teacher or lecturer, more critical-minded than ever before? Is this affecting the writing at all?

Cowley: It may easily affect the writing. It may have a constipating influence. Of course, the writer should have his critical faculty developed as highly as possible. The trouble comes when the two faculties, critical and creative, get out of balance. If the critical faculty is built up too soon and too fast, then the writer becomes constricted and his work may lack any sort of freedom. A good many novels that come out of the academic background seem to me to be too tight.

The whole novel was figured out in advance. You can see where every chapter drops into the slot. It is all fine, but it is dead.

Stegner: Full of mythical patterns.

Cowley: And meanings on different levels.

Stegner: It used to be said that it was virtually impossible to make a living solely off writing. Considering the tremendous boom in the publishing industry in paperbacks and so on, is this still strictly true?

Cowley: It's still true that very few people make their entire livelihood out of writing books. A few people make enormous livelihoods out of writing, like Truman Capote, who spent five years on *In Cold Blood,* which will bring in about two million dollars. Well, that's a living. Even after Uncle Sam gets most of it, it's still a living. But there are very few jackpot authors and very many people who keep on paying their nickels into the slot machine and never getting anything back. The average book still sells two or three thousand copies. That means that the average royalty on it is about a thousand dollars.

Stegner: It seems as though there are more jackpots now than ever before.

Cowley: There are more jackpots now and the jackpots are bigger; they have never been so big. For those who don't make a living by writing books but nevertheless do write them, there are more subsidiary sources of income at the present time—lecturing, for example, and the foundations, which seem to be eager to help promising writers. That situation has developed so fast and far that at the present time you have a new profession in this country. It is the profession of being a NOT-writer. Sometimes it yields more in actual cash over the years than the book would yield. I don't know what the qualifications are for being a not-writer. I've been tempted to study them because of all professions it seems to me to be one of the most attractive. Somehow or other you have to start out by letting the rumor get around that you have a great deal of talent. Then you become a little bit mysterious about the talent. Preferably you don't show anything you write to anybody else, and if you are not writing anything anyway, then it's easy not to show your not-writing to not-readers. But the foundations hear of this, and they hear that the book that you are not-writing is going to be a great book when it is finished in ten years to twenty years, so they come across first with modest stipends of two to five thousand dollars, then ten thousand dollars from Guggenheim or Rockefeller—and I have no doubt that sometime in the not distant future there will be a Nobel prize established for the man who has not-written the most ambitious book.

Canzoneri: Please keep on.

Cowley: It goes beyond this, though. Among professions followed by the not-writers is teaching writing, or not-writing, on a college campus. Sometimes the not-writer on a campus is a very good teacher, but sometimes he is also twisted by his own experience, so that he teaches his students to despise anybody who is low enough, commercial enough to publish a book and expect royalties instead of foundation grants. So in that case the not-writer produces a whole little flock of not-writers following in his footsteps and also besieging the foundations for grants for these outstanding projects they always have that will be not-finished in 20 years. The other side of this is just a little bit deplorable for a simple-minded person like myself, because I've always felt that one of the things a writer has to do is write, and it seems to me that sometimes the writer who in spite of various obstacles does get books written, and gets them published year after year, is a little bit neglected in comparison with the not-writer who is not-writing James Joyce's *Ulysses*.

Stegner: You told a very funny story the other night about a woman (whose name we will not mention) who was not-writing a book for years and years . . .

Cowley: Yes, we better not bring names into it. I could bring one name into it, though, because the example of this one name had terrific effect on foundations and publishers. Katherine Anne Porter, a writer of high talent and great seriousness, was not-writing a novel for twenty years. In the course of those twenty years she got very substantial advances from publishers and very substantial grants and very substantial jobs from various universities. Then finally she spoiled everything by finishing the book and publishing it. Now, in this case, the book when finished and published received extraordinary reviews and was a best seller and was sold to the movies. This one example filled everyone else with the idea that he too could not-write a book for twenty years while living on grants and then have it be a great success. But I know of two or three other books that are being not-written at this time which are not going to be successful, which in fact are going to be sad duds.

Canzoneri: Do you think that the fact of the foundation grants, the patronage of universities, and the new government grants will be a detriment to literature?

Cowley: Oh, no, I think it is fine. I think that the more money that is poured into writing the better. For example, we are having a considerable production of works in American scholarship at the present time. Those works simply would not be funded without various forms of subsidy from universities and from the Guggenheim Foundation. One would have to be crabbed and bitter indeed to say that those works have not been useful; some of them have been exceptionally good. At the present time the English, who were ahead of us in scholarship for a long time, very much envy the work of American scholars, except they don't think it's very well written. So far the foundations have done less, I think, for fiction, because it's harder to pick out the writers in that field who are not only serious and promising but also are actually working.

Canzoneri: You can show progress better on a scholarly work than you can on a novel.

Cowley: A scholarly work can be judged better. Also I think the foundations' juries or committees have been a little anxious to make discoveries, so that they have granted their money in many cases to authors who are not only unpublished but perhaps never will be published.

Canzoneri: Haven't the foundations and these other sources had other effects which are less direct on the current literary situation?

Cowley: Well, the whole prosperity of the publishing business at the present time is dependent very largely upon grants from the foundations and the United States government to the libraries, which have increased the sale of books almost across the board, except for the cheaper varieties of entertainment. But the sale of serious books has probably . . . well, it has certainly increased. I would hate to set a figure on the increase, but for certain types of books it has been at least a hundred percent over the last ten years.

Canzoneri: Is this also increasing the range of titles published?

Cowley: It opens up publication possibilities for books that would have been rejected immediately by trade publishers ten years ago.

Now they say, "This sounds interesting. This will have a college-library sale, and perhaps it will even have course adoptions and be valuable in paperback." When I look back at my book *The Literary Situation,* finished in 1954, I see many things I missed in it and some that I didn't foresee at the time. The book was written just before the era of the so-called quality paperbacks; bookstore paperbacks would be a better term for them. They first became established through Jason Epstein, who edited Anchor Books for Doubleday; then Viking and Knopf went into the field, with Compass and Vintage books, and Harcourt Brace has the Heritage Library—there is a whole collection of these "libraries" now. The result is that a serious book which would have had a sale of two thousand copies and then have been allowed to go out of print is now, after that hardcover sale, reprinted as a quality paperback and will go on selling year after year. In some cases the sales are extraordinary. I know that *The Great Gatsby,* for example, which had a sale of twenty thousand copies in its first year, now has a sale of close to a quarter of a million copies *every* year. Charlie Scribner says it has taken the place of the *Mill on the Floss.*

Canzoneri: How does this quality-paperback situation affect the new novel, if at all?

Cowley: So far it's had almost no effect on the novel. I explained all this once in an article for the *Reporter.* The question is why new novels aren't brought out in paperback. The answer is that paperbacks are cheaper than hardcover books not primarily because they are in paper covers. That makes some difference, but not the big difference. The big difference is the author gets a lower royalty. The lower price of paperbacks comes out of the author's hide. In most cases, not always, if the publisher is to pay a respectable royalty to a new author and at the same time pay for the cost of promoting his work, the idea of selling the first edition of a novel for a dollar-and-a-half to two dollars, or now even two-fifty, in paper is rather presposterous. The publisher could not sell enough additional copies at that price to make it profitable. But at the same time the existence of the paperback has built up a great deal of resistance on the part of the public against paying five and six and seven and eight and ten dollars for a book. So we'll see a gradual movement in several directions. This is a fairly safe prophecy: paperbacks will continue to go up in price, authors will get higher royalties on paperbacks by fighting for them, and more and more often the original edition of the novel will be published simultaneously in hardcover and softcover. Then we shall see what the public likes best. If it really prefers the softcover book, perhaps in the end that will be the form that wins out. But this is not going to be a rapid process.

Canzoneri: I wonder if you could talk a minute about the situation with the different forms—the short story, the novel, non-fiction, poetry—as to the market, the possibilities.

Cowley: The short story had a tremendous development in this country, largely because of American magazines and because of the international copyright situation. There was no international copyright until 1891—I go back into history instinctively. The result was that the English novelist in this country got not a damn cent for publication of his work. He lost, and the American novelist lost, because the American novelist could not withstand that competition of absolutely free work. In the meantime American writers supported themselves by writing short stories for magazines. Most of the magazines in the '90s and the early 1900s created enormous markets for short fiction. An author like Jack London would make fifty thousand dollars a year out of writing stories at a time when that was equivalent to at least two hundred thousand a year now—not only because the dollar has depreciated in value, but also because there was no income tax in those days. You could live right well on fifty thousand a year.

Stegner: You could have a ranch in the Valley of the Moon.

Cowley: It is curious how magazines publishing short stories have gone out of business or have gone over to publishing non-fiction. Usually they have gone out of business. I don't know what the explanation is for those magazines still in business not publishing many stories, but they have gone more and more from stories into articles, and more and more of the magazines that are successful at the present time are not written by independent writers contributing articles, but are staff written from beginning to end, like *Time* and *Newsweek* and many others too. So the market for short stories has been contracting steadily. It comes down now to essentially the *New Yorker* plus one short story per issue—one per month—in *Harper's,* one per month in the *Atlantic,* and one or two per issue in each of the literary quarterlies. It isn't a very large market. And that has naturally led to an emphasis on the novel at the expense of the short story. The novel is not a dying form, or rather it is the fabulous invalid—it dies every year a horrible death and is resurrected on Easter Day and goes on for another year. In fact, the short story writer is urged by his agent or his publisher to write novels—except for one thing, that the mass-market paperback has been a market for stories to some extent. Stories sell better in newsstand paperbacks. The newsstand paperbacks have replaced the fiction magazine, and of course TV has partly replaced the general magazine. But non-fiction in this country has had a considerable development. I agree with Capote that there is such a thing as the non-fiction novel, except that he didn't invent the form; there always have been non-fiction novels. He practiced the form admirably, but there had been dozens and dozens of non-fiction novels before his time. I might even point to *Exile's Return* as a non-fictional novel.

Canzoneri: Right.

Cowley: It was done rather deliberately in that form. Not every good biography, but almost every good one might be called a non-fiction novel, and through using the technique of fiction and drama, non-fiction has become a more sophisticated medium. Then for the rest, poetry has always had the reputation in this country of being something to practice if you wanted to get into the poorhouse. It has yielded less money to its practitioners than any other form; and it still does. Nevertheless, there are higher financial rewards for poetry at present than there have been at any time in our past history. Not only because of foundations, which often help poets, and because of prizes, but also because of the government's stepping in with the National Endowment for The Arts—something which might not survive if the country elected a conservative Congress.

In the meantime the government has been trying to encourage poetry forums and reading trips by poets over the country. One thing it hasn't been able to encourage is the book publication of poetry. For a publisher to issue a first book of poetry is equivalent to the publisher's saying, "I shall now donate four thousand dollars to the arts"—and publishers do this quite deliberately. But then when the next poetry manuscript comes in they are likely to say, "Well, I paid my ante last year." In other words, book publication is still the weak side of the situation of poets. There are cases in which a poet has been unable to publish a book, but in which the University of Texas or the University of Buffalo library has bought the manuscript from him for more than he would have earned from it if it had been published. This is actual. I have heard of other cases in which the book was published and then the printer's copy of the manuscript was sold for more than the poet's royalties on the book.

Stegner: Maybe we can get up a new profession of NOT-publishing.

Cowley: That might very well be. Another factor in the literary marketplace that I don't think attention has been called to—and as the wife of the salesman who died said, attention must be paid—is that literary papers, roughly speaking, weren't worth anything ten years ago, and now may be worth considerable sums. I think of the nephew of Queen Victoria who wrote to her asking for a pound to buy sweetmeats. She sent him a letter explaining why a boy his age shouldn't have a whole pound. When they asked him, "What did you do?" the nephew said, "I took the letter down the street and sold it for a pound." That's what is happening with some poetry manuscripts.

Malcolm Cowley: Literature was a Substitute for Religion in the '20s

Joseph Haas/1971

From the Chicago *Daily News*, April 24–25, 1971, pp. 4–5, 10.

You can't call a muster of the great literary figures of the American '20s and '30s without listing the name of Malcolm Cowley. Renowned poet, critic, editor, literary historian, Cowley is all of that. And yet, modest man that he is, he is perhaps best known for having assumed the role of Boswell to his generation—Faulkner, Hemingway, Pound, Fitzgerald, Cummings, Crane, Wolfe, Steinbeck . . . and so many others.

Most of them are gone, their work absorbed by the curricula in American literature. But Malcolm Cowley, at 72, remembers them as they were, as the vibrant, profligate talents of as exciting an era as American letters is apt to produce.

The distinguished elderly critic, with his full head of silvered white hair and the well-clipped mustache of an English country gentleman, was in Chicago recently for the opening of an exhibit of the letters, papers and books he has donated to the Newberry Library.

The evidence of his lifelong fealty to literature filled every case of the Newberry exhibit that closed this week.

There are letters to and/or from James Thurber, Jack Kerouac, Scott Fitzgerald, W. H. Auden and Stephen Spender, Edmund Wilson and Katherine Anne Porter, Margaret Anderson of the *Little Review* and Nelson Algren, Hart Crane and Eugene O'Neill, William Carlos Williams and Burton Rascoe, Robert Coates and Kenneth Burke.

That was Malcolm Cowley's world, the life we wanted to discuss with him. First, how does he compare the writers of the '20s with those of today?

"It seems to me now more than ever that the writers of the '20s were all people of extraordinary personalities, the whole lot of them.

105

If you brought them together in one room," and his voice warms with love as he recites some of the names, "Fitzgerald and Hemingway and Faulkner, Thornton Wilder, Glenway Wescott and Cummings, Dos Passos and Pound—well, imagine the strength of that gathering of personalities! And each with a sort of devotion to the art of writing that you don't find so much today, I think.

"You found it in Thomas Wolfe. You can find it in *The Faulkner-Cowley File* (a collection of their exchange of letters over nearly two decades) or that interview with Faulkner in *Writers at Work* (which Cowley edited). You can see it in Hemingway's remarks about writing, this devotion to writing and the idea that it was the most important thing in life."

If the writers' attitudes have changed, what does Cowley believe caused this?

"My students at the University of Minnesota last winter kept telling me that one difference between the generations was that the present generation is more social-minded and less art-minded. They feel they have to change society and this is more important.

"But the '20s, that was such a vibrant generation. And at the present, they're still discovering new writers of that period. For goodness sake, take my old friend, Ramon Guthrie. His life nearly ended in September, 1918, when some goddamned fools sent his squadron out on a mission over the German lines in junky planes that were too slow and with machineguns that would always jam. They started with eight planes and two of them got lost in the clouds. The remaining six were jumped by 17 Fokkers from the Red Baron's squadron (although von Richthoffen had been dead for a month by then, it was still considered his squadron). Well, the Germans got five of the six planes—Ramon was the only one who got back to base.

"And now, after serving in World War II as a lieutenant-colonel in OSS, after being a professor at Dartmouth for 30 years, being retired and," and Cowley's voice indicates that this is an ultimate ignominy, "even being dropped from *Who's Who,* finally as he writhes on what everyone thinks of as his death bed, he writes an extraordinary book-length poem *(Maximum Security Ward).*

"There are others from the '20s who are unjustly neglected. The poets John Brooks Wheelwright and Phelps Putnam. Novelists like Robert M. Coates and, from the '30s, Nathan Asch. Nathan, Sholem

Asch's son, had four books published in the '30s and then went off to serve for four years as a bomber-sergeant in World War II. When he came back, he couldn't get anything published.

"He died about four years ago of lung cancer, leaving behind great piles of manuscripts of which I've read several. The trouble is that, as he finished 'em up, there is no single book. But if some good editor got to work on them, there would be a tremendous book in that abandoned mass of writing. When he was good, he was awfully good."

How does Cowley feel *The Literary Situation* (the title of a book he completed in 1954) compares today with the way it used to be?

"Any time is a good time for a writer or a bad time. The problem of staying alive is somewhat easier now for writers, with so many prizes and awards and fellowships and university posts. Why, even a poet can keep himself alive by giving readings today.

"It was very hard for the writer in the '20s—hard to keep himself alive while he was getting started. It was not a boom time in culture despite the economic boom."

Which does he feel helps the writer produce his best work, hard times or easy times?

"I'd be a damned fool if I answered that question . . .

"But I've seen a lot of people corrupted by easy times. And I saw a lot of writers corrupted by the movies in the 1930s. Faulkner said, though, that if a man loses his soul to the movies, he never had one to lose. He kept his.

"You know, Faulkner was hired by Warner Bros. on a long-term contract. They didn't know who the hell he was, but he could write dialog on the set, so they kept him on. He actually wasn't as good on plot as he was on dialog. He had a tendency shared with Scott Fitzgerald to overplot a story. But he got screen credits for several films, of which his favorite was one called *The Southerner* with director Jean Renoir. He also did the adaptation of Hemingway's *To Have or Have Not*, which had absolutely nothing to do with Hemingway's book when Faulkner was finished with it—but it was a good movie."

Which books does Cowley feel were the great books of the '20s and '30s?

"Well, one that is not considered great today, Hemingway's *For Whom the Bell Tolls,* is his best book, but it's unfashionable to say so.

"It's a tremendously complicated book, not about what people think it is about. It is actually a mystical book on at least one of its aspects, about the conquest of time, turning time into an eternal present by a sort of mystical experience: Living as richly in 70 hours as you could in 70 years. That theme is played out against the background of the Spanish Civil War, which also goes in, and you finally end with Hemingway to some extent making Robert Jordan a Christ figure. The whole thing is very rich and complex."

Why, then, is *Bell* often put down as a lesser book and *The Sun Also Rises* hailed as Hemingway's masterpiece among the novels? Did *Bell's* popularity tend to diminish its stature with the critics?

"Yes, there is some truth to that. Another reason, however, is that it offended all of the political sects absolutely, from the right to the left. There was something in it to offend everyone when so much criticism was politically oriented.

"Another great novel, an extraordinary book that was also an enormous success and that has been much ignored, is John Steinbeck's *The Grapes of Wrath.* People tended to think of it in terms of the Okies and their plight, and when they were hired by the aerospace industries or began to own garages or pump gas, people felt the reason for the book was gone and abandoned it.

"But this is another very complicated book with all sorts of symbolic overtones and parallels with the Bible. The critics began to cop on to this aspect of it about 10 years ago and, since then, it's coming on like mad; it's back for teaching again. But that was the peak of Steinbeck's career. He didn't continue to do good work after that.

"As for Scott Fitzgerald, I was in an argument yesterday with a young man from the University of Miami who plans to do his dissertation on my work. But for him, the great Fitzgerald book is *Tender is the Night,* and I argue, yes, that's a book that gains one's affections, but if you want a book that is beautifully put together, that stands as a unity, you have to go back to *The Great Gatsby.*

"With Faulkner, the greatest single things he wrote are the stories, 'The Bear' and 'Spotted Horses.' Otherwise, my feeling is Faulkner is great for his over-all story, carried on through book after book, with some tremendous writing."

Faulkner, then, is the pre-eminent literary figure of Cowley's period?

"I think he is, as far as total production is concerned. But I always find a great difficulty in comparative ranking of authors. It seems to me like trying to compare a pound of beans with a bushel of feathers. I mean, what common ground has Faulkner with Fitzgerald? Or, if you get beyond this country, with Joyce or Proust or Mann, who's not getting the attention in this country that he ought to? Why try to rate them comparatively?"

Does he feel a sort of proprietary interest in Faulkner because of his role in restoring the author's works to print?

"No, by God! This man is too great for me or for anybody else to claim any credit for. What I did essentially was to read all of the books and see the connections between them, the whole cycle of Yoknapatawpha County, and to get that into the *Portable Faulkner*. And the reason that collection had such an impact was simply that I wasn't alone, other people had been feeling the same thing about Faulkner, so as soon as the *Portable* came out, it was widely reviewed. You don't expect a Viking *Portable* to get the front page of the *New York Times* Book Section, but it did. And Robert Penn Warren wrote a splendid essay for *The New Republic*. So the *Portable* was the turning-point, but only that. But it did give me great satisfaction to play a role in it."

The *Faulkner-Cowley File* seems to indicate that Faulkner was given to straining the truth at times?

"Not with me. But he did tell a lot of lies to interviewers. It was sort of a grand disdain for them, a putdown.

"I'm not sure that all the stories he told me about his adventures in New Orleans were 100 per cent true. I'm waiting for Joe Blotner's biography to find out whether Faulkner really ever was a rumrunner. That's Joseph L. Blotner of the University of Mississippi,* who is writing the more or less authorized Faulkner biography. Watch for that one; it should come out next September."

*Blotner was a visiting professor at the University of Mississippi, but he has been at the University of Michigan for many years.

How does Cowley feel about the "new biography" that leaves no area of an author's life sacred, such as Carlos Baker's *Ernest Hemingway,* Nancy Milford's *Zelda* and Michael Holroyd's *Lytton Strachey?*

"I haven't been very much in favor of it in some biographies. It seems to me too much of the weak side of people is pointed up. Carlos Baker distinctly played up the Mr. Hyde side of Hemingway and de-emphasized the Mr. Jekyll, and Hemingway was tremendously generous.

"For instance, in the Baker biography, there was none of Hemingway's generosity to other veterans of the Spanish Civil War. And he helped them all, substantially. And Hemingway was absolutely charming. He was modest and attentive and he would listen to you, to one person at a time, and completely. I think he was really shy, too, in a way.

"Once, out of nowhere, I received this large envelope from Ernest and inside there was a letter and a manuscript. He wrote, 'I'm enclosing the manuscript for the introduction I just wrote for *A Farewell to Arms,* and I thought you might like to have it.'

"And I said to myself, 'What do I want with this manuscript?' Well, Ernest added in his letter, 'Perhaps sometime you'd like to sell it.' About 15 years later, I had an appraiser over to my place to look at my papers and books and he looked at that manuscript and said, 'I'll put that down for $1,500.' That was Ernest, simply turning over to me something that was worth $1,500."

What about *Zelda,* which was a much more revealing book about Scott Fitzgerald and the odd relationship with his wife than Arthur Mizener's *The Far Side of Paradise?*

"I thought Nancy Milford did a very good job. And there was new information. It cast light on Scott that I never had known before.

"Scott was a volatile mixture. He was extremely likeable, but he could get drunk and do crazy or offensively brutal things. I didn't know Scott as well as Ernest and Bill Faulkner, but I found him most of the time tremendously thoughtful, polite, interesting and charming.

"Hart Crane was another Jekyll and Hyde, the Mr. Hyde coming out mostly when he was drunk. Sober, he was tremendously thoughtful. He got my first book of poems published for me—he took them from me, put them togther and found a publisher and all at a time, you would think from other stories, that he was on a continuous revel. But then, he'd drink heavily and become violent, throwing furniture out, reeling around the country house with an oil lamp. To be at a party with Hart meant that some time the phonograph would be turned on and Hart would begin dancing, dancing, with everybody. It was the most athletic, frantic dancing, like savages around a fire."

He laughs, remembering those parties. When his laughter ends, Cowley says, "Such good times! Such roars of laughter!

"No, those men weren't average people in any way. They were great individualists. And they had their moments of madness.

"But their devotion to writing! For the contrast with today, read something like Norman Podhoretz' *Making It.* He sounds essentially like a dentist in Queens in his attitude toward his 'career.' "

How did Cowley come to help Kerouac get *On the Road* published?

"Oh, there were sometimes people I helped to get past the editorial board at Viking. Kerouac turned in the manuscript and Viking turned it down. I got *Paris Review* to print part of it and, when he finally resubmitted it to Viking (after several other rejections), I managed to persuade the other editors to go ahead with it.

"Later, I think Jack was corrupted by the notion that every word that fell from his lips was more or less sacred. Automatic writing is a fine theory for the writer, but why in hell should anyone have to read it?"

How much help did he give to Kesey with *One Flew over the Cuckoo's Nest?*

"He was writing it while he was in one of my classes, though it was started before I went out to Stanford. But Kesey does his own writing. I had a hand in it to this extent: I persuaded him to omit some sections because they seemed to me repetitious, over-drawn. So there wouldn't be a word in the book that is mine, so to speak.

"I haven't been in touch with Ken in a long time, but I've heard he was off drugs and living quietly in Oregon. I hope he comes back to writing. When he was in my class, he told me he had a half-dozen novels he had all planned and wanted to write."

And what about Cowley's writing? Is he working on his memoirs or his collected papers and criticism?

"Oh, I write episodes from my memoirs now and then, but I doubt if I shall try to bring them together. I might do a book about the '30s—in fact, I have one about half-written. As for the papers, I won't do anything with them—someone else might."

How does he feel about much of the new experimental writing being done today, the "new novel" and "anti-literature"?

"I was just reading an anthology called *The Anti-Story*. I think that's cockeyed because the story is a fundamental form and what distinguishes it is the sequence of events. What the editor of this collection is saying, in effect, is that a great many current writers are trying to disregard events. It puts me off—puts me to sleep.

"There was a story in there, however, by Joyce Carol Oates. It had the distinction of being a real story and it was superb. No, I haven't read her novel, *Them*. I read Doris Lessing's *The Golden Notebook*, too, and I was crazy about it. I thought it was the most extraordinary book I had come across in a long time. But I haven't gone on to read the rest of Lessing.

"I'm becoming such a bad reader."

The Importance of Knowing Ernest

Denis Brian/1972

In Ernest Hemingway's Story *My Old Man,* a son overhears two men talking about his dead father. "Well, Butler got his, all right." . . . "I don't give a good goddamn if he did. . . . He had it coming to him on the stuff he's pulled." Another man comforts the son, "Don't you listen to what those bums said, Joe. Your old man was one swell guy." When Lillian Ross wrote her Profile of Hemingway in *The New Yorker,* a lot of people thought that "Papa," as they called him, everyone's old man, had "gotten his." Opinion was divided as to whether he "had it coming" or was a misunderstood "swell guy."

Twenty years after Lillian Ross's Profile appeared in the May 13, 1950, *New Yorker,* Denis Brian visited the reigning Hemingway authorities to get their views of Miss Ross's view of Hemingway. What he found was that each one had known a different Hemingway, and each seemed to feel that his was the real one. The same rivalries obtained among the Hemingway hunters as among the hunters in their hero's stories: each one claimed to have brought back the best head.

Brian interviewed Miss Ross; Malcolm Cowley, the distinguished literary critic who once interviewed Hemingway for *Life;* George Plimpton, who interviewed him for the *The Paris Review;* A. E. Hotchner, author of *Papa Hemingway;* Carlos Baker, author of *Ernest Hemingway: A Life Story;* William Seward, one of the few academics to ever befriend the writer; John Hemingway, Ernest's eldest son; and Mary Hemingway, his last wife. The interviews taken together provide a *Rashomon* vision of the writer, which is in itself another portrait of Hemingway.

Brian was interested not only in Hemingway but also in the art of the interview. He began by asking each person what he or she felt about Miss Ross's Profile. In that Profile, Hemingway is quoted as

saying: "I started out very quiet and I beat Mr. Turgenev. Then I
trained hard and I beat Mr. de Maupassant. I've fought two draws
with Mr. Stendhal, and I think I had an edge in the last one. But
nobody's going to get me in any ring with Mr. Tolstoy unless I'm
crazy or I keep getting better."

When it comes to interviewing, who was the champ? Was it Miss
Ross, "the girl with the built-in tape recorder," as one *New Yorker*
writer described her, or one of the others? Malcolm Cowley helped to
persuade Ernest Hemingway to be interviewed for *Life* magazine's
January 10, 1949, issue—an interview which tended to perpetuate
the Hemingway legend. Cowley proved a man with views of his own,
one of which was that Ernest Hemingway's official biographer,
Professor Carlos Baker, was not sympathetic toward his subject.

Brian: Were you startled when you read the piece on Ernest
Hemingway by Lillian Ross?

Cowley: Yes, I was.

Brian: What was the surprise? How did it fail to show the man you
knew?

Cowley: If you take a stenographic account of what a man says at
a certain time, that does not necessarily give you the impression of
what the man was. Lillian's piece gave much more of the impression
of a playboy and a snob than one ever actually got from Ernest.

Brian: And you don't think he had those qualities?

Cowley: I don't think it was a true impression. In other words,
something much more was here. There were other interviews with
Hemingway, for example Hotchner's whole book, although a lot of
that was fake. You know what he did? I could spot it because
[chuckles] I knew the sources. When he said "Hemingway said,"
actually he was quoting Hemingway's letters to him. Because Hemingway's will said: "You must not quote from my letters. They're
protected by copyright." So Hotchner just put the letters in place of
the conversations.

Brian: Apart from that, did Hotchner's book strike you as a vivid,
truthful account of Hemingway?

Cowley: Of his last days, I thought it probably was. The early stuff
was ignorant.

Brian: Although Hemingway called you the best critic in the U.S.
and you spent two weeks in Cuba with him, afterward he's quoted as

calling your piece about him as "not awfully accurate." Did he ever tell you what he considered inaccurate?

Cowley: The one inaccuracy Hemingway picked up against me, according to Hotchner, was that I said he carried one flask of vermouth and one of gin. And Ernest said: "Who would waste a whole flask on vermouth?" But this information came from, I think, Buck Lanham or John Broth, so somebody else made the error and I simply repeated it.

Brian: Hemingway praised your honesty in withholding some material he didn't want used. What was that?

Cowley: He didn't like my saying, which was absolutely true, that at Oak Park he was a literary boy, not a sports boy.

Brian: Did he ever tell you why he hated his mother?

Cowley: I never asked him the question. What would this be? You can see from the story that she made a worm out of his father. She was one of those arty women who ruled the roost.

Brian: You knew Scott Fitzgerald personally. Did you think Hemingway's portrait of him in *A Moveable Feast* was fair?

Cowley: It was a caricature to some extent, but the whole thing rests, not on Fitzgerald, but on Zelda. Hemingway did not like Zelda and he blamed Zelda for the ruin of Fitzgerald. And, also, to tell the truth, Hemingway was a man who could not bear rivals; essentially couldn't. And, except for Maxwell Perkins, who was out of the field, he very often couldn't forgive anyone [chuckles] doing him a favor. That was the bad side of his character, but too much of the bad side got into the Carlos Baker book. I'll tell you the one thing about the book, since I had also done research on Hemingway's life. At times there were good stories and bad stories about what Hemingway did. And I caught Carlos Baker using the bad stories and leaving the good stories out, in cases where I knew that both were accessible to him. For example, I showed Baker my letters about Hemingway and out of those letters he chose the uncomplimentary [laughs] things and omitted the complimentary things of which the letters were mostly composed.

Brian: Do you think any essential mystery remains about Hemingway?

Cowley: Yes, I think there's an essential mystery about him. Even in Baker's book there are stories that certainly aren't told. I don't

intend to tell you about them now. If you ask me the question. . . .
No, I won't even give you an example.

Brian: Can you give me a clue without actually stating it?

Cowley: The clue is (actually nobody would know this as far as I
know) what happened in Italy between, I think it's July 8, 1918, when
he was wounded, and the time when Hemingway went home. Baker
doesn't know.

Brian: You once called Hemingway the proudest man in the
world. Was he the proudest man you ever knew?

Cowley: Absolutely.

Brian: Do you think if one combined your interview with those of
George Plimpton, Lillian Ross, and Leslie Fiedler, it might give a fair
picture of Hemingway?

Cowley: You know, they might. They'd catch him at different
periods and with different feelings. But the most vivid things I've had
said to me about Hemingway were by a man now dead, Nathan
Asch, who knew him in Paris in 1924–5. And they would have to be
thrown in.

Brian: Could you say one vivid thing Asch had told you about
Hemingway?

Cowley: Asch's was the picture of a younger man in Paris when
Hemingway was already the leader of the young people. And Asch
did admire him. Here's something Asch wrote about Hemingway:
"Once in Paris he had a dinner-table argument with another young
writer" "—that was Nathan Asch—"about their respective talents.
Later when they were walking toward the Dôme for coffee, Hemingway fell into a boxer's crouch and began feinting and jabbing. That
was something he often did in those days. The other young writer
began shadow-boxing too. He hit Hemingway accidentally and
Hemingway hit back, knocking him down. His mouth gritty, tasting
bits of teeth, the other picked himself up and stumbled back to his
hotel room. Later that night there was a knock at the door. It was
Hemingway. 'I couldn't go to sleep until you forgave me,' he said.
'You know of course that I was wrong in the argument. You've got a
lot of talent. You've got more of everything than any of us.' . . . It was
an event when this towering figure passed the sidewalk tables at the
Dôme. Arms waved in greeting and friends ran out to urge him to sit
down with them. The occasions were charming little scenes, as if

spontaneous, although repeated. In view of the whole terrace Hemingway would be striding toward the Montparnasse railroad station, his mind seemingly busy with the mechanics of someone's arrival or departure. And he wouldn't quite recognize whoever greeted him. Then suddenly his beautiful smile appeared that made those watching him also smile. And with a will and an eagerness he put out his hands and warmly greeted his acquaintance, who, overcome by this reception, simply glowed and returned with him to the table as if with an overwhelming prize . . ."

Brian: Is there one word you could use for Hemingway?
Cowley: Complicated.

PW Interviews: Malcolm Cowley

Roy Bongartz/1973

Publishers Weekly, 204 (September 17, 1973), 20–21. Reprinted with the permission of *Publishers Weekly* and Roy Bongartz.

Malcolm Cowley, the sensitive and enthusiastic critic of American fiction, celebrated his 75th birthday last month (August 24) with a party for friends and neighbors in the converted Connecticut barn he's been living in for nearly 40 years. Cowley and his wife Muriel went up there from New York City to find a good place to work, and he has been writing there ever since, his delight with the dedicated, self-challenging prose of the 20's exiles undiminished.

A tall, comfortably built man with jowly cheeks, a neatly trimmed salt-and-pepper mustache, and a full head of white hair, he could pass for an exceptionally distinguished Santa Claus. There is a shrewdness in the guileless blue eyes, a carefulness, a valuable *attention* to any idea presented for consideration. Describing his approach to his work for a recent *PW* interviewer, he says, "I try to start with a sort of innocence—that is, with a lack of preconception about what I might or might not discover. To preserve the innocence, I try not to read the so-called secondary or critical sources until my own discoveries, if any, have been made."

Cowley is again reminding American readers of the marvelous but flawed masterpieces of the 20's in another new book, out a few months ago: *A Second Flowering: Works and Days of the Lost Generation* (Viking). In it he updates a series of virtually definitive essays on writers, many of whom his criticism first brought into prominence: Fitzgerald, Hemingway, Dos Passos, Cummings, Wilder, Faulkner, Wolfe and Hart Crane. And he still talks about the old reception his first book received from established literary thinkers. The book, *Exile's Return,* was the first to take the younger post-World War I writers seriously. "They said I was dealing with writers who would never amount to anything. 'Hemingway and his friends

118

are growing dim,' one of them wrote. Not a single critic over 35 spoke well of that book. But then that same book was reissued in 1951—to 'a chorus of critical applause,' as the cliché goes. Now it's in its 15th printing."

The 20's writers, Cowley says, "were much more ambitious to produce a masterpiece than writers today. They were ready to sacrifice their lives to producing it. Ambition like that is rare now. And the work of writing was more separate from the writer's personality. But now the importance centers around creation of a *persona*. It was harder, financially, too, in the 20's; there were none of the present opportunities for being supported by a foundation grant. There was only the rare publisher's advance, where an editor might take a gamble on you for $300. Well, on that you could live on potatoes for six months in Connecticut in those days."

As for complaints that he's looking backward too much, Cowley says, "I confess to sharing the weakness often imputed to members of the generation, Dos Passos and Hemingway in particular: that of living too much in the past. 'But we had such good times then,' I find myself saying with others. We thought of ourselves as being wise, disillusioned, cynical, but we were wide-eyed children with a child's capacity for enjoyment. Did other generations ever laugh so hard, or do crazier things just for the hell of it?"

Cowley has kept the flame of the 20's burning bright in many ways, one of the most telling being the Viking *Portable* series of anthologies that have caught the passing fame of a number of authors and helped to make them permanent fixtures in the literary scene. For example, Robert Penn Warren says that the Faulkner portable "marked the great turning point in Faulkner's reputation in the United States." But Cowley is quite alive to what is going on today and in more recent years as well. He was responsible for getting Ken Kesey's *One Flew Over the Cuckoo's Nest* into the *Portable* series. A student of Cowley's at Stanford, Kesey "was a natural," Cowley says. He was also responsible for publishing Jack Kerouac's *On The Road*.

On the health of writing, Cowley says, "Don't talk about the decay of American fiction, talk about the decay of family-style magazines." He sees "category" paperbacks taking over the former role of magazines—sci-fi paperbacks, Gothic paperbacks, masturbation-daydream, confessional, lesbian, gay. The recent proliferation of these paperbacks surprises Cowley: "I went into an antique shop in California last year; it was run by a couple of dykes, and there were two whole shelves of lesbian novels in paperback, and I had never heard of a single one of them except *The Well of Loneliness*." With the short story market "shrunk like a sandspit in a typhoon," the avant-garde "little" magazines increase their influence—"That's why so much new fiction is fantastic or ambiguous," Cowley suggests.

Cowley recognizes that traditional fiction is being increasingly outsold by non-fiction, but he believes that the strengths of fiction will prevail by insinuating themselves into the so-called "personal reporting." "Mailer will go off to make a novel out of what actually happened, but it is much more interesting from the fiction aspect of it than it is from the reportorial." Cowley sees a strong continuing market for what he calls "panorama" novels about life in the U.S. as a whole, where a particular segment of society—Hollywood moguls, the jet set, for instance—makes the background. "They still hit the jackpot; even the fake ones will sell enormously."

Cowley has little sympathy with wildly imagined novels of impossible scenes unrecognizable in ordinary life. He sees also a wide gap between books praised by reviewers and those bought widely by the public. "The public still reads novels to find out what life is like," Cowley says, "but it is hard to find this out from a novel that would be flatly impossible. People like to find a pattern in life, to see evil punished and good rewarded. Thus every story becomes a fable with a moral. Even if a good man is ruined or sacrificed in a novel, there's a moral—that life is meaningless, perhaps. People will not like this moral, but it is there. Now if you subtract the story from the writing and make it a phantasmagoria of events, there will be no satisfaction in it at all."

A Pennsylvania native, Cowley began writing on his high school paper and was editor of the Harvard *Advocate* in 1919. In Europe in the 20's he studied French literature and wrote poetry and "portraits real and imaginary" for a couple of little magazines of the time, *Secession* and *Broom*.

He became literary editor of the *New Republic* during the 30's, and recalls publishing John Cheever's first story, written at 17, entitled "I am Expelled From Prep School." (Cowley's son has now married Cheever's daughter.) Since the Second World War he has been editing the *Portables* and other anthologies, as well as producing his criticism, doing book reviews for the New York *Times* and Washington *Post* and teaching. He has just returned from six months at the University of Warwick, England. Of modern educational theory, he says, "There is a tremendous lot of crap about that word *elitism*. If you say John is a better student than Jake you're condemned for elitism! How are we going to get along without an elite? Are we going to have four billion absolute equals? Equal opportunity, O.K., and maybe even equal living standards, O.K., too, but not everybody is qualified for top jobs."

In his faded blue shirt and chino slacks he strolls out into a little wood of tall, straight pines that he tells visitors he planted himself as seedlings when he first moved up to his barn. He's a gardener, too, proud of his corn, rhubarb, lettuce and tomatoes, and he looks ruefully at the sharp green meadowland of the farm next door that, because of the economics of land prices, has just gone out of business.

But he is really more at home in his study, where, he complains, he has been made into an information service by every student or scholar in the country who wants to know some fact or other about a 20's writer; they are forever telephoning or writing to him and he says, "The government ought to subsidize me, provide me with a secretary so I could handle all this work." He is already well into his next book,* memoirs of the 30's in which he will recall, among other things, the disillusionment among American liberals with Communism. He has in fact given all his letters to the Newberry Library in Chicago, and so will have to move out there this winter in order to get a look at them; the library is presently arranging living quarters for him and his wife.

It is the youthful energy of the 20's, though, that still most animates Cowley's spirit, and when he has any advice for young writers it is this taking-the-world-by-the-hair dedication of the authors he admires that underlies it: "For God's sake, write a great deal, and get it published!" he says. "Many young writers simply don't spend enough time and ingenuity in getting their work published. You can always find somewhere to get it printed, even if you don't get paid."

*The Dream of the Golden Mountains

To publish a lot, you have to write a lot, of course, but, he says, "I've never known a man develop a good style who didn't write a good deal." Cowley's last word, for those who would emulate him as a critic who has had a large part of forming the literary taste of his country, is: "Your judgment must be subjective—but with a great deal of objective information, or order to be persuasive."

I Wish It Were 1900

Arthur S. Freese/1975

NRTA Journal (January–February 1975), 9–11. Reprinted with
the permission of the NRTA Journal. Copyright by the National
Retired Teachers Association.

Not many writers can enjoy the satisfaction of seeing their work
reissued nearly a half century after it was first published—and receive
much more acclaim the second time around.

With his recent book, *A Second Flowering,* Malcolm Cowley—
poet, author, editor, literary critic and historian—has had another
flowering of his own, along with that of his beloved *lost generation.*
And recently his book, *Blue Juniata,* has resurrected the best of his
poetry, which critic Allen Tate describes as the work of "one of the
finest poets of his generation."

This was the man I visited a few weeks ago on his seven acres in
Sherman, Connecticut. Malcolm Cowley is a tall, heavily-built man
with blue, twinkling, humorous eyes. He looks the perfect grand-
father with his full head of handsome, curly white hair, his precisely
trimmed mustache, his plump cheeks and his pipe.

The Cowleys are a warm, friendly, good-looking couple—the kind
of people you'd want to know. Their charming house was originally a
barn: The living room in which we sat had been the hayloft; the
workroom, a tobacco barn.

They rebuilt the farmhouse some 40 years ago when, as the poet
recalls, "It was farmland—not a tree anywhere except a single elm."
His land now has many trees 50 feet high. Nearly everywhere you
walk you find fruit trees or vegetables growing—cantaloupe and corn,
succulent grapes, enormous tomatoes and lettuce and rhubarb.

Malcolm Cowley was born on August 24, 1898, the son of a
physician in a Pennsylvania town whose name, Belsano, is no longer
on the map. He grew up in Pittsburgh where, at the age of three, he
met four-year-old Kenneth Burke, now a famous literary critic,
philosopher and translator. That friendship, which began in the very
first year of this century, still goes on.

During his long career, Malcolm Cowley has had a single goal: "I always wanted to be a man of letters—and words have always been my business. I've been connected with all sorts of magazine and book publishing—as a reviewer, editor, poet and author, and as a literary historian trying to help and explain other writers.

"Poetry was my first love, although I haven't been writing many poems for the last half-dozen years. I got into book reviewing early and eventually became the interpreter of the writers of my own generation."

I asked what writing was like in the first years of our century.

"In the 1900's and the 1910's," Mr. Cowley said, "this country was provincial—the real standards were in England. If you wanted to make it as a writer you had to make it with the English public. The big ambition was to write 'The Great American Novel'—as if there could be such a thing. Very often this, too, was judged by the reaction to the book in England."

During this period a whole generation of American writers began their revolt against the genteel tradition. Theodore Dreiser, Sherwood Anderson, Eugene O'Neill and Sinclar Lewis laid the groundwork which, after World War I, finally produced a native literature and native standards.

The war to end all wars proved a watershed for American fiction writers. In Mr. Cowley's words: "It was a huge event in American literature as in other things. The war shook the writers loose from their moorings: They had different ideals of writing and wanted to make it all new, to set down the world as it was. There was literary ferment before the war but not much of a public to read it—the genteel tradition was so strong that the radical writers (in a literary sense) couldn't even be published in New York."

The World War I generation of writers and poets are the group commonly known as the *lost generation*—but, as Mr. Cowley points out, they would better be called the *lucky generation*. The critic presents a representative sample of this group—all of them born between 1894 and 1900—in *A Second Flowering:* F. Scott Fitzgerald, Ernest Hemingway, John Dos Passos, E. E. Cummings, Thornton Wilder, William Faulkner, Thomas Wolfe, Hart Crane.

He points out how this generation was lucky in that it managed to find the best of all worlds: "As small boys they witnessed the coming

of the automobile and the airplane, yet still knew the countryside with
its fields and woods. They were trained in the Protestant ethic and
were taught English and grammar as no youngster has been for a
long time now. They matured in the '20s which welcomed young
beginners and was generous to them."

This was also Malcolm Cowley's background. He graduated from
Harvard in 1919 and went to New York to free-lance. *The Dial,* then
a monthly magazine, gave him a half-dozen novels to review at one
dollar a review. Then came another review for *The New Republic* for
ten dollars. Once the novels were perused, there was a bookdealer
who gave the young writer 35 cents for each review copy.

In 1920, young Cowley earned enough money to keep afloat: "I
had to use my wits—writing for all sorts of funny little magazines and
papers; doing book reviews and all sorts of things." Henry Seidel
Canby gave young Malcolm some books to review for *The Literary
Review,* and ten dollars a week. This made him something unique in
New York—the only salaried book reviewer!

Offered a fellowship to a French university, the young writer and
his wife went abroad in 1921. On a total of 3,000 dollars they were
able to live in France for three years and had enough to travel in
Europe and pay for their return trip to New York in 1923.

The Depression proved a good time for Mr. Cowley: "I was very
lucky. All through the Depression I was literary editor of the *The New
Republic* and our salaries weren't cut. I earned 125 dollars a week
then and I could live like a lord."

The *lost generation* writers were established then and suffered less
from the Depression than younger writers. In 1934, Malcolm Cowley
published his book *Exile's Return* about the *lost generation* of writers
whose qualities he, more than any other critic, recognized and
affirmed. The book was condemned by every critic over the age of
35, but its reissue in 1951 brought uniform praise and recognition.

World War II produced a far different effect on the American
writers. It took a major toll in casualties among them and left the
survivors drained after long years of fighting. So the '40s and the '50s
were still dominated by the *lost generation* which didn't fade out until
the '60s with the deaths of Hemingway, Faulkner, Cummings and
James Thurber within a year.

What bothers Malcolm Cowley is this: "There's less fiction being

written and published today—although the quality is better because
the audience is more sophisticated and demanding. But a great many
of the novels today are self-indulgent—the author is trying to do his
own thing and to hell with the public . . . the result most often is that
the public says to hell with the author."

Returning to his own career, Mr. Cowley said he has been a visiting
professor at many universities: "I did my first teaching when I was 52
years old, in 1950, at the University of Washington. Students then
were very conventional and looked forward to a secure job with
retirement pay. That lasted until the '60s and the student revolt at
Berkeley. In 1970, the revolt became universal because of Vietnam.

"The rebelliousness is gone now, but the great trouble is that
interest has shifted from English and American literature to practical
subjects that might lead to jobs after college."

As one of the closest and most thoughtful observers of our lifetime
scene, Mr. Cowley offered sharp answers to other questions:

Freese: You've lived through our entire century—how do you
regard it?

Cowley: My dear sir, don't ask me such big questions! Remember
the king who wanted his scholars to reduce all knowledge to one
sentence? By the time they finally returned, the king was old and on
his deathbed, so they whispered it in his ear: 'Man is born, he suffers,
and he dies.' This century has changed a great deal and it's going to
change more—I'm afraid for the worst on account of the energy crisis
and the population crisis.

Freese: Are we better or worse off than when you were a child?

Cowley: The country is worse off. Life has become much easier,
we've become more mobile, better educated, more sophisticated, but
the actual quality of life is visibly deteriorating and will continue to do
so because we're using up the resources of the planet.

Freese: What do you consider the world's greatest danger?

Cowley: That we'll continue to go downhill this way!

Freese: What do you believe is the world's greatest hope?

Cowley: That more and more people will withdraw from the
commercial system and learn to be self-subsistent, using a minimum
of energy and getting that from the sun or wind, growing their own
vegetables. I'd love to see that.

Freese: What do you think is its greatest need?

Cowley: Self-subsistence is the moral imperative. That's why, instead of retiring to Florida or California or a desert community near a gold course maintained at enormous expense, I'm going to continue living in Connecticut as long as I can.

Freese: If you had your life to live over, what would you do differently?

Cowley: Lots of things. I spent the first twenty years of my life trying not to be a success—I wanted to stay out of the rat race and that's why I free-lanced and took unpopular positions. Now I think I'd try to do what I didn't do then—make an earlier reputation as a writer.

Freese: What is the most significant lesson you've ever learned?

Cowley: In dealing with people whether young or old, always preserve their self-respect; never say or do anything to make them feel degraded.

Freese: Is true happiness possible?

Cowley: There is no such thing as true happiness in this world and I've never used the word. The nearest one can come to happiness is in satisfaction with a job well done by oneself.

Freese: What goal should one seek in life?

Cowley: It's the same thing—self-respect.

Freese: If you could look at the world in 2075, what would you most like to see?

Cowley: I'll be candid—I'd like to see it as it was in 1900. We grew up in a more friendly, free and open world than the one we're in today. Now there are too many people and they move around too fast. I like a world that doesn't move so fast; where there are more trees and fields and better food to eat. I must admit that bred into me and still sticking with me is that old-fashioned Protestant ethic, which means that if you want anything you have to work for it.

Freese: Which individuals you've known have you liked and respected the most?

Cowley: My oldest friend Burke and I still conduct an enormous correspondence with him. The prominent literary figure I felt most affection for was William Faulkner. It was a distant affection. He was not a close friend, but I had great sympathy for him. Ernest

Hemingway was the most charming person I ever met but also one of the most difficult.

Freese: How important is money?

Cowley: Damned important! Enough money so that one feels free to do things is one condition for self-respect—without it, contentment is destroyed.

Freese: How important is friendship?

Cowley: It's the most important when one is younger, for it is then that one depends most on friends and is most influenced by them. After 50 or 60, you'd better be good friends with your wife—with your neighbors, too. I feel affection for a host of people—not always the people I see most often; but that feeling of affection is important to me.

Freese: How important is freedom?

Cowley: Freedom is what is truly important.

Freese: Have you found most people in the long run to be good?

Cowley: Most people in the long run *intend* to be good. But they're deflected by selfishness and cowardice, so that finally many of the things they *do* are evil. They're also deflected by want of sympathy, so they only carry out their code of ethics with people with whom they identify.

Freese: Is there any special advice you want to give to younger people?

Cowley: Nobody can be given advice—except to do their own thing, with respect for others and for the future of the world, not to leave the world poorer.

Before we said good-bye, Malcolm Cowley called my attention to a poem he wrote six years ago, which he ended with a prayer. It reads, in part: "I pray for this . . . to love the earth, to be sparing of what it yields and not to leave it poorer for my long presence."

Excerpts from "Two Gentlemen on Literati Road"

Tom Wood/1975

Lost Generation Journal, III (Fall 1975), 3–5. Reprinted with the permission of Tom Wood.

A rural artery called Church Road winds about the beautiful Connecticut countryside near the small town of Sherman. The traveler sees neatly etched valleys and can relax along the road in deep shadows made by the vaulted roofs of foliage formed at intervals by huge trees that are so grand that they make a plainsman's heart ache with joy.

This road runs past the homes of two men of letters who are closely connected with the history and criticism of the Lost Generation. Their homes are located about a mile apart. They and their wives visit back and forth like country folk who have much to do, but must break into their routines to be neighborly.

The men are Malcolm Cowley, the No. 1 critic-historian of the Lost Generation, and his friend of many years, Matthew Josephson [the subject of Wood's other interview], who likewise is a critic and historian of the same group. Both men have channeled their literary talents in other direction, Cowley sticking close to works about the Americans who went abroad between World Wars I and II, but adding poetry and broader literary criticism to his efforts, and Josephson applying himself to biographies and socioeconomic interpretation.

Cowley's most noted work, *Exile's Return,* forms the frontispiece of his life's work and establishes the anchor for his extremely busy career as poet, critic and historian.

Although both men have passed their mid-70's, their signature works were formed when they were young men. *Exile's Return* came out in 1934 and was revised and reissued in 1951. Cowley was 36 years old when it was first issued.

Cowley is about to be favored by a bibliographical work by Diane U. Eisenberg through the Southern Illinois University Press. The work, called *Malcolm Cowley: A Checklist of His Writings (1916–1973)*, should be in the bookstores about the time this issue of the *Lost Generation Journal* hits the newsstands and libraries.

The Eisenberg work, with an introduction by Cowley, is exquisite in detail. The section on books starts with *Racine*, a work privately printed in Paris in 1923, and *Blue Juniata,* Cowley's first book of poetry. She also lists Cowley's works that have been translated into several languages, including Japanese and Croatian. Through her work, one sees immediately that Cowley has displayed magnificent scope.

During 11 years with the *New Republic* (1929–1940), Cowley's book reviews gave him an unusually keen literary judgment and a tremendous exposure to the major works of his time. . . .

The average man or woman of letters will be intimidated long before getting to Eisenberg's listing of Cowley's introductions to the works of other authors and his contributions to books edited by others in the literary vineyard. Once the shock wears off, the value of Cowley's contributions to American and world letters hits the reader and envy turns to admiration.

Cowley has introduced a galaxy of books. A sample includes *A Thornton Wilder Trio, Great Scenes from Great Novels, Madame Bovary, Miss Lonelyhearts, The Outlaws on Parnassus, The Ordeal of Mark Twain,* and *Anna Karenina.* His contributions to books and to periodicals were numerous and diverse. Poems, books reviews, essays and articles show the reach of the man.

Wood: About how much time have you spent in France? I went back and listened to the tapes I made with you about this time last year, and it seems you were there the first time in the Twenties—the early Twenties—for about two years.

Cowley: Yes, I was first in France as a member of the American Field service during the War. Actually I was in the French Army for six months, and got French Army pay. I got five cents a day and a quart of wine—every day—and a quarter pound of tobacco every month.

Wood: You knew [E. E.] Cummings then?

Cowley: I knew Cummings. No, I first saw Cummings at Harvard. He was still in Harvard when I was a freshman. I saw him at meetings of the Harvard Poetry Society, though I didn't meet him then. I didn't meet him till New York in 1918.

Wood: What years were you with the American Field Service?

Cowley: 1917—six months. I came back when the American Field Service was taken over by the American Army.

Wood: This may not be a fair question, but what made you decide to become a critic-historian? You started with the *New Republic*. Was this your first big move in the career sense?

Cowley: Well, my first big move in the career sense was when after coming back from France I decided I could make it as a freelance writer. That switched me over into book reviewing a good deal because that was the most dependable source of income for me. I'd already been reviewing books and I also wrote magazine articles. And then finally when I was taken on the *New Republic* staff, I gravitated naturally to the book department.

Wood: Did you join the staff of the *New Republic* in 1929?

Cowley: 1929. Just three weeks before the Wall Street Crash.

Wood: How long were you with the *New Republic*?

Cowley: Actually working in the office, eleven years.

Wood: You became an editor then, didn't you?

Cowley: I was the literary editor which means I ran the book department and also did reviews while helping to edit the rest of the paper—very busy eleven years.

Wood: Now, from there what was your next big move?

Cowley: While staying on as critic for the *New Republic*, the next move was into literary history. I received a five-year subvention.

Wood: A five-year what?

Cowley: A subvention is sort of a fellowship. It gave me five years to study and write about American Literature.

Wood: *Exile's Return* was 1934, wasn't it?

Cowley: 1934, that's after most of it was published in the *New Republic*.

Wood: Most of it was published prior to the issuance of the book? Would you consider *Exile's Return* one of your early great triumphs or not?

Cowley: It wasn't a great triumph at the time. I think it had a total sale of 950 copies the first year. It attracted a good deal of critical attention—not all of it favorable, by any means.

Wood: I would say you've had a remarkably balanced career in literature, criticism and writing in general. You've got what I think is a tremendous spread—poetry, reviews, essays, books, translations. There's a tremendous diversity in your work. So, I just wonder how posterity will remember you or how you want to be remembered?

Cowley: First, I am a poet, critic and literary historian. They all come fairly close together.

Wood: Do you have any second thoughts about your views of why people went to Europe or to Paris, for instance, in the Twenties? Are you still with yourself on that?

Cowley: I still have the reasons I stated earlier. And do not forget, among those reasons was simple finance. It was much, much cheaper to live in Europe. For example, I went to Europe in 1921 because I received a fellowship of 12,000 francs a year amounting at that time to a thousand dollars. I went to Europe. The fellowship involved half-fare on the French Line. I went with my wife. Lived there a year; the fellowship was renewed another year. During those two years I earned around a thousand dollars or more by writing for American magazines. That would make a total of three thousand dollars. Then, we came home and I landed in Hoboken with five dollars in my pocket—and no debts. We lived in France for two years on three thousand dollars.

Wood: I wonder if you would mind comparing the views of youths today with those of the Twenties. I think you told me last summer that they had differing causes. There are thousands of young Americans who are abroad right now and I wonder if they went abroad for the same reasons your own group went abroad?

Cowley: The financial reason has pretty much disappeared and as a matter of fact this age group, or generation, contrasts in many ways with that of the 1920's.

It's a curious phenomenon of history—literary history—that the same group of attitudes is likely to recur about every thirty years. That is, in some ways the 1920's reviewed the 1890's. And the 1950's in some ways reviewed the 1920's. The 1960's in some ways repeated the 1930's, an era of social rebellion. The social rebellion was more widespread in the 1960's than in the 1930's.

Wood: Would you say that the youngsters of the 1950's were reviewing a cultural interest abroad? As was your own group?

Cowley: Yes, they were seeking personal fulfillment. And in the 1950's it was also cheaper to live in Europe than in the United States. That changed. At present it's most expensive to live in most of Europe.

So, going abroad has to be out of romance, desire, adventure, self-improvement, self-discovery and joining the drug scene in Amsterdam, for example. Although at present there's no marked age group since the 1960 Love Generation on the generational scale. American young writers seem to be marking time and looking for direction—for a new spokesman.

Wood: You think they're marking time now, right?

Cowley: Right now, yes.

Wood: Do you think each generation of young people as they come up go through processes similar to the 1920's although they might not have the same objectives; that is, they're seeking a fulfillment that is natural to each generation—or do you have any feelings along that line?

Cowley: You're getting on a subject that I could talk on for hours and hours—the subject of successive generations.

The important thing to note is that every age group has its own sense of values. It has a whole different set of values, aspirations, antipathies and it strives to express these in its writings. Now some generations show more differences than others, and those are the ones that become remembered generations. For example, the Lost Generation of the Twenties and the Love Generation of the 1960's. But they have to find leaders or spokesmen, Fitzgerald said. Very often, what these leaders or spokesmen lay down is what their generation tends firmly to believe.

Wood: I, of course, arrived a little late on the scene, but I've done quite a bit of reading in your particular spectrum and consider you the Number One cultural historian, certainly of that era. I can't think of anyone who has a stronger reputation or who has done more work that has been better received than your own work. I don't feel that I'm being too far off by calling you the Number One historian.

Cowley: Well, I'd always accept that. [laughs]

I want to explain one thing before hanging up about generations and age groups. A new age group, a cluster of writers and artists, appears at irregular intervals, but somewhere around every ten to fifteen years. Of course, a biological generation is thirty years. But usually the successive age groups oppose each other. That's why the sway or return of the pendulum occurs every thirty years. It occurs after two age groups.

Wood: One of the things I wanted to ask you and was about to forget is this. Since you were yourself part of the generation and were very intimately involved in a great deal of it, how do you look upon your value as an interpreter of your time and your people? I would think it would be an asset, but it might also get you into some difficulties.

Cowley: No, no. I think that the man most conscious of his generation was Scott Fitzgerald, among writers. He was the one who always spoke affectionately of "my contemporaries."

But it seems to me that I had a great deal to do with forming the notions that we hold of the so-called Lost Generation, which is really the World War I generation. I followed their careers right from the beginning.

Wood: Well, you've had a nice long career and you've had a chance for reappraisal and yet your first large appraisal seems to be holding. And strangely enough it seems to be holding in the mind of the public. We had talked about that earlier last summer. I had asked did you think perhaps you had misled the public in some areas? Rather an inelegant question, but I felt that rather than their making a huge cultural push, that if I were going to be the historian, at this late date, that I would have to stress the adventure and desire for maturation above desire for cultural accretion. I recall that at the time you evidently didn't agree with me.

Cowley: Well, the watchword in the 1920's was experience. A great many of the adventures of that World War I generation was a search for experience on which to build writing. The feeling that a rich personality depended on having wide experiences and adventures. And thirty years later in the 1950's, the watchword was identity. Who am I? How can I find who I am? So, in that respect, you might say, maturation and experience.

Wood: In reading people like Glenway Wescott, there's such a heavy emphasis on the American's great desire to find a culture of his own, to find some sort of cultural identity. However, I've talked to a lot of old people who were not part of this movement to Europe and back. They didn't seem to feel the same deprivation, not to the same degree at least that Westcott stressed and the other historians of that era and I'm just kind of testing it for my own mind.

Cowley: Well, go ahead and test it. Keep testing it. The reactions were different, but there was a strong feeling in the year 1920 and before that American culture had been disappointing and that something richer and freer was to be found in Europe.

Wood: Do you have any feelings about whether the intelligentsia of a generation stands apart from its own tribe so to speak? I mean for instance, do you think those who went abroad probably had the advantage of a better education than the average American. It seems sort of natural that they would have different views from those of the general public. I just wonder how far apart they stood from the tribe.

Cowley: They stood very far apart in 1920. Because the younger generation of writers was more sophisticated, more urban, I suppose, than the mass of the American public. And I think that's why the bourgeoisie was very hostile. There seemed to be a sharp division between the intellegentsia and the public. But that was also a moral differential. Because the new generation of that time had much freer morals than the general public.

Wood: Well, you know it's a little difficult for me to interfere with things sometimes because we have seven or more million students going to college or universities now, and during your own era I don't know what the figures were, but they were quite low.

Cowley: It was quite low. It certainly wasn't one million.

Wood: And so this, I feel, had to produce some sort of massive differential.

Cowley: It did for a time, but you must also remember that the young writers were a minority in college—even at Harvard.

Wood: Now, where did this hunger for culture come from? Did it come strictly from universities in your judgment, or did it come from the lower grades? As a Harvard man, I expect you had—and I don't mean this in a rude sense—a natural feeling of superiority, particularly for that day.

Cowley: Oh, no, no, I don't have a feeling of superiority.

Wood: Do you think you had an advantage then?

Cowley: This starts with middle-class people, but I was very fond especially of farmers, because I lived a great deal in the country and always got along well with farmers.

Wood: There must be a feeling of accomplishment that has to be recognized, like the difference between having and not. A guy has a good job; then obviously he has security and a feeling of certainty that he can get a job done as opposed to a man who has nothing to spend. And so if you have something in your mental bank to spend I don't see how you can avoid having some feelings or—maybe superiority is the wrong word—but something in the mental bank where you would have security in feeling, a base for accomplishment.

Cowley: Oh, no no. I think you're going off on a dangerous track here. And also it's a track that doesn't have particularly much to do with the Lost Generation. If you could get the social attitudes very well from Fitzgerald's early stories, even *This Side of Paradise,* with the snobbery of Princeton at that time, the social lines were drawn fairly distinctly. The intellectual lines not so much so. And being a serious writer of the younger generation in those days was more like belonging to a secret society.

Wood: You mean you really have no feeling of advantage relative to the people who were educated and went abroad?

Cowley: Feelings of superiority were lacking, but feelings of brotherhood were quite strong, among people who had the same experiences.

Wood: That wouldn't necessarily carry you up and down the full spectrum.

Cowley: No, no.

Wood: Well, it's very possible that I'm off on the wrong track on that and I agree with you. It's still a point of curiosity as to where the hunger and desire for cultural exposure came from. I would assume that it came primarily from college, based on what I've been able to put together.

Cowley: Oh, no, it went back. Mostly it started in high school.

Wood: Do you recall any specifics in your life where this hunger began?

Cowley: Hunger? My goodness, I can remember the time when my older friend, James Light, later the director of the Provincetown

Players, introduced me to modern literature—Ibsen, Bernard Shaw and Oscar Wilde and so on. Goodness, how I read in those days. That was in high school.

Wood: Do you make any distinction at all in the different capacities of those who went abroad, particularly those who became a part of the *literati?* I find it difficult to think of the real producer as not being exceptional or even superior. Whether they felt that or not, their mental capacities must have differed.

Cowley: Oh, yes, but there's always a degree of pardonable snobbery in the literary world. People who write look down on the people who would like to write but can't. That's always the case for every generation.

Wood: In the Lost Generation group, those who went abroad, there was such an outpouring and such a sunburst of activity that there seems to be cause to believe that there would be something identifiable that would explain why they rather than their predecessors or people who followed produced so much.

Cowley: There is no explanation why so much was produced by one group and much less by other groups who are not even groups. If you look at the history of American literature, good writers appear in clusters with empty years between the clusters. Did you ever happen to think that Emerson was born in 1803, Poe in 1809, Longfellow and Whittier in 1807, I think.

Wood: Can you explain these things in cycles?

Cowley: Writers appear in cycles. We can't find any genetic cycle, but one thing is that talent tends to produce talent. A great deal is simply emulation, rivalry, and learning from one another.

Wood: It doesn't seem to be quite as haphazard or accidental as we think. I keep looking for an answer; maybe there is no answer.

Cowley: The answer is no answer—except one thing—talent breeds talent in such groups, so that a great man has not only his own talent, but that of all his friends.

Malcolm at Eighty

Patrick Hynan/1978

Broadcast by the Canadian Broadcasting Company on 18 August 1978. Printed with the permission of Patrick Hynan.

At the age of nearly eighty Malcolm Cowley represents, in his dogged steadfastness, the last of a dying breed—the man of letters. For nearly sixty years he has devoted himself to literature, first as a critic of French literature and later of American literature, where his perceptive insights into some of the best-known American writers of the century have made him famous. He is best known for his criticisms of the writers of his own generation, those born during during the 1890s. They include Scott Fitzgerald, William Faulkner, Ernest Hemingway, Thornton Wilder, John Dos Passos, Edmund Wilson, Archibald MacLeish, Hart Crane, and Thomas Wolfe, most of whom became known through Gertrude Stein as the "lost generation."

Later, Mr. Cowley wrote about a number of them in his classic *Exile's Return,* an account of ex-patriates in the 1920s. In many ways Mr. Cowley's career has closely paralleled many of those writers. Born in August 1898 in Pennsylvania, he graduated from high school in Pittsburgh and later studied at Harvard. In 1917 he quit Harvard to join the French ambulance corps. In 1921 he won a scholarship to the University of Montpelier. In Paris, in the early 1920s, he came for a while under the influence of the Surrealist movement, and came to know well some of its leaders such as André Baton and Tristan Sala. In Paris he met Ezra Pound, Hemingway, E. E. Cummings, and Ford Madox Ford. He also helped edit *Broom* and *Secession* magazines, when many of the writers of that era were first published.

Returning to the United States in the late 1920s he lived in Greenwich Village where he eked out a living as a freelance book reviewer, while writing at the same time poems and essays. In 1929 Mr. Cowley's book of poems, *Blue Juniata,* was published and on the recommendation of his friend and sometime colleague, the late Edmund Wilson, he became his successor as literary editor of the

138

New Republic. In the 1930s he became active in many left-wing
political causes, though much of his writing during this time was still
being done for magazines.

In 1944, at the suggestion of Viking Press, he became involved in
the first of the Viking "Portables." The first one he compiled was a
selection of Hemingway's writings, and then in 1946 appeared his
now-famous Faulkner Portable which Robert Penn Warren said
"marked the great turning point in Faulkner's reputation in the United
States."

During a long visit to his home in Sherman, Connecticut, where he
lives with his wife Muriel, Patrick Hynan first asked him whether he
had ever consciously set out to become a literary historian and critic,
one of the best American critics of this century.

Cowley: Not in the least. I wanted to talk about my own
generation of people who seemed to me distinctly different in their
aspirations, their ideals, everything else, from the generation immediately preceding them. In fact, as always, they were in revolt against
that generation, in revolt against the fathers. So all during the 1920s
there was a battle going on of generations. The generation of Sinclair
Lewis, Sherwood Anderson, and Willa Cather was very much in the
dominant position at that time. The people that I spoke about had
different ideals of literature and were trying to be heard.

Hynan: What is very interesting about those writers such as
Hemingway, yourself, E. E. Cummings, Hart Crane—to some extent
Hart Crane—John Dos Passos and the rest, all came from the
country. You were all very much country boys, or young adults . . .

Cowley: Not so especially. We may have come from the city, but
we all had a double life. What we liked was to live in the country 50
miles, 100 miles, from a convenient city, preferably New York or
Paris. And there was always this double life. For example, E. E.
Cummings to the end of his life spent half a year in Patchen Place in
Greenwich Village and half a year at Silver Lake, New Hampshire.
Faulkner was the exception there. He was a country boy who
remained a country boy. He didn't much like the city for long visits.
But everybody else—Hemingway was the same way. I could under-
stand his boyhood because he was the son of a doctor in Oak Park
who spent very long summers in the northern part of the southern

peninsula of Michigan and lived in the woods, as I had lived in the woods as a boy.

Hynan: Also, many of you had served, which is also another curious coincidence, in the war, the First World War, around 1917 in of all things the Ambulance Corps. Cummings was in it, you were in it, Hemingway was in it, John Dos Passos was in the Ambulance Corps. Robert Coates—was he in the Ambulance Corps?

Cowley: No, he was in Naval Aviation for a while.

Hynan: Faulkner was in Toronto as an Air Cadet at the University of Toronto in the Royal Canadian Air Force there. I find this another very remarkable coincidence.

Cowley: It wasn't so much of a coincidence. The Ambulance Corps was the way to get abroad fastest. They didn't go into the Ambulance Corps because that was a non-combatant service. In fact, many of my friends transferred from ambulance driving into aviation later. But the Ambulance Corps was the *fast* way to get abroad. For example, I decided to go into the Ambulance Corps in I think it was March 1917, before this country declared war. By April I was in Paris.

Hynan: The decision to go into the Ambulance Corps by yourself and so many other of these writers who weren't writers at the time, of course, but later became very well-known writers . . . but your decision to go in there, was that also tied in with a sense of what you called an exile's return, the sense that all of you later shared, deracination—a lack of roots. You were looking more toward Europe, rather than America.

Cowley: I don't know how conscious that feeling was, and yet the Ambulance Corps was especially an uprooting experience because you weren't even serving in the American Army. You were serving the French for French Army pay of at that time 5¢ a day and a quart of sour wine, and a quarter of a pound of just awful smoking tobacco once a month. That was the French Army and we learned to drill, un, deux, trois, quatre, un, deux, trois, quatre! And we were spectators of the war, for the time that we were in the Ambulance Corps.

Hynan: In talking to a lot of these writers later, after you got to know them very well, particularly in Paris—perhaps some in New York, but certainly in Paris—in the '20s, did you get from them an impression that they all felt something . . . had been let down, they'd let themselves down, or they had been let down, or they felt some sense of alienation coming from Europe after the First World War, coming back to the United States. Was it a matter that they wanted to race back to Europe as quick as possible?

Cowley: The chief thing was that America had turned away from them. This is something that is hard for people to realize, but there was close to a counter-revolution in the United States in the year 1919. A reaction against Wilson's policies of liberalism; every approach to State ownership was put down as an approach to Communism, so that the political atmosphere was repressive then, almost as during the McCarthy era later. But we weren't politically very much awakened. Chiefly we objected to a sort of moral kind of revolution. The atmosphere in that respect is hard to realize now. If a woman smoked a cigarette on the streets of New York in 1918, she was likely to be arrested as a prostitute. And then came Prohibition, and Prohibition seemed terrible to us, so that life in Paris, even in Berlin at that time, was so much more easy-going, so much more adapted to art, and cheaper, too. Much, much cheaper. The cost of living in France at that time for an American with dollars was unbelievable. I went to France in 1921 with a scholarship of $1,000. I earned perhaps $500 during that year by writing for American magazines. On that $1,500 my wife and I paid our passage to Europe, lived there in comfort. The sum total was that we came home after two years and I had five dollars in my pocket after finishing tipping the stewards on board the liner. So the two of us lived in comfort for two years on about $3,000.

Hynan: Were there any writers, any of those writers of the '20s, yourself included, admired? Those who had been in the past . . . ?

Cowley: There were hardly any American writers of the past admired at that time. Well, a few friends . . . Allen Tate and I admired Edgar Allan Poe. A few people admired Whitman. Melville was almost unknown in 1918; he was discovered during the 1920s, but nobody read Emerson, Hawthorne, or, of course, nobody read Whittier or Howells, or any other of the American worthies . . . so that our admirations were largely French at that time.

Hynan: And what of the French writers?

Cowley: Of course, the admiration would be at the beginning for Flaubert, and then for Proust, with occasional divinations into other writers. Jeffrey Wolf in his *Life of Harry Crosby* said that the

Americans in Paris were ignorant of French literature. That's simply because he knows so little about them. He should read some of the correspondence of that time, with the mentions of French writing and the importance of carrying on the discoveries of a writer like Proust.

Hynan: But to get back to Paris, from Berlin to Paris, all the magazines there: *Transatlantic, Sweep, Broom* magazine, *This Quarter* . . . the writers who were there. Now there must be something serious going on, that you were detecting, that you were seeing . . . what was happening to these people with Pound and with Hemingway . . .

Cowley: Much more seemed to be happening at that time with the French writers with whom I consorted a good deal than with the American writers. Americans have always been hesitant in speaking about intellectual matters. They will write about them sometimes in letters, but it seems to me that most of the conversation I heard was about personalities rather than about literary issues.

Hynan: What about Pound, for instance?

Cowley: Oh, Pound—Pound had at that time his curious way of always finding the "lowdown." He took me to the back of his studio and showed me some huge folio volumes and he said, "I've found the lowdown about the Elizabethan drama. It's all cribbed from those books." Those books were the Venetian state papers. Actually, the plots of several Elizabethan plays do come more or less out of the Venetian state papers, of the same episode as told there.

Hynan: You kind of liken, you do liken, Pound to a fox—you have likened him to a fox, who's always running away from his own admirers . . .

Cowley: His own admirers. He wanted to keep a running broad-jump ahead of his own admirers, so he always had to change his style. I liked the earlier Pound, I was much impressed by that. He lost me after about Canto 20 . . .

Hynan: But are you talking about the earlier Pound, say, in the London days?

Cowley: Yes.

Hynan: Did you often get taken around to Gertrude Stein's famous apartment?

Cowley: Several people wanted to take me to see Gertrude Stein, but I didn't like the idea of Gertrude Stein.

Hynan: That's curious . . . why?

Cowley: I thought she was, shall I say, tremendously . . . man-
nered, and really had less talent than she thought she had. It would
be *impossible* to have as much talent as she thought she had. She
had a tremendous lot of astuteness in summing other people up. But I
stayed away from the apartment . . .

Hynan: Of course, she coined the phrase in a letter to Hemingway
or in a remark to Hemingway that you were all part of the "lost
generation," but really looking back more than 50-odd years later, do
you think there really was a "lost generation"?

Cowley: I think it wasn't a lost generation; I think it was a
tremendously lucky generation, even with all the tragedy that we
have learned about in the case of so many of its members. Those
tragedies are more or less to be expected, and it was a lucky
generation in the way it got rather early recognition, the way it felt a
freedom to experiment in life and art, the way it had an audience
which enjoyed reading what the members of the generation wrote
because they were reading about themselves—they belonged to the
same era, too. And then after the '20s and '30s . . . in the '50s
people began looking back to the '20s with nostalgia—these were the
days when writers took risks, as indeed they did. They took them
because they were full of an absurd self-confidence.

Hynan: Why is it that some of the writers you've known, whom
you'd believe have as much talent as the famous writers . . . why is it
that they never became famous?

Cowley: It's a very complicated question. To become famous you
have to *want* fame, besides everything else. I don't think that Bob
Coates, Robert M. Coates, really wanted fame. Oh, he would like it if
it came to him on a platter, you know . . . it's always convenient. But
he wouldn't put himself out for it because he'd seen close friends of
his, notably Hemingway and Jim Thurber, become famous and it
seemed to him become monsters at the same time, because they
always had their fame in mind. So he wasn't going to do that, he was
going to remain a decent human person and never put himself out to
gain the fame that his talent might well have gained him. Another
one, Conrad Aiken, who is one of the major writers of twentieth-
century American literature, had a feeling that he always ought to
remain off-stage, behind the scenes, so that every time he threatened

to become famous he would offend some critic who was going to review his book or have a fight with some publisher, so the fame was always deferred. And then by the time he was eighty years old he began to miss this fame which he thought should have come around on a bicycle and rung his front door and said, "Mr. Aiken, I want to tell you that you're famous." But the others, like Norman Mailer for example, set right out to become famous . . . they couldn't *live* if they weren't famous.

Hynan: Is this related—this pursuit of fame—related somehow to an American disease. Is it a peculiarly American disease, or is it a disease suffered only by artists?

Cowley: I think it's a universal disease. And I think that much of it is made up over the years. People who should become more famous in their desserts will end up becoming less famous, and somebody else who was always staying in the background will be resurrected after death. There's a rough justice in this, but even posterity is not infallible.

Hynan: Had Faulkner been famous when he was very young, would that have affected his work? Because in your latest book, *And I Worked at the Writer's Trade,* this is what you are really trying to burrow into, to get at—what is the effect of fame or what you call the image the author constructs for himself and presents to the public?

Cowley: His talents were such that in his early books he had gained quite a wide reputation, and then of the books, and his best books, he wrote later in the 1930s and up to 1942, people turned away from them and his reputation had fallen to nearly zero by about 1942. And that was a sorrow to Faulkner, and yet what he wanted to do was to write the books, not to be famous. Then when fame descended upon him like an avalanche from a high mountain, that in part made things more difficult for him because he felt that he was not only a man writing, but he was also Faulkner the world figure.

Hynan: Well, you had much to do with that, though, didn't you?

Cowley: I had something to do with it, because at a time when his reputation was in eclipse, I managed to write about him and have published the *Portable Faulkner* in '46, which happened to restore his fame for a special reason. And the special reason was that there were other people who admired Faulkner and the appearance of the *Portable* gave them a chance to put their admiration into print. One of them was Robert Penn Warren who had a very high reputation academically, so from that time on Faulkner began to be studied by the academics and he already had a wide reputation in this country by time he won the Nobel Prize.

Hynan: In your present book, which has just been published—*And I Worked at the Writer's Trade*—you try to get back to who is famous or why it is that very good writers have been neglected; you try to bring them back, you try to resurrect them, resuscitate them. But even despite your efforts, valiant as they are, probably they won't be; yet did it give you any great pleasure that Faulkner, who was neglected for years and years and years, now becomes known to a new public as a result of what you wrote about him.

Cowley: That gives me a very great pleasure. It gives me the pleasure not of discovery, but of rediscovery, and discovery of the design back of all of Faulkner's writing. He is a very great author and he would have been reestablished to fame at some time. I perhaps had a great deal to do with hastening the discovery. He always felt there was a huge distinction between Bill Falkner the neighbor of many good neighbors in Oxford, Mississippi, and William Faulkner the writer who turned out these novels. They weren't the same person at all. His genius was something alien to him; it was something that he couldn't depend on and sometimes he stood back and looked at it. He said, "My God, I can't understand this. I wrote these books. Just I, Bill Falkner, wrote these books? I can't understand it."

Hynan: Well, let's get back to this question, because it is a very important one, the one you pose yourself, and I will pose it to you. What is the effect on an author's work, of the image he constructs of himself and presents to the public? Would Hemingway be a victim of this?

Cowley: Hemingway was somewhat a victim of it. He had to construct a false image of himself. He wasn't at all an essentially great sportsman, a great boxer, a great shot. He was an extraordinarily good wing shot, but he wasn't the greatest marksman in the world, but he always had to be first. And this necessity rather falsified his whole life, I think, at the end. And in *Islands in the Stream* you find out that at the end he was using his *persona,* his projected image, to the public, as the hero of his novel instead of the man himself.

Hynan: Were there any other writers you know or that you've studied of this century who also suffered from this?

Cowley: I think that many, many writers suffer from it. One special point at which the suffering becomes quite, quite obvious is the author who writes a book which is saluted as a masterpiece. Then it becomes a terrible, terrible task for him to write another book, because he's afraid of the critics saying, "This isn't as good as the last book. After Fitzgerald published *The Great Gatsby,* which *he* thought was a masterpiece, and which is a masterpiece, it took him nine years to publish another book, which was an extremely interesting book but not a masterpiece. One writer after another has gone down under that strain.

Hynan: What about Hart Crane?

Cowley: Hart Crane was a very special case and he's been written about a great deal. He was a difficult man, he was a difficult man to live with because every once in a while he would get drunk and do terrible things—throw your furniture out of the window, for example. And yet, once again, he depended on the talent that he felt within him that he wasn't sure of possessing at every moment. It couldn't be a trade with him—writing couldn't be, writing poetry—it had to be a discovery, a manna from heaven. And sometimes the manna wouldn't fall.

Hynan: I love that quotation in *Exile's Return* which you wrote in 1934: "Hart tried to charm his inspiration out of its hiding place with a Cuban rumba and a pitcher of hard cider."

Cowley: That he would do, but he couldn't always charm his inspiration out of its hiding place. Sometimes it stayed obstinately there.

Hynan: But he was an obsessive reviser, wasn't he?

Cowley: Oh, he would revise poems endlessly, endlessly. And before writing the poems he would make for himself long lists of words and phrases that ought to go into the poem. Some of them would go into it. He prepared for the moment of inspiration; after the moment of inspiration, he revised endlessly, but the moment of inspiration wouldn't always come.

Hynan: You published *Exile's Return* in 1934. Today it is, to my mind, a classic. It's a classic. It holds up still very, very well. And you had it revised in 1951 with a new foreword and the rest of it, but in

1934 when you published it, what was the reaction to it? Was this
book something new for a lot of people?

Cowley: It was something new and it was something *condemned*
in general. Younger reviewers rather liked it, but older reviewers were
absolutely furious. They said this generation that I was writing about
hadn't produced anything, Mr. Hemingway was growing dim and so
were the other people mentioned in the book. It was as if a ton of
bricks had come down on my head, and you know the book, after
being a most widely reviewed late spring book of 1934, sold 983
copies. And during the next ten years it may have sold another
hundred copies. It was quite different when I revised and reissued it
in 1951—it was almost universally praised and it has gone on with a
regular sale since that day. I don't know how many printings its gone
through . . . twenty perhaps.

Hynan: Why is it that it seems every so often critics and reviewers
miss something. They always seem to unite on something being bad
or something being very good, but when it's bad, it's very, very bad
. . . I mean, they've missed by more than a country mile. Why does
this happen among critics and reviewers? Is it a sense of imitation,
following each other or what?

Cowley: Oh, I wouldn't lay the fault entirely on critics. It's on
human nature—aren't we all sheep essentially?

Hynan: In a sense, yes.

Cowley: We follow the bellwether and go on . . . critics will do
that. It was very clear in the case of *Exile's Return*. This was a case of
generational conflict which is going on at all moments.

Hynan: Yes, and this is very important because you've said of the
1920s, it was a generation of "ions." What about the 1950s, when the
'50s became more sympathetic, highly sympathetic, to the '20s?

Cowley: Highly sympathetic to the 1920s? But that's part of the
alternation of mood in generations or, I prefer to call them age
groups, because a generation is supposed to be thirty years, a
physiological generation, whereas these alternating moods of age
groups come in intervals of about 15 years. Fifteen is the convenient
figure; it doesn't mean anything. But there is an alternation of mood
between the outward turning, the idealistic, the we-ness of the 1900s,
the 1930s, the 1960s, and the inward turning, the I-ness, the me-

ness, of the 1920s, the 1950s, and now the year 1970s. We're in the middle of another "me" period right now.

Hynan: Without any way of being as creative as the 1920s was, or without having something so clearly defined, you know, because surely, to your generation, the First World War was an absolute pivotal event. It was something of enormous importance.

Cowley: It was extraordinary for the creative person . . . they were very lucky at that time. We've had good writers since; we have good writers today whom I'm not going to mention because I hate to get into names, but there's a lot of vitality in American writing at the present time, as in Canadian writing . . .

Hynan: Which I would like to talk to you about very briefly because I know you don't know a great deal about it; you haven't followed it that closely, but there is one writer you've often mentioned to me, and I have in turn mentioned to others because we've both read him very well—John Glasgow.

Cowley: Oh, yes, I was crazy about John Glasgow's *Memoirs of Montparnasse,* and that is one of the truest books about Montparnasse around the late 1930—

Hynan: Late 1920s, around 1930, close to that, yes.

Cowley: —that I've ever come across, and I've been interested in Glasgow's career since then. He had been one of the few uniting points between the French poetry of Canada and the English poetry of Canada. He did a great anthology of French Canadian poetry in English translation.

Hynan: You likened the 1920s to an age of islands, your contemporaries in that age you likened to islands. What was the difference in the '30s when you became literary editor, succeeding Edmund Wilson, of the *New Republic?* Was that a different age from your contemporaries?

Cowley: That was a completely different age. The interest had turned outward. There was not so much interest in producing a masterpiece, which was the aim of writers in the 1920s, to making a personal success, not financial but artistic. And in the '30s there was more interest in comradeship, in changing and saving the world, in people working together, linking arms with hundreds and thousands of others as they marched toward the golden mountains across a bridge. That was the interest in the '30s, and the '30s as a period for

younger writers produced fewer masterpieces. They produced a
number of interesting works and then even now one's interest has to
be aroused in these works for historical reasons. It wasn't—except for
the survivors of the '20s, as for example Faulkner—it wasn't a great
age in new writers, although some of the new writers who appeared
in the '30s later did produce masterpieces.

Hynan: Didn't you become politically aware yourself during the
'30s? You became very much identified with left-wing politics in the
United States.

Cowley: I was involved in left-wing politics, first in the effort, you
know, to save the American economy—it seemed so important in the
first four years of the 1930s—and then in the effort to save the world
from fascism. It did seem in the later 1930s that fascism was sweeping
over one country after another and that unless we did something,
worked very hard, it would capture the world and thrust the world a
thousand years backward.

Hynan: What is your biggest complaint right now about yourself
and about how people use you? Are you used a lot by people?

Cowley: Oh, dear, dear, I'm used too much. You asked in one
earlier period about what is the effect of the academic life on writers.
I'll tell you one effect—they have to get a Ph.D. before they get a job.
In order to get a Ph.D. they have to write a dissertation, whereas in
the 1920s they would have written a poem. In order to write a
dissertation they have to do some original research. The original
research, if it's about some figure of the 1920s or 1930s involves
getting hold of people who knew that figure. And simply through the
accident of having lived so long, as Archie MacLeish said of himself
and me, that we're two of the last leaves on the oak tree—they write
me a letter and practically ask me to write their dissertation for them,
most of the time not even enclosing return postage. And I get
resentful, I get angry at being used, shall we say, as a national
research facility by people trying to write dissertations without the
nation having funded me even to the extent of getting me a secretary
so that I can answer these letters. Edmund Wilson had a card printed
up saying, "Mr. Wilson does not give interviews, does not supply
information to Ph.D. students, does not write blurbs for books, does
not . . ." He would check off the proper "does not" and send the
printed postcard back. I'm sometimes tempted to follow Wilson's

example, but being naturally, by inheritance, by family background, humble and helpful, I try to write letters to these people telling them where they can go for their information.

Hynan: You write in *And I Worked at the Writer's Trade* that over a period of sixty years or so you were involved in literary activity but that you feel now increasingly alone and beleaguered. Why is this?

Cowley: I feel alone and beleaguered to some extent because literature in this period has taken a turn, an antihuman turn, that doesn't excite my interest. It seems to me that so many fiction writers of today are practically in effect saying, "Look, Ma, no hands!" They're boasting about their technical facility and forgetting the fact that literature has to do with people and has to do with life. They think it has merely to do with technique. So these principles that were inbred in me, that literature deals with people, deals with human life, deals with the life around you that you know, are being increasingly defied by writers of talent who simply want to display their technical virtuosity. It also limits their subject matter so that the "academic novel" so-called is likely to be one of the dullest forms of writing one can imagine. When I open a book and find out from the first few pages that this book is about a 40-year-old professor falling in love with one of his 20-year-old students, I close the book—softly, reverently—but never to be opened again.

Hynan: Has this been a good age for you to live in? Has the twentieth century been a good one for you?

Cowley: I couldn't imagine a better century to live in, but then I never did live in another century and I don't have that imagination. I might very well have been happier had I been fifteen years older, had I been able to go to Paris in the Belle Epoque before World War I—I would have loved to have seen that life. But it seems, on the contrary, that life has been continually interesting and eventful during this twentieth century.

A Conversation with Malcolm Cowley

Diane U. Eisenberg/1979

From *The Southern Review,* 15, (April 1979), 288–98. Reprinted with the permission of Diane U. Eisenberg and *The Southern Review.*

Malcolm Cowley and I have something in common. We both have read each and every one of his literary contributions, made over a career that spans some sixty years. No easy feat, that . . . his pieces number more than thirteen hundred! Nevertheless, with his generous and remarkably accurate guidance, we were able to locate, list, and annotate the Cowley "oeuvre" the poetry, the books, the book reviews, the short critical pieces, the longer essays, the translations, and the short fiction. The result, after a period of several years, was a publication which pleased us both: *Malcolm Cowley: A Checklist of His Writings, 1916–1973* (1975).

Cowley has been accessible to younger scholars in a pleasant, responsive way. When he agreed to this interview I was delighted, but not surprised. "Let's work together to make it a good one," he wrote. "The best place for us to meet is the Harvard Club. I'll blow you to lunch. There's a room upstairs where we could talk quietly afterwards." And so, we met in New York City on one of the few lovely springlike days that we have in March. We lunched on cold red salmon and white wine and then went upstairs to talk.

This is what was said.

Eisenberg: What part does your new book, *And I Worked at the Writer's Trade,* play in the total work, the "oeuvre" of Malcolm Cowley?

Cowley: I have always been interested in doing a history of American letters and the literary life in my own lifetime; this book picks up some aspects of it that I'd neglected before. It deals with friends, whom I haven't written about; it deals with sudden surges of emotion in the literary world, changing fashions, and finally with the sixties and with the resurgence of the religion of art in the 1970s. It is in many ways autobiographical. I love to write memoirs. In fact, the easiest parts of a book for me are the parts when I'm really collecting my own memories of something that happened.

Eisenberg: Why is this book called *The Writer's Trade?* Why not the writer's "profession" or "vocation"?

Cowley: In this book, I refer to the trade of letters as distinguished from not the profession, but the vocation. The priestly vocation of writing is a little different from the trade of writing things, getting them published, and getting adequately paid for them. This book is more or less about the trade in as far as I can see. For example, I have often wondered why it is that some authors of as great talent as others, very famous, never get recognized for the true extent of their talents. I've tried to answer that question in this book with something that is true in some cases at least. You know, there are authors who really don't want to be famous. They think they want to be famous; they'd like to be famous if it came to them without working at all to be famous. They're willing to work at writing but they want their privacy; they want their honest work. S. Foster Damon was one of them. On a larger scale and with greater talent, Conrad Aiken is another who has never been recognized for the great poet and man of letters he truly was.

Eisenberg: Where did you learn "the writer's trade," the business of writing?

Cowley: In the trade I'm an autodidact. I learned from bitter experience. I could always write clean English and the editors of the magazines I wrote for always appreciated that, because they hate to go through a manuscript and mark it up. So I could always get my things published one way or another. But very often I didn't get much money for them. *Usually,* I didn't get much money for them. I've never had that talent and I've never had a regular literary agent. I don't know why; I suppose it is because I have always liked to deal directly with editors, having been one myself and finding that we spoke the same language.

Eisenberg: Do writers have an easier time of it now than they did when you started out? How has the trade changed?

Cowley: It's easier and harder. The trade of free lance is harder today. I don't think there are so many free-lance fiction writers. There are not many magazines that publish their work. As late as the 1920s and 1930s there were dozens of magazines that published short stories and paid for them. *The Saturday Evening Post* paid Scott Fitzgerald $4,000 per story for a while in the early thirties. On that, Fitzgerald could live, like a spendthrift prince. And I think there were others who were paid up to $5,000 by the *Post* at that time. That doesn't exist now; there's one magazine that pays well for stories and that is *The New Yorker.* I don't think there's another one. Many magazines pay well for articles and so most free lancers you meet today are article writers, not fiction writers. On the other hand, at the popular top of the profession it is novelist fiction writers who hit the jackpot.

Eisenberg: You say in your new book that you are unhappy about fiction writers who write "anti-stories" and in effect abolish the audience. Would you comment on this?

Cowley: That is true. Take Kenneth Burke's definition of literary form which he wrote at least as early as 1930. He said, "Form is the arousing of the expectation in an audience and the gratifying of that expectation." In other words, you raise the expectations, hopes, curiosity of your reader and then by the end of the story, in the course of time and by events of the story, you satisfy that expectation or curiosity. The reader plays a part. The reader determines the form. If, on the other hand, you say "Go to, I will abolish form; form is not true to life," well then you limit your readership to other people who are interested in fiction and technique. The ordinary reader doesn't want to read a story in which things happen, seemingly by pure accident, by arbitrary choice or whatnot. They like a story that moves from a beginning through a middle to an end. Those writers who took up the anti-story were really saying "Go to. Abolish the audience." Furthermore, there is an absolute lack of any feeling of playfulness or sense of humor in the anti-story. They're show-off stories. See how clever I am! See how I fooled you! See what a great man I am! Certainly some of these writers are very good indeed and I don't mean to imply that I have any objection to fantasy. Fantasy can be a story as anything else can. I simply object to the anti-story in which the beginning is no different from the end.

Eisenberg: "Good writers try to follow a special code of ethics,"

you tell us in *And I Worked at the Writer's Trade*. How did you arrive
at it?

Cowley: It's a long story. I tried to state something that I'd
observed for all of my adult life. I first came across it in Paris in 1922
through a number of French writers, among them Louis Aragon, who
was my particular friend at that time. I noticed that a great many of
their literary judgments were really moral judgments. "This man is
betraying literature; this man is catering to the public; he's just an
artist; he's not a poet," they would say. And so I tried to analyze for
myself, "What are these people basing their ethics on? Flaubert,
Proust or somebody else? What do they really think are the moral
standards for writing?" I came up with a sort of pentalog. What I
worried about was the fact that a man can observe all the command-
ments that writer or artist is bent on observing and yet mistreat his
family, fail to pay his debts, drink or have various other vices. The
artist's code of morals doesn't protect you from ordinary day-to-day
or neighborly vices but, nevertheless, it is a moral code and it has
produced actual saints of literature—who weren't saints in life.

Eisenberg: In the opening chapter of *And I Worked at the Writer's
Trade,* you quote Henry James: ". . . every man works better when
he has companions working in the same line and yielding the
stimulus of suggestion, comparison, emulation." Were you thinking in
part of the very good friendships you have sustained over the years
with other writers?

Cowley: In part I was thinking of my own friendships but I was
thinking of other people too. For example, I'll give away the subject
for a book that ought to be written. I'd like somebody to write a book
about the young men who were on the staff of the *Nassau Literary
Magazine* at Princeton in the years 1915 and 1916. Now those young
men included Edmund Wilson, Scott Fitzgerald, John Peale Bishop,
and some others whose names are not so well known, like T. K.
Whipple, John Biggs, who became a very much respected federal
judge in Delaware, and Henry Chapin, who wrote his autobiography
at the age of eighty. They had, with the exception of Chapin, a very
close relationship and grouped together for a long time. There were
other people also, such as Alex McCague. They were always writing
letters and asking each other's advice about their new book or new
poem. John Peale Bishop, who was one of the most talented of the

group, although his full talent was never realized, wrote to Edmund
Wilson from France at a time when he was struggling with a long
poem, saying, "Dear midwife, I need your services. The baby refuses
to be born."

There was another Harvard group at just exactly the same time
that included John Dos Passos, e. e. cummings, Robert Hillard, and
others whose names aren't so well remembered like Dudley Mc-
Comb. They wrote letters to each other in which they talked about
literary truths and about what they were trying to do. It was a
continual emulation. When one of them wrote a good book, all the
others were proud and also envious because, there is this double
thing among writers. They're terrible rivals, one of the other, and yet
they're all addicted to literature. So when one of their number does a
good thing they're proud of him and that raises their own stature.

For myself, I've been fortunate in friends. For example, I went to
high school with Kenneth Burke, whom I first met when he was five
years old. And beginning in high school we exchanged a huge
number of letters in which we would talk at times about ourselves
and what we were doing and what we had read. At other times we
talked about literary problems and in this case that exchange has
gone on down until yesterday. My most recent correspondence with
Kenneth was the night before last when I wrote him a long letter
upon hearing about the death of Matthew Josephson. Matty
Josephson and I had also known each other since 1916, I think, when
he was a sophomore at Columbia and I had come down to see
Kenneth, who was also at Columbia. Josephson and I were very
close in the 1920s and 1930s. He was an engaging young man with
large ideas and definite opinions about almost everything. He has a
talent for meeting great people in the world of letters and then
introducing his friends to them. Also for working on new magazines.
Then, he got to work on a life of Zola in the late 1920s. He showed
his other talent then and that was for a large, imaginative conception
on which he would spend, if necessary, years of work. It was not
enough years. He wasn't as good a stylist as Kenneth. His thought
didn't go as deep. But he had a broader grasp of conception.
Although our relationship had somewhat cooled during the last years,
nevertheless, it made me very, very sad to hear about Matty's death.
You asked, though, how much was I thinking of my friends and our

influences upon each other. The curious thing is that in most cases this rubbing of elbows and emulation is strongest during one's twenties. After that, people go off in their own paths and haven't so much to gain but nevertheless, the emulation remains.

Eisenberg: Would you explain the concept of "generations" or "age groups" that runs through your writings from *Exile's Return: A Literary Odyssey of the 1920's* to *And I Worked at the Writer's Trade?*

Cowley: Every fifteen years or so, the young people growing up are marked by a different sense of life from the sense of the age group before them and after them. For example, the period from 1960 to 1973 is distinctly different from the period in which we're living today. These kids grow up listening to different music, with a different sort of family structure. Sometimes the mothers are home, sometimes they're away at work. They receive different sorts of schooling. Sometimes they get left behind. Sometimes they get social promotion, whether they can read and write or not.

All these things differ for each age group. They have their qualities more or less stamped into them by the time the members are about twenty years old. Mauriac said, "It sometimes seems to me that all my career as a novelist is based on things that happened to me before I was twenty." So these new age groups come up one after another. They associate with each other, and not so much with older or younger people. They have an ideal of what the good life should be. They have their aversions and aspirations and these are all a little bit different than the aversions and aspirations, the catchwords, the music, the games, everything else of the age groups a little younger and a little older. And there are always, at any given time, oh, perhaps five age groups coexisting all at once; the children up to fifteen, the youths up to thirty, the rising generation age thirty to forty-five, the dominant generation, forty-five to sixty, and then the older generation from sixty to the end. And all these, each one of these age groups, has a different sense of life. And each of them tries to make its own sense of life prevail so that you find at times that there is a great deal of conflict between age groups.

Eisenberg: Can the writers of an age group avoid "the destiny of the age," those strains that run through a culture during a particular era and are experienced by all those alive at the time?

Cowley: Those strains affect everybody alive at the time but since there are always several different age groups coexisting at that time, they affect each age group in a different fashion. The Second World War was not the same war for Hemingway that it was for Norman Mailer; it was not the same war for Norman Mailer that it was for Donald Barthelme, who was a kid while it was going on. Those great events and those moods of the time affect different age groups in different fashions. But at times you find the different age groups picking up the same atmosphere or you find a younger generation converting an older generation. For example, in the 1960s you began to see faculty members joining rebellious youths. They always seemed to me to be faintly absurd, like fat businessmen dressed up as babies. They weren't really doing their own thing; they were doing the students' thing at that time.

Eisenberg: Is there always one literary generation or age group within a given decade that has the ascendency and is more vital?

Cowley: That's really two questions. There is always one age group in a given decade that has the ascendency. For example, in the 1920s which we think of now as the time of the Lost Generation, the dominant age group was composed of Sinclair Lewis, H. L. Mencken, Willa Cather, and Red Lewis, and especially all the people who were then in their forties. But the more vital generation at that time was what afterwards came to be known as the Lost Generation . . . of young people in their twenties, born just before the turn of the century.

Eisenberg: In what period does a writer or an artist, for that matter, make his greatest contribution?

Cowley: I'm sorry to report, I wish it were otherwise, but it seems to me now that the thirties for a man or woman is the key period. Yes, between thirty and forty-five. And that has been especially so in American letters. You take one author after another and you find that his or her real contribution has been made between the ages of thirty and forty-five. Novelists usually hang on longer than people in many other fields. They may do their best work a little later. But on the whole, as I go over the biographies of American writers, it seems to me they've said their big say by the time they're forty-five.

Eisenberg: And then what happens?

Cowley: Well, their craft continues to improve and if they have been truly interested in the subject, their writing may continue to improve for a long time. But the new thing that they were going to bring forward is likely to have been contributed before they were forty-five.

Eisenberg: The role of women has changed dramatically in your lifetime, hasn't it?

Cowley: Ah, what a change, indeed! I was just writing a little section of another new book which had to do with the International Writers' Congress for the Defense of Culture, in 1935 in Paris. The organizers of the Congress tried to get the most famous anti-fascist writers they could find to sit on the same high platform to deliver speeches. It occurred to me as I wrote about the Congress. "My God, how few women." The only woman's name that I saw was Anna Seghers, a very talented, exiled German novelist. She was the only one on the platform wearing a skirt. If they were to have such a Congress today, which they wouldn't do, it would be made up of perhaps one-third women. And when we think of very distinguished writers these days, or distinguished writers in the new generation, there are many, many more women among them.

Eisenberg: Do you have some favorite women writers?

Cowley: Of course I have favorites among women! You don't expect me just to love the whole damn sex, do you? I think Doris Lessing is awfully good and I think her novel *The Golden Notebook* is one of the classics of our time. In American writing today, Joyce Carol Oates and Joan Didion are very good. There are many other gifted women writers, whereas in the generation of the 1920s they were almost all men. I think Katherine Anne Porter was about the only woman at that time whom you thought of. Also Louise Bogan.

Eisenberg: I recall that you collaborated with women in different of your efforts. I know that you worked with Hanna Josephson on the dramatization of Aragon's war writings.

Cowley: I collaborated with her, oh gladly. I'd work with the devil himself if he had a good prose style.

Eisenberg: An interview with Malcolm Cowley would be incomplete if it didn't have a question or two about William Faulkner. Have you ever wondered what might have happened to Faulkner if you hadn't brought him back to the public's attention in the early forties with your now famous introduction to *The Portable Faulkner?*

Cowley: Yes, I have, but I have no conceit about what I did for

Faulkner's work, not for Faulkner, but for his work. My *Portable Faulkner* wouldn't have had the effect it did, were is not that several very able novelists were crazy about Faulkner. He had never lost his reputation among some of his fellow novelists. It was the critics, especially the academic critics and journalistic critics who had gone sour on his work because it was hard to read. When the *Portable* came out, it was an opportunity for some of his novelist admirers, notably Caroline Gordon and Robert Penn Warren, to write very long and featured reviews of the *Portable* which no *Portable* had received before. Warren had very high standing in the academic community and that helped move Faulkner over there. Faulkner's work made Faulkner famous, not any treatment of his work. Even if I hadn't edited the *Portable,* he'd have been very famous at some time. I think the *Portable* hastened his fame by two, three, four, or five years.

It also meant that when he got the Nobel Prize for different reasons, the American public was at last prepared to accept his getting it. Although there were some very angry editorials about this "degenerate novelist," he would have been famous without any help from me simply because the work deserves to be famous. It takes time and time heals.

Eisenberg: You distinguish between Faulkner's genius and his talent in an interesting way. Could you explain that distinction?

Cowley: Faulkner didn't make that same distinction in words but he, too, at times spoke of his genius. Once, in a conversation with an older woman in New Orleans, when he was about twenty-one, he said, "You know ma'am, I'm a genius." But he really didn't mean, "I *am* a genius." He meant, "I *have* a genius." That means that something in him, when he wrote and gave full rein to it, would produce things that he didn't expect to be produced. Those things came out of his subconscious mind, not directly out of something he had figured out. And coming out of the subconscious mind, they had a truth, call it a primitive nature of man. Things happen in one of Faulkner's stories, not by logic, but by magic. Actually, in some cases it's fairytale. His great story "The Bear" is a fairytale, as I said in *And I Worked at the Writer's Trade.*

Then you have to distinguish from this "genius" the fact that Faulkner also had a great "talent." He was an intelligent critic of his own work and he could take a story drawn from the unconscious and revise it in certain ways that would turn a touching, affecting, powerful story into a really great story. He also showed his talent when he was working in Hollywood. That was talent, and he showed it when he was writing a sort of detective story at times. That's talent, not genius.

Eisenberg: Why have you steered certain authors away from writing book reviews, although it has been the art form which you used most often?

Cowley: I gave this advice to Erskine Caldwell who had what impressed me as a very great natural talent for telling stories. It seemed to me that if he got into the sort of analytical work that is required in a book review, he might weaken his natural talent for writing stories. I certainly wouldn't have given that advice to Alfred Kazin, for example, who had a natural talent for criticism. Later, it turned out that he also had a natural talent for reminiscences. I think it was perfectly sound advice for Caldwell. It's an individual matter, depending upon in which direction your talent lies. I learned to write book reviews because when I was so poor in New York City, in the twenties, book reviews were the only things I could get paid for. I didn't get paid very much, but, still I was paid something. So I wrote book reviews and then I wrote more book reviews and that really stopped me from writing fiction. It did have that effect on me. I wrote some stories when I was younger and I would have written more if I hadn't taken so much of my time with book reviews. But since chance more or less had dictated that form to me, then, as with anybody else, I began pouring all of myself into that form and it became my sonnet sequence.

Eisenberg: "I am a revisionist by trade. I hate to write, but I love to revise." That's a Malcolm Cowley quote. And I know it's true, having traced your poems in their many revised states. Would you comment on the revising that you do?

Cowley: I've fallen into very bad habits of writing. I write one paragraph at a time, and until that paragraph is in fair shape I can't even transcribe it. So that a great deal of my revision has to do with making sentences work. A great deal of it has to do with striking out long words where I find a short word makes the same sense. A great deal of it has to do with avoiding the trite phrases that are so difficult to avoid, because some of them were once, in the beginning, the best phrase for that thing. So you have to stop and ask yourself, "What really happened? Now, how can I put that into the simplest language?" Or, once again, the revision has to do with varying the sentence structure.

Eisenberg: When does a revised poem, one that you've made several changes in over the years, become a new poem?

Cowley: Why, Diane, that's an absolutely metaphysical question. They used to ask in a philosophy course: they'd say, there's a little boy who had a jackknife. He lost one of the sides of it, and had that replaced. Then he lost the other side and had that replaced. Then he broke the blade, and had that replaced. Then the frame got lost, and he had that replaced. Was it the same jackknife? Well, you can ask that about any number of machines. Is it the same car after you get a new motor and a new body?

Sometimes you retain the title, sometimes you change the title in the course of the revision. I ran into that as a practical question, in getting together *Blue Juniata: Collected Poems* because there were some poems that I changed so much that I thought they were new poems and they ought to be published again. Were they new poems or weren't they? Once I sent off a poem to *The New Yorker.* It was accepted and then I wrote to them and said, "I've been thinking about this. This was published once before in another form and although the form was completely different I think that bars it out this time, so I'll have to withdraw the poem."

Eisenberg: What are you working on now?

Cowley: I am trying to extend *Exile's Return,* or that sort of book, through the 1930s. But it's going to be a very different sort of book because I can't any longer use "we" so freely as I did in *Exile's Return.* In *Exile's Return* I was conscious of speaking for many other people I knew. In the 1930s there was more difference of opinion and I have to be a great deal more objective. But that is what I'm working on now; I am carrying that story through to the beginning of World War II.

Eisenberg: You say, "The hardest problem for any writer, no matter what his medium, is getting to work in the morning." How do you get started each day?

Cowley: Ah, I don't, Diane. I can spend days trying to get started on writing a piece. The hardest thing is writing the first sentence.

Edmund Wilson once said to me, "I used to worry about the first sentence; I don't any longer. I just write the first sentence. Then I go on." But I can't do it like that. I have to see the shape of a piece before I start to work on it. So I spend most of my time glooming over what I'm going to write. Then once I get started, writing goes at a normal slow speed, much slower now than it used to be.

Eisenberg: Are you doing it all in your head or are you making notes?

Cowley: I very often make notes, even voluminous notes. Once, on the essay I did on Faulkner, I took ninety pages of single-spaced notes. It must have amounted to, oh certainly, fifty thousand words on Faulker before I even started writing the essay. Then the essay wasn't hard to write.

Eisenberg: What is the process through which you go as your thoughts are coming together?

Cowley: It goes slowly. Very often, in the close criticism of a longer piece, you find things out on a second reading of the book. I begin marking passages that seem to be significant. Then I'll type off many of those passages on separate cards. Then I'll sort the cards and very often, by the time the cards are sorted, I'll find that I have the form for my essay.

Eisenberg: How long are you working each day?

Cowley: I'm not working as long as I used to. I used to be a sprint runner when I was doing reviews for the *New Republic*. When the final review had to be written, I would work on it from twelve to twenty-four hours. I actually have written for twenty-four consecutive hours on a piece, but now I can't do that any longer. I have to write longer pieces and two or three hours a day is about as much as I can do while my head is still clear and fresh.

Eisenberg: Do you find time to read for pleasure?

Cowley: Little, little time to read for pleasure. The pleasure reading that I do has to do with one of our family pleasures at night sometimes . . . watching the serial as novel on TV. When they put Trollop on TV, we read Trollop, after falling in love with Susan Hampshire, the star of that performance. "I, Claudius" set us to reading "I, Claudius" or "The Twelve Caesars," which, by the way, is selling very well in paperback as a result of "I, Claudius." Now that they're putting on *Anna Karenina,* I started reading Tolstoy again.

Trollope, Tolstoy, Dickens. I like the serials but they are mostly on public television and mostly imported from England.

Eisenberg: What other kinds of things are giving you and Mrs. Cowley the most pleasure these days?

Cowley: We enjoy watching television serials and features and we enjoy meeting friends.

Eisenberg: Are you satisfied with what you've accomplished, with the Cowley "oeuvre"?

Cowley: No! Distinctly dissatisfied! It goes back to a long and bad error that I made during my twenties. That is, partly influenced by French friends, I decided, "Well, I just have to keep at this thing honestly and if I make any great success in my twenties or thirties I'm not going to keep at it honestly," so I actually *tried* not to make a success. I was the anticareerist at that time for myself. And a part of the result was that I didn't drive myself to write some big work that was really expected of me. I had chances, too, but I didn't drive myself to finish it. And the fact that I didn't drive myself hard enough in my twenties is the big error I made. I should have been looking much more at the big overall pattern . . . keeping at producing bigger books. That was an error.

Eisenberg: In appraising your life you've said, "No glitter, no jackpots, just one man's struggle through changing times with the laborious, lovely, but unpracticable task of putting words into patterns that he hopes will be permanent"; through the years you've observed, chronicled, and lived through a century of dramatic change. What hasn't changed? Is there anything that remains the same?

Cowley: Well, that same statement, which was true when I was young, is true today. I mean, the writer's trade is a laborious, tedious but lovely occupation of putting words into patterns. I love that trade, profession, and vocation. And that is something that persists over time.

An Interview with Malcolm Cowley

Warren Herendeen and Donald G. Parker/1981

From *The Visionary Company: A Magazine of the Twenties* (Summer 1981), 9–21. Reprinted with the permission of Warren Herendeen and Donald G. Parker.

In late April we accepted an invitation from artist Peter Blume and his wife Ebie to visit them—in order to interview Mr. Blume—at their Sherman, Connecticut, home on Church Road, where they have lived, opposite Muriel and Malcolm Cowley, for the past fifty years. After our tape-recorded afternoon interview was concluded (printed in part in this issue), Mr. and Mrs. Cowley arrived for cocktails and dinner. We were then regaled with fascinating recollections of the Twenties, and after—of both the famous and the forgotten—told with narrative skill, wit, and humor.

The following day, after lunch with the Cowleys in their picturesque, almost French-seeming country house (actually a converted barn), Mr. Cowley led us on a tour of Sherman. He had recently heard that the new owner of Addie Turner's house had found some Hart Crane "papers" in the attic . . . investigation of this rumor was the impetus for our tour. At the Turner house we looked into its now legendary rooms, gazing out the window from which Crane threw his recalcitrant typewriter, glancing for a moment through another window across the countryside—and the years—to "Robber Rocks," where Crane once lived with the Slater Browns. (Peter Blume and Allen and Caroline Gordon Tate had also lived at Mrs. Turner's during the Twenties.) The present owner of the house showed us the "papers"—two recently discovered items: a postcard to Crane from Gorham Munson in Germany (asking the poet if he had received the art books Munson had mailed to him) and Crane's tennis racket, in need of restringing and woefully warped, still inside its cover, Crane's name (still "Harold Hart") and his Cleveland address printed on the canvas.

Finally that afternoon, back at the Cowley residence, America's foremost literary historian treated us to a wide-ranging interview in which he moved from the question of nineteenth-century influences to a discussion of his future plans. (Part of the interview is published here; the other part will appear in the *Dictionary of Literary Biography's Update*.) A gracious, witty man, filled with years worn comfortably and thoughtfully, Mr. Cowley was immensely well-informed, quick of mind, and decisive. He seemed the kind of realist the century had need of, one intellectually and passionately engaged in its great ideas and movements—steadfastly a humanist, a man of good will and clear vision. He was eighty-three in August.

Interviewer: As you know, we have been speaking with Peter Blume about the Twenties and about our new magazine, and we wonder if you would respond to a few queries about the Twenties, once again. You said recently in a letter to us that you preferred the name "World War I generation" as opposed to the "Lost Generation" for the Twenties. Would you explain?

Cowley: It wasn't the Lost Generation any more than several other generations have been "lost." Or, perhaps one should say, any more than *every* generation is lost when one measures its small achievements against its dreams. So I would rather say that this is the generation of people who came of age around the time of World War I. They seemed to have had—like every age group (the new word is "cohort") . . . they had certain ideals, a certain sense of life that was different from that of people a little older or a little younger. I sometimes think that in *Exile's Return* I gave about as effective a statement of those ideals as has been made and thus helped to shape not the generation but the public concept of it.

Interviewer: Do you agree with what we have said in reference to our magazine, that the Twenties was the seminal decade in American literary culture in the twentieth century?

Cowley: It was a seminal decade, but perhaps there have been others. I think that it produced unusual numbers of persons of marked individuality, and of marked talent too, so that it really did set that impress on American culture for a while—to the extent that people somewhat younger fell into the same patterns. A succeeding generation really didn't appear until the 1950s, except in poetry, where a number of very interesting poets appeared at the end of the 1930s. There were five or six of them—Delmore Schwartz, Randall Jarrell, Robert Lowell, John Berryman, Theodore Roethke—five of them. All of them were manic-depressive, with marked manic phases. Two of them committed suicide; they all died young; and they were all highly talented. I think perhaps Ted Roethke was the most talented poet of that group, even more than Robert Lowell. Somebody ought to do a book on the group. They weren't friends, but call them a group of talented poets, all of about the same age and all with rather tragic or sudden ends. Roethke and Lowell died of heart failure. I think, more or less, that Delmore Schwartz died because he wasn't Shakespeare. That's what his first wife said: "You know what's the trouble with Delmore? He isn't Shakespeare." So he got discouraged by not being Shakespeare. And then Berryman and Randall Jarrell both committed suicide.

Interviewer: Did you read *Humboldt's Gift?* about Schwartz?

Cowley: That's about Delmore, yes.

Interviewer: In another letter to us in 1978 you compared the Twenties and the Thirties and essentially referred to the Twenties as having "me-ness" and the Thirties as having "we-ness"; to the Thirties as having political and communal interests as opposed to the Twenties as having a dream of individual success.

Cowley: That's true, the "me" and the "we." I think there has been a sort of alternation of "me" and "we" periods in American literature and even in American life. I think during the "me" periods the ideal has been individual success, whether in money, in literature, or in electric lights on Broadway. Always it's the success of the individual, and the most, the *greatest,* sacrifice the individual makes is the sacrifice of his life to his art. Then that will be succeeded by a "we" period in which the dream is of a new society that all of us join together in creating. "We" periods always end in (well, almost always end in) some public event that leads to disillusionment. For example, the Twenties ended with the Wall Street crash; the Thirties ended really with the Stalin-Hitler Pact in 1939. Nothing clear came after that until we were in World War II. I've said "Twenties" and "Thirties," but remember that these periods aren't equivalent to decades; they very often last a little longer than decades. After the war we have this era of the turtleneck sweater. The individual once again. The "I" period of individual security and don't-take-any-risks, which was the 1950s, sometimes called "The Silent Generation." Remember *that* succeeded to what we call the 1930s. The decade pattern doesn't work out at all. We leap over decades. The Fifties lasted until I don't know when—I suppose until the Kennedy assassination in '63, isn't it? when you had that brief and crazy period, from '63 to '73? Always this alternation of "I" and "we," or perhaps I'm wrong on that, perhaps I'm riding a theory too hard, but it does in strange ways seem to work out like that. You could expand the thing backwards and forwards; for example, the generation with enormous interest in social causes, followed by the World War I generation, as I'd call it, which had absolutely no interest in social causes till after the Wall Street crash.

Interviewer: From the vantage point of *The View from 82¾* does your reading of manuscripts or of the American scene at the moment suggest we are in a social-minded era, now—more of a "we". . . ?

Cowley: No, I haven't seen this appear, though I'm pretty sure it will appear. That is, you could take a risk and predict the course of history, but you can't give dates to the future. At some time the "me-generation" that we have been witnessing for the past ten years or so will give way again to a "we-generation," when and because of what events I don't know.

Interviewer: Some of the remarks you made in *The Dream of the Golden Mountains,* which we were talking about last night at dinner, especially your description of what President Hoover was doing just before Roosevelt took over, seemed to have a rather peculiar similarity to some activities going on today. Does it seem a little like historic repetition?

Cowley: Oh, yes, we get those repetitions. I look forward with trepidation to what's going to happen in the next four years. And what a cabinet Reagan has!

Interviewer: Did we misunderstand you last night? We thought we heard a reference to the fact that you had written something recently about Caroline Gordon's death.

Cowley: No, I haven't written anything about her death. I got an account of it from her granddaughter—very touching. No, I wouldn't undertake to write that.

Interviewer: Concerning our title, with the key word being "visionary," is that an apt term for the Twenties?

Cowley: "Visionary Company"?

Interviewer: We think especially in reference to Crane it is, but we wonder about the whole decade.

Cowley: Peter Blume is a visionary; for example, if you look at the collection of his paintings over the years, you can see vision finding expression in them. I think he's better for your thesis than some other people. Kenneth Burke has been speculative rather than visionary. He has produced in the course of his long career an extraordinary number of new ideas, many of which have been accepted, even down to the Structuralists and Deconstructionists. It isn't true that they took the ideas from Burke, but he was the precursor of many of them, especially in his emphasis on the *word*. He speaks of his system as "logology." So that becomes a little aside from this concept, "visionary," which often seems to me to promise a vision of a new earth and a new heaven, a little bit toward being utopian, or else toward the mystical apprehension of the world, in terms of Whitman's "Song of Myself." Hart Crane, yes, he is part of a visionary company. Hart Crane and Peter Blume, but I think that for myself I was always much more realistic. I had visions of the ideal life at times, but, except for a brief period in the early Thirties, I wasn't actively working to enforce a vision.

Interviewer: Among the people we've been talking to or mentioning, of course we find sympathies of interest and shared concerns. Some of them have become very well known over the decades, but they also seem somewhat overshadowed historically by the influence of T. S. Eliot. We would like to focus a little more on the visionary people to see them as they were in and of themselves, apart from Eliot.

Cowley: Of those whom you might be interested in writing about, not many of them were affected by Eliot. I must say I was a little affected by Eliot. I could point out the influence in various poems, but other poets reacted strongly against Eliot, among them both Crane and Cummings, in different ways; Cummings at the end of his life was a sort of transcendentalist, as I tried to make clear in the essay I did on his work. Wanting to document the "visionary company," perhaps you should bring in Thornton Wilder, who was visionary in a curious fashion, although not close to the other people that you thought of writing about.

Interviewer: Was *The Bridge of San Luis Rey* discussed much among the people you knew at the time it appeared?

Cowley: No, that didn't affect my immediate friends. There's Allen Tate to mention here, simply in point of geographical focus. It is possible also to mention Matthew Josephson and Robert M. Coates, whom you've left out of your reckoning and you shouldn't leave him out. He's a much better writer than he's been given credit for being. Cowley, Blume, all those on this little one-mile stretch of Church Road in Sherman; then across the state line there was a house where Blume, Hart Crane, Allen Tate, Caroline Gordon, and a forgotten figure, Nathan Asch, all lived in one house, and half a mile away at Robber Rocks, Slater Brown and Sue Brown. John Wheelwright came here for a couple of summers. And who else?

Interviewer: Did Kenneth Burke ever come up this way?

Cowley: He never stayed here. He settled in New Jersey, but he came here for parties. Several of his friends corresponded with Kenneth so voluminously that it almost became a close companionship. As you know, Burke and Sue Brown and Jimmy Light, of the Provincetown Players, and I all went to Peabody High School in Pittsburgh, and that led to a sort of reassembling of the Peabody High School group in Greenwich Village in 1919. In fact, Jimmy Light was the one who made friends easily, so that when I first came to New York as a boy of twenty, immediately I was more or less friends with the old Village characters, including Gene O'Neill and Dorothy Day, besides many others whose names have passed out of currency. Kenneth Burke and Matty Josephson were classmates at Columbia for a year. Oh, Bill Brown was also in that class, so that this formed a somewhat closely-knit group. I thought your idea there had a good basis in actuality.

Interviewer: We plan to pursue that idea. You've mentioned several writers of the Twenties that you thought were ignored or passed over and ought to be further considered—Foster Damon, for example.

Cowley: One of them is Dawn Powell, who was an extremely witty novelist; one book I recommend is *The Wicked Pavilion.* Her last novel, *The Golden Spur,* is quite interesting too, besides all the

novels before that. Each novel has a superb chapter in it. She was
actually wittier than Dorothy Parker. Now she is almost totally
forgotten. Ramon Guthrie, I think, should have received more attention. There are others that I think of from time to time—I've
mentioned Coates—who never got just recognition for what they had
done.

Interviewer: Could you tell us a little more about Nathan Asch?

Cowley: Nathan was the son of Sholem Asch, who was an
enormously popular Yiddish novelist; all his books were translated
into English and many of them were bestsellers. Nathan started out
quite young with a novel called *The Office,* which received very good
reviews here. Didn't have much sales, most first novels don't have,
but for some surprising reason it sold better in Germany during the
Weimar Republic. Then he wrote a second novel that was disappointing to me, called *Love in Chartres,* and a third novel called *Pay-Day,*
which was more or less suppressed on moral grounds. That was the
best of his novels. *Pay-Day* was also the day of the Sacco-Vanzetti
execution, so he worked that into the novel. After that he wrote a
book called *The Road,* about traveling over America by bus, and he
wrote a novel about this area, called *The Valley.* That ended his
publishing career. During the war he was a sergeant in the Air Force,
really in their public relations, a P.R. non-commissioned officer. Not
having to do it, he nevertheless flew a large number, a dozen or
more, of bombing flights over Germany, and he wrote letters that
were extraordinary. I used to get them. He came back and lived in
Mill Valley and wrote. His wife had a job and supported him. He
wrote, and nothing he wrote was published. Each of his manuscripts
would have been accepted if it had been a new book by a new
author, but his bad record in the bookstores frightened publishers,
and they wouldn't take his other novels. Then he started to work on
memoirs. . . . He wrote an extraordinary memoir of his father,
Sholem Asch, which he gave to *Commentary* and Podhoretz printed
it, after cutting the heart out of it. Then he died of lung cancer. I think
he was almost a paradigm of the failed author, but he had loads of
talent. He was in Paris with Josie Herbst, another author whom they
are making efforts to rescue from obscurity, and John Herman and
also Hemingway, who was the great star of Paris in those days (he
was cool to his rivals even if they were younger and not much of

rivals). You find Asch mentioned in Hemingway's *Letters*. I was a
better friend of Nathan's than most of the other people around him,
and sorrier about his lack of recognition and rather early death. I
don't think Peter Blume liked him so well; they lived for a time at
Addie Turner's house.

Interviewer: You once suggested to us that there was a story to
tell about how you happened to write *Exile's Return*. You said it
started with a sort of house party at Yaddo and the suggestion was
that, given the opportunity, you would tell this story.

Cowley: Elizabeth Ames, the director of Yaddo, suggested to me
that I organize, for the week before the mansion opened, some sort
of conference of writers, and Matty Josephson may have suggested
that we make it a conference about writing memoirs of Paris in the
1920s. I don't know, that idea was very much on my mind, so we got
together, Kenneth Burke, Evan Shipman (another forgotten writer of
the 1920s), Bob Coates, Jack Wheelwright, Matty Josephson, and we
went up there and had the mansion to ourselves for a week. I wrote
the beginning of *Exile's Return*—I think the beginning was an account
of my adventure with the proprietor of the Rotonde. That was written
first and I got that underway before I left. Nobody else wrote anything
as far as I know.

Interviewer: What year was this?

Cowley: This was in May 1931. In 1933 I decided to go ahead
with the story and by that time I saw it as a book. I took a leave of
absence from *The New Republic* for ten weeks and went down to a
farm on the state line between Tennessee and Kentucky, a farm
called Cloverlands, owned by cousins of Caroline (Gordon) Tate. The
Tates were living near at hand that summer and I worked hard on the
book. By the time I came back in July, I must have had a manuscript
of close to 150 pages. The funny thing is that when I look in my
notebooks for the periods, I don't find anything but complaints about
how slow I'm going along with this. But I had several inspirations in
the course of the writing. What I did first was go right back to the
beginning and write about my youth in Pennsylvania, then Harvard
and then Ambulance Service, so I could bring it up to having me in
Paris in the summer of 1923. I had from then on the problem of
finishing the book. It was Harry Crosby's suicide that gave me what I
regarded as the end of the book because I thought Crosby summed

up a lot of things that I'd been talking about in the earlier parts of the story. And that thing, the Harry Crosby long chapter, I wrote in two weeks in the little town of Riverton, Connecticut, where I had room and board for $22.50 a week. This was really in the depths of the depression—March 1934. So that's the story of the writing, except that the book was finished on May 1, 1934, and it was out before the first of June. They handled things fast in those days. Now it takes at least six months to get a book through the press.

Interviewer: Did you say somewhere that you had removed the number one . . .

Cowley: Oh yes, I finished on May Day, May first. I thought it was too ostentatious, so I changed the date simply to May.

Interviewer: You seem to have worked continuously through decades.

Cowley: No, no, at certain points I became blocked on some piece that I couldn't finish. If you went through my notebooks, you would find projects for books I never wrote, including at least two novels, as I come to think of it, and other summaries of collections of essays, and yet I've published more books since I was seventy years old than I published before I was seventy. That's rather unusual, isn't it? One reason is that partly they were collections and rewritings of things I had done in my fifties and sixties. In my notebook I find several times, "Time for another book." Well, let me see, what do I have for it . . . *And I Worked at the Writer's Trade* started out as a collection of essays pure and simple. And then as I worked on it, I began typing it together. Before that, *A Second Flowering* was essentially a collection of long essays I had written on authors of my own generation which. . . . When I got the book together I wrote four or five new chapters to fill out the plan.

Interviewer: From what you just said, it sounds almost as if things accumulate and suddenly a pattern seems to emerge. Is that how it works?

Cowley: Pattern doesn't "seem" to emerge, but I find it. The pattern is likely to be chronological, not by date of writing, but by date of subject matter. I do have a feeling that things that happened in 1960 couldn't happen in quite the same way in 1961 or 1962. I have the feeling that the world is a continuing—on-going, they now say—process in which, existing in time, any event is irreversible.

Interviewer: From this point of view would you say that some of the people who write to you asking questions about the 1920s aren't sufficiently oriented toward ideas or events or historical patterns? Are they too oriented toward subjects, personalities . . . ?

Cowley: Well, very many of them have theses that they want to prove; too often the theses are without relation to the actual sequence of events. What produced this frame of mind? Was it produced by a series of experiences, an irreversible series? There is a point at which the attitude, the frame of mind, begins to emerge from it.

Interviewer: When you answer these questions, do you find any compelling reasons to think that we are like the World War or post-World War I generation?

Cowley: No, I find no compelling reasons. One thing was that the post-World War I generation had more confidence in a strange way. That is, a new world seemed to be opening up in literature. Each of them felt he could contribute some new book, if possible a masterpiece, to the picture of American literature. Some of them did, a few of them did, a very few. They had confidence and it seems to me each had confidence in his own talent.

Interviewer: Novelistically, does Faulkner, in your mind, reflect very well the feeling, the atmosphere, of the 1930s?

Cowley: I've never read a novel that reflected the atmosphere of the 1930s properly. When I came to read the books they always seemed simplified. They gave us the picture perhaps partly the way it was, but gave such an abstract, simplified version of it. The characters became simpler than they were in actuality, so that in a way I mistrusted the historical novel always. Life is more complicated than the historical novel makes it out to be.

Interviewer: Your own writing is characteristically precise, dramatic, and clear, and yet at the same time you admire Faulkner, whose novelistic style can certainly be sometimes described as difficult and complex.

Cowley: Well, Faulkner's style is difficult at times and simple at times. When he comes to the climax of a narrative, his style becomes as sparse, as simple, as Hemingway's. Sometime, for narrative technique, re-read his story, part of a novel, "The Bear," with a firm structure and everything happening once again in a graded series.

Almost always in Faulkner you are continually building up toward a climax; then you reach the climax and he likes to end the story on a tangent, or by shooting off in some way. It's like the Greek dramas which we're told were performed three at a time, in trilogies, and were followed by a satyr play. Faulkner does that instinctively.

Interviewer: You've even gone to the extent of saying that, in your respect for prose, you would work with the Devil if he had a good prose style. At the time you were studying in France in the Twenties and afterwards, you maintained an interest in French literature. Were there some French writers that seemed to you to have a prose style that . . .

Cowley: My interest in French literature, by the way, came to a strange stop with the fall of Paris in 1940. From that date I haven't truly kept abreast of French writing. I'm rather disappointed by the fashion in which French critics and philosophers have become so Germanic. But in the interval before that, for style I truly admired Maurice Barrès. I translated one of his books, but others I simply read with admiration for the way he always surprised you. That is one feature of a good prose style—you can't read a page of it without being bouleversé—without being surprised and upset by a choice of word at one point or another. Barrès was marvelous at finding the word that surprised you. And of course there was always Flaubert for the fact of making so damn few blunders in his rhythms and his choice of words. in prose I was taken by many writings of my friend Louis Aragon; he had that same ability to surprise. As I say, I kept up with French literature until the fall of Paris and then, what was it? I became a little deaf to it. Of course, Racine and Baudelaire were my great enthusiasms.

Interviewer: You have spoken of Emerson as one of your heroes. What special quality is it in Emerson that makes him a hero?

Cowley: He's a hero of prose. I think that Emerson's style at his best is one of the most admirable in American literature. Outside of that is his perfect integrity and the fashion in which this boy of a poor family, really, in one fashion and another, gave up the pastorate of a wealthy church and went out to see if he could live . . . by writing. He wrote his essays, and the income he got from them was from reading them to an audience, reading them beautifully. You could always trust Emerson. He did so much for so many people in a quiet way, if he believed in them.

An Interview with Malcolm Cowley

Randell Watson and Michael T. Guinzburg/1981

From the *Sarah Lawrence Review,* (Fall 1980–Spring 1981) 42–48. Reprinted by permission.

Interviewer: We had questions but we decided we wouldn't be too formal about it, and so I guess we're going to ask you to start rolling.

Cowley: Well, what if the wheels are square?

Interviewer: Is there anything that you would like to talk about?

Cowley: Start rolling in what area? On what highway?

Interviewer: The highway of American literature of this century.

Cowley: That's a big highway. Very broad. Eight lines of traffic both ways.

You know, when I went to college a great many years ago, class of '19, as far as I know there were no undergraduate courses in American literature at Harvard. I think there were a couple of graduate courses, maybe a seminar in Emerson, but not one undergraduate course. I went through six semesters at Harvard with scarcely a suspicion there was such a thing as American literature.

Then in the inter-war period, in the nineteen-thirties, there were signs of interest. After the war, when they were putting together the *Literary History of the United States,* the contributors had great arguments and they weren't going to pay much attention to twentieth-century American writers. I remember popping up in my seat and arguing about this; and finally they did give attention to twentieth-century writers. Then gradually the courses proliferated. Now you can't go to a big university without getting more courses in American literature than anyone has use for.

The professors started out by establishing a canon. Certain books were in the canon and certain books weren't in the canon. About the first book to be unanimously elected to the canon was *Moby Dick,* and that is very curious because *Moby Dick* had been out of print in this country from approximately 1880 to 1920. It was discovered

around 1920 and suddenly there were more and more editions of
Moby Dick and more and more critical essays on *Moby Dick.*

After the Melville period T. S. Eliot was the canonical author. For a
while there were more dissertations on Eliot than on anyone else, and
that kept on. It look a long time before the Faulkner boom started,
but that has gone to amazing lengths at the present time. Whitman is
coming as the next object of attention, and I hope Emerson; but
always the focus shifts. One author is canonical and one author is
outside the pale. Everybody writes about the canonical authors. Why
not write about the uncanonical writers, some of whom are actually
very good?

Well, that's enough going down the center of an eight-lane highway. Ask me another question.

Interviewer: Do you think Hart Crane's poetry has held up over
the years?

Cowley: It has held up very well. There's a moderately big battle
going about Hart Crane's *The Bridge* between two sides that I call
the integrationists and the dispersionists. The integrationists believe
that *The Bridge* is an extremely important work for its overall form as
a unified poem. The dispersionists say, "No use wasting time on
whether *The Bridge* is a failure; it *is* a failure. What we should do is
find the remarkable riches that Crane distributes over the length of
the work." In this great argument I fall between two stools. There's
absolutely no doubt that Crane himself was an integrationist; but
there's also no doubt that some sections of *The Bridge* are better than
others. There are two sections which I think would improve *The
Bridge* if they were removed. Those are a poem called "Indiana" and
another called "Quaker Hill." Still another poem, "Cape Hatteras,"
teeters on the edge of greatness while continually threatening to fall
into absurdity. But other sections of *The Bridge* are undeniably great
poetry. Those sections are "Ave Maria," "The River," "The Dance,"
"The Tunnel," and "Atlantis." In those sections you do find an
interweaving of themes and the poem does have a unity.

So I think it is going to last for a long time. One reason is that
Crane could use the English language. Just take three realistic lines,
not highfalutin' lines, about hoboes:

"There's no place like Booneville, though, Buddy,"

One said, excising a last burr from his vest,
"—For early trouting."

Now take those three lines. Nobody else could do that. It seems absolutely simple.

One said, *excising* a last burr from his vest.

The amazingly right word. And when Crane comes to the name of the town it's the right name, too, Booneville, recalling Dan'l Boone, because he was drawing a parallel between his hoboes and the pioneers. And that phrase "early trouting" is beautiful! The lines go on like that. "Trains sounding the long blizzards out" and "Papooses crying on the wind's long mane." That's beautiful stuff. There is a simple line in his hymn to the Mississippi at the end of "The River." "The River lifts itself from its long bed." It is a beautiful picture, a beautiful marriage of sound and sense. So that thing going on through almost the whole poem is simply admirable.

I've gone on about Hart Crane; ask another question.

Interviewer: In the letters you exchanged with Faulkner when you were working on The Viking *Portable Faulkner,* you seem to have a real burr in your foot about the difference between the pear tree and the gutter pipe.

Cowley: Oh! Indeed I did have a burr in my shoe and a bee in my bonnet about that question, but I decided that I had better just follow Faulkner and what the devil if Miss Quentin climbed down a pear tree in one book and a gutter pipe in another? That was Faulkner's business, not mine. I like the pear tree because one of the abiding pictures in *The Sound and the Fury* was the pear tree in blossom in early spring in Jefferson. That also made a fitting use of the pear tree for Miss Quentin's escape. But all right, he says gutter pipe, let him have gutter pipe, and let him not correct the pear tree in the earlier book. It was a long argument.

Interviewer: Do you have any idea why he was so insistent about leaving the two versions unchanged?

Cowley: No, I don't. His imagination worked in certain ways. He said at one time, "I know more about events now than I did when I wrote the first version of *The Sound and the Fury.*" Jason's money is hidden in a different way; in the second book it's beneath the boards of a closet. All these things shift a little, but it doesn't matter a damn. That's Faulkner's business. He doesn't have to be totally consistent.

Now, if Faulkner were a student named Smith I'd make him be consistent.

Interviewer: You talk about Hemingway's shadow side. Could you discern something like that in Fitzgerald?

Cowley: No, I don't think you can infer it in the same way with Fitzgerald. His trouble was alcoholism. With Hemingway it was much more complicated. I think he was an accredited alcoholic at the end, but he didn't really graduate with honors until he was fifty-six or seven. Up until that time he could ingest more alcohol than any other living person and still carry himself with sobriety.

It was a terrible thing with Hemingway, to have this shadow side. He had very high moral standards for himself and he was always violating them and then he had a bad conscience. If he had a bad conscience, the man with whom he had violated his standards often suffered. Hemingway wouldn't talk to him.

He did a mean thing to me one time. I had done the Hemingway *Portable,* which was a great success and which introduced a new level of criticism on Hemingway. The Viking Press just had the rights to the Hemingway material for five years and at the end of five years Scribners took back the rights and the book went out of print. Now, Hemingway could have stopped that if he'd written to Scribners; they'd do anything he asked them to; but he didn't. And this was in contrast with Faulkner and the *Portable Faulkner,* where after five years, Faulkner said, in effect, to Random House, "Yes, let Cowley go along with the *Portable Faulkner.* I am grateful to it." So it did go along and had quite a substantial sale over the years; it must be close now to three hundred thousand. I felt grateful to Faulkner for standing up for the book.

Interviewer: Do you have any idea why Hemingway didn't?

Cowley: He said, "I think it's better for all my work to be under one roof." So he got Scribners to do a *Hemingway Reader* which was very much like the *Portable* but actually wasn't as good and didn't have as wide a sale either.

Interviewer: You've listed thirteen books you've published and seven of them were published after you were seventy.

Cowley: I thought that was pretty good; making a fast finish instead of a fast start.

Interviewer: Your most prolific period has been the past twelve years. . . .

Cowley: As far as books are concerned. But in many cases those books were largely written before the twelve years, written but not finished; then after seventy I finished them off and published them. The exception is *The View From 80.* That was all new.

Interviewer: In *The View From 80* you talk about the relative vitality of different people. To what do you owe your seeming great vitality?

Cowley: There is a change in just simple vitality between one man and another man. For example, Hart Crane had enormous vitality, more vitality than stamina. He would put himself all out in a debauch, and then he couldn't come back and work the next day. Hemingway said that, "I've been selling vitality in one way or another all my life." When you met him it was very much like coming up to a fire that was burning brightly because he would throw out these vital rays. And Fitzgerald, too, had a good deal of vitality. In fact I think plain vitality is one of the greatest components of talent and genius.

I have other theories in here too. Many of the well-known writers were manic-depressives. Now, it's funny, you would think that poets would always be, not manic-depressives, but schizophrenics. But no, they're manic depressives. When they're in their manic stages they begin working like mad. For example, Hart Crane wrote most of *The Bridge* in about thirty-five days on the Isle of Pines. He had it all prepared. He'd been working on it for three years. He knew what he wanted to write and then when he ran into this manic mood he turned it all out in about thirty-five days. That was enormous because his poetry is so close-textured. His thousand lines in those thirty-five days would be like someone else's five thousand.

I don't know. I've always felt that I had too little vitality, although I've had a great deal of persistence. I have to nerve myself up to do a streak of very hard work.

Interviewer: How do you prepare yourself for work?

Cowley: You lie down for a while; then you drag yourself to the typewriter; then you read over what you wrote the day before; then, with immense pains, you write another sentence. Then it begins to go faster.

Interviewer: How much of a part did you have in the editing and publishing of Kerouac's *On The Road?*

Cowley: I had very little part in the editing of that book. When it came to me it had already been re-typed in conventional manuscript order. I had a part in getting it accepted by Viking Press, definitely. I thought Jack wrote very well. He wrote a good flowing style. It was really modeled on Thomas Wolfe. Like Wolfe it just swept everything in front of it.

I had not great interest in changing commas or words; but I thought that in the structure of the book he'd done a weak thing by having it swing back and forth across the country like a pendulum. One suggestion was that he should telescope two-thirds of the trips across the country and have simpler movement. I think he did that. He certainly didn't rebel against anything I told him. After I finished with the manuscript it went to a copy-editor and the copy-editor had ideas about commas, sentences and so on, and changed some of Jack's precious prose. He was furious.

I find it very amusing that I was intimately connected with two of the Beat Generation novels. One was *On The Road* and the other was *One Flew Over the Cuckoo's Nest.* Ken Kesey was writing that in my class at Stanford.

Kesey wasn't like Kerouac at all. He didn't insist on *every* separate word or episode being left unchanged. He would take suggestions from me and his fellow students so that there was a good deal of rewriting in the early parts of *One Flew Over the Cuckoo's Nest.* I thought it was brilliant. I never ran into a book quite like it.

Interviewer: What about the modern experimental fiction?

Cowley: I belong to the generation or group of writers who believe in stories. So many of the new generation of writers believe in nonstories, what they call spatial form. I think it's a lot of bullshit. In the end a story is the only way you can present a person or a life. Each of our lives is a story. So, I think that puts two strikes on some of the new writers, the anti-story people.

In the meantime, on the pessimistic side, most young writers aren't learning enough about the English language. That's a terrible thing. The actual junctions, smoothness, logic of the prose has deteriorated. This doesn't hold for everybody. For example, John Cheever's prose is alive. If you put your hand on it, it squirms like a snake.

Interviewer: How do you feel about Paris these days, Mr. Cowley, as a city of inspiration?

Cowley: Well, it was a place you could go to live cheaply and come into contact with another culture, as I did; and for some people, for those who were willing to work, it was a very fine experience. For those who weren't willing to work and who just sat around cafes it was the prelude to going to pieces. But when you think of all the American writers of the twenties who were connected with Paris in one way or another, not only writers but musicians, painters and so on, on the whole it was a good thing.

There is an old Japanese fairy tale about a tigress. One moonlit night a Japanese wandered up into the mountains, looked across a cliff and saw the tigress carrying out her cubs from the lair. She carried them all to the cliff and dropped them over, one after the other. Then the she-tiger went down the cliff and looked at the cubs she'd thrown over and just one of them was still alive, and that was the one she brought back to her lair and would spoil ever afterwards. Paris was something like that. It carried a lot of people there as if it were a mother tiger and it threw them over the cliff. If they survived, then they were treated very well, but many of them didn't survive.

Malcolm Cowley: Countryman

Robert Cowley/1983

From *Country Journal* (October 1983), 62–70. Reprinted with
the permission of Robert Cowley and *Country Journal*.

At times I have difficulty associating my father, Malcolm Cowley, with
his most famous book, *Exile's Return* (1934), his account of American
writers in the 1920s. I'm glad to find that it has acquired something of
a classic status, but I'm far prouder of the fact that some of his best
work—*And I Worked at the Writer's Trade, The View from 80,* and
The Dream of the Golden Mountains—was written in the last few
years. It can't have been easy. He was eighty-five this past summer.

Chalk one up for country living. My father and my mother—she
recently turned eighty-one—own 7 acres in Sherman, Connecticut, a
village some 70 miles north of New York City. We came there in the
summer of 1936, when a trip to the metropolis and back was not just
an excursion you made each weekend but an adventure. As a child
growing up in New England, I found the great divide was still this: are
you a native or not? Though I was hardly two, and though I might
live in Sherman for the rest of my life, I could never hope to attain
that distinction. My family were considered outsiders, doomed to be
"city people" forever.

It has been a long time since Sherman was one of those *Ethan
Frome* places where old folk lingered at the end of a remote road
with a cow, a few chickens, and a presumed burden of memories.
Perhaps the town never was like that; certainly it hasn't been in my
lifetime. But there was another Sherman that *has* disappeared,
something of a self-sufficient arcadia. My father will point out his
study window at the long hill that crowds the western horizon and
recall that six sawmills were once in operation on it. Today, you can
stumble on packs of wild dogs up there. The roadside platforms with
their early-morning freight of heavy metal milk cans are gone: about
twenty years ago, the big dairies announced that farmers must store
milk for pickup in expensive glass-lined tanks holding 10,000 gallons.

It was a requirement that immediately wiped out all smaller dairy farms in the town.

If Sherman has managed to preserve some of its rural character, my father is partly responsible. I don't think that it is too much to say. As chairman of the zoning board for twenty years, he tried to keep Sherman from surrendering to the patternless subdivisions and garish commercial sprawl that have spoiled so much of the American landscape. From an airplane you can see the result: the suburbs actually end and the country begins at the south end of town.

In 1968, when he turned seventy, my father retired from the zoning board. That was the year when his collection of poems, *Blue Juniata,* appeared, and one night he gave a reading for the town. Then came a surprise. He was presented with a silver plate engraved with the words:

TO MALCOLM COWLEY
In grateful recognition of many
years of service
to the town of Sherman

"I was a native now," he told me, "But it had taken a long time." You might say that the process of becoming one is what the following discussion is all about—beginning in Pennsylvania at the turn of the century.

Robert: I find it somehow fitting that you, of all people, were born in the country. You arrived in the summer of the Spanish-American War, didn't you?

Malcolm: Yes, I was born August 24, 1898, in a farmhouse near Belsano, Pennsylvania. The town was 70 miles from Pittsburgh, where my father was a doctor.

Robert: That first experience with the country was almost your last, as I remember.

Malcolm: My mother was alone because my father had been summoned down to Norfolk, Virginia, where his younger brother was supposed to be dying of camp fever. He recovered. So Mother, alone in the big house except for my Aunt Margaret—virgin and slightly crippled—was in labor for two days. Tanny, as we called my aunt, became so terrified that she shut herself in a closet. Finally, my mother's moans attracted somebody passing on the road in a horse and buggy—there was no telephone at the time. He drove to the nearest mining camp and came back with the company doctor, who arrived during a thunderstorm and saved two lives.

Robert: There's something I've long meant to ask. What is your earliest memory?

Malcolm: Oh, my earliest memory is being brought in to my grandmother, who was deaf and used an ear trumpet. She was sick in the parlor, which was the room I had been born in. She died when I was four.

But for the rest, the earliest memory would be the first time I wandered off into the woods and found the Vinton Lumber Company had just cut out big timber. The woods were all covered with peeled hemlock logs.

Robert: In one of your poems you describe "the woods cut twenty years ago for tanbark/and then burned over, so the great charred trunks/lay crisscross, wreathed in briars. . . ." I take it that the countryside was being ravaged even then.

Malcolm: Even then. And more then. In my earliest childhood there were still great tracts of first-growth hemlock and beech and maple—some of the loveliest woods I've ever seen. The Vinton people got in there with a logging railroad we called "the stump dodger." At the foot of our hill a train with six carloads of logs would go down every afternoon, until finally the whole area was logged clean.

But the coal mines hadn't sulfur-poisoned the streams yet, at least not near us. The streams were still full of fish. I spent all my time barefoot, going fishing. I would go barefoot from the middle of May until the middle of October, when we went back to Pittsburgh. At the end I would have to walk a mile to school in my bare feet over frozen ground. I still remember that.

Robert: You seem to have been left alone a good deal of the time.

Malcolm: I was a fortunate child in that I was moderately neglected. It meant that I could run as wild as a weaned colt in an unfenced pasture. I would disappear from the house after breakfast—or sometimes without breakfast—go into the woods, and be gone all day. I came to feel that the countryside belonged to me and that I belonged to the countryside.

Robert: For someone growing up in rural America around the turn of the century, how was life different? Was there something special about it?

Malcolm: Well, there *was* something really special. In the first place, poverty. Real poverty in that area. In the second place, people ate what they could produce. Potatoes went into the root cellar. Apples were gathered, pressed into cider, and the cider boiled down into apple butter, which would stand on the shelves in the pantry. They even had flour ground from their own wheat. They'd have a cow and a couple of pigs. In the fall you'd hear the pigs being killed by having their throats cut, their terrible wails going over the whole country. But by the end of the winter people actually didn't have enough to eat. And they would have lots of children. I pity those farm wives. The farm wives didn't wear shoes, except on Sunday. They had bare feet, huge slabs of bare feet like slabs of bacon, and usually wore calico dresses. It was all truly primitive and truly a household economy.

Robert: What do you think were the best things about the country when you were growing up?

Malcolm: Absolute freedom was the best thing—I mean, for a boy. There was hardly a No Trespass sign in the whole of Cambria County. You could go anywhere your legs would carry you—or, if you had a horse as I did, you could go anyplace the horse would carry you. You could go into anybody's woods and hunt, you could go into any stream and fish; you could wander over old fields anywhere. The only rule was you had to be home for supper.

So, freedom was the first thing—that sort of scope and possibility. And the second was self-dependence. If you wanted to live well, you had to live well on food you grew yourself.

Robert: Do you think we've lost that sense of freedom?

Malcolm: Yes, that is something in the past of this country that has disappeared. I watch children being brought up—including you, you know—and they aren't allowed to do dozens of things that I was allowed to. Your mother wouldn't let you disappear in the woods for the day.

Robert: I think it's even more constricting for kids now than it was for me.

Malcolm: It's *much* more. Starting out when they're three years old, in nursery school, they have to learn a form of communal living. We're always rubbing elbows with people now.

Robert: How has the end of that limitless freedom you once knew affected American life in general?

Malcolm: That is a thought that is very hard to develop. But the increasing lack of freedom has most certainly produced a mass instinct by which any sort of new fad will spread all over the country and everybody will become affected by it—and then suddenly the fad will disappear. It's the same way with political reactions, when suddenly the country changes its mood and our whole government is actually overturned. The development of the "mass man" is one of the most threatening things that is happening to us. Of course, the most threatening is the destruction of natural resources. The land itself, the air, the water. Minerals. Everything is being used up.

Robert: Let's go back to Belsano for one more moment. How has it changed since you were a boy?

Malcolm: One thing is the road. With the road being widened and surfaced, the houses all stand within ten feet of it. There is no more of this business of barefoot boys scuffling in the dust of the road or hanging around the porch of the general store. The creeks have turned yellow with sulfuric acid from the mines—though I hear that some of the streams have been cleaned up. All the big timber is gone. The fields are overgrown; there are hardly any fields left any more.

Robert: What happened to the house where you were born?

Malcolm: That was a terrible thing. It was taken over for a roadhouse. The big room where I was born was the barroom. In the summer of 1968 I went in there and had a beer. Then I drove on without looking back.

Robert: You started coming to Connecticut in the mid-1920s. What attracted you here to Sherman?

Malcolm: Sherman filled a sort of pattern in my mind. If you take American literary history, the pattern is Concord: somewhere that is a couple of hours from the metropolis and yet out in the midst of fields. Sherman was like Belsano, only not so poor. You could live here in quite a primitive fashion. Most of my friends were—you might call them Thoreauvians. When the writer Slater Brown was beginning to remodel his farmhouse, old Charlie Jennings, from whom he had bought it, came over to watch the work. "Well, Mr. Brown," he finally said, "I'm glad to see you ain't putting in one of them bathrooms. I always said they was a passing fancy."

Robert: What did Sherman look like when you first saw it?

Malcolm: The main road in the valley was not paved. It ran through very prosperous farms, lush tobacco and cornfields. The hills in back were pastured so that the woods you see now were not woods at all. It was a little vision of Arcadia. Connecticut was almost all farmland in those days. Sherman was all farmland.

Robert: Move ahead to 1936. You'd been living in New York City for five years when you decided to settle in Sherman for good. The way you managed it still seems unbelievable.

Malcolm: I was determined to live in the country, so I kept looking for a place up here. Peter [the artist Peter Blume], who had a house for rent of $10 a month, said that there was an empty barn across the road, and why didn't I buy that? Finances became an obstacle. I had in the bank $300. So here is the how-to recipe that nobody could carry out today.

My secretary offered to lend me $1,000 without making a record of it. So I accepted that loan. I paid $1,300 for the old barn and seven acres, and then I had an equity. On this equity of $1,300 I could at the time borrow $6,500 from the local bank, and with that we could set out to rebuild the barn into this house. But houses always cost more than you think they should: I had to take out a second mortgage of $1,600 from a generous woman in New Milford, Connecticut. Then the house was still unheated, so to buy a furnace and radiators, I made a further loan of $1,300 from another bank. In a little more than six months, I ended up with a house, a cornfield, a briar patch, a trout stream, and an enormous aggregation of debts. Figured out, it came to about $10,800 in all, on my original investment of $300. Credit was so cheap at that time. Just imagine having a 5½-percent mortgage today.

Robert: Well, you got your wish, but what about Mother? She'd spent her whole life in the city.

Malcolm: There was one time when the three of us were driving to New York. We came to the state line, and Muriel said, "Rob, never forget that you were born in New York City."

Robert: I take it, then, that life in the country was hard on Mother at first.

Malcolm: It was unnecessarily hard. She came to the house one summer and said, "I can't stand it any longer. I was crossing the bridge and I saw a rat as big as a small dog." "How did you know it was a rat?" I asked her. "It had a bare tail." And I said, "That was a possum." But she still didn't like it.

Another time she had to put up the bars at the gateway to keep cows from getting in, and she had laid the bars down by the side in the grass, but the grass was really poison ivy. Well, she knew poison ivy after that.

Slowly she became adjusted to the country. Now she finds trouble readjusting herself to New York. But she never learned to share my idea of subsistence living. I could never tempt her into chickens.

Robert: How did a place like Sherman take to newcomers in those days? It was still very much an old New England town, isolated and self-sufficient.

Malcolm: When strangers moved in from the city, they were not greeted warmly, but neither were they greeted with the hostility that they met with in some places. The senior Mrs. Osborn said to Muriel at the meat counter of the old village store, "Oh, the city people. I don't mind them as long as they don't try to *help* me." Later, Mrs. Osborn was asked about a newcomer to Sherman. She said with distaste, "She's the *friendly* type."

Oh, those wonderful New England remarks. Old Mrs. Edmonds was talking about her daughter, and Muriel said, "She had a hard time having her baby, didn't she?" Mrs. Edmonds, still ironing, said: "*She* thought she did."

Robert: I remember, as a boy, how people in this town always seemed to look after one another. Do they still?

Malcolm: They don't because they don't know one another as well. For a long time they did, though. If a barn burned down, there was immediately a benefit held for the farmer who'd lost it. If a farmer was sick at harvest time, the other farmers would pitch in to get his harvest in.

Robert: That sounds quite different from Belsano eighty years ago.

Malcolm: Yes, it was. Sherman had much more community spirit. In Belsano, nobody ever went up the back roads to see whether families had enough to eat during the winter, which they didn't. Here the town would take care of destitute people. The first selectman would give them an order for groceries.

Robert: How do you account for the difference?

Malcolm: It's something in the whole New England system which settled towns. A town was built around a church, and a church was a community of the faithful. Politics, the town government, and the town meeting pulled everybody together. For people who were thought of as belonging to the community, there was always that helpfulness in New England. I think much more than in Pennsylvania. Tremendously more than in the South.

Robert: What are the biggest changes you've witnessed since you moved here permanently in 1936?

Malcolm: Farms going out of business, in the first place. There may have been forty in Sherman that year; at present there are three. Fields that used to be pastures become overgrown, first with brush and then with trees. Not with good trees. Other farms have been subdivided. The whole land has gone into a mixture of subdivision and scrub forest. The great problem besides the decline of farming is just keeping the land open. Once the land grows up into scrub forest, there are no more views. People come to New England for the views, and then they use up the farmland and there are no more views. There are more woods in New England now than there were fifty years ago.

Robert: I believe they call the phenomenon "woodland sprawl." Do you ever envision all that scrubland being made into field again?

Malcolm: Yes, I do, but it's one of the dreams I have to shove aside. As the pressure for food grows, I can imagine whole suburban developments being bulldozed down and turned back to farmland.

Robert: What about the people who choose country life now— have they changed, too?

Malcolm: They're not so homogeneous as they used to be. These days you get so many executive types who move from one part of the country to another that the sale of a house isn't permanent any longer. It will have to be sold again when the owner is moved to California. Or Texas. But there are also social divisions arising between white collar and blue collar. We have some very serious ruckuses over taxes and zoning. All this results in less social cohesion.

Robert: Zoning has always been a touchy subject here.

Malcolm: I feel that zoning is often carried too far. You know, when I was head of the zoning commission in Sherman I had a simple formula for suggesting what the regulations should be. I drove around town and asked what people were doing. Anything they had been doing for years was legal. For example, Edna Barnes had a rooming house up on Barnes Hill. I said, "How many roomers has she?" Somebody said six. So the regulations permitted rooming houses with not more than six roomers. The zoning law passed and didn't meet with a great deal of resistance.

Robert: Do you think people go overboard in an attempt to protect the environment?

Malcolm: You can't go overboard in actually protecting the environment. But it ought to be that people can earn their livings in the town. I also find myself on the side of those who want to hunt and fish—especially when it comes to controlling two terrible pests. One is deer, and the other is raccoons. Now, in a farming community deer and raccoons are both kept within reasonable limits. But the suburbanites who don't have any gardens come in and say, "Aren't the deer sweet? People should be forbidden to hunt them"—forgetting that people as well as deer and raccoons have to live in the area. A sort of balance of nature should be maintained, and that's where environmentalists are likely to go too far.

Robert: You cited the fights over zoning—and I know you would add stringent protection of the environment—as manifestations of class division in towns like Sherman. Do you feel that the country has become too much the province of the well-to-do?

Malcolm: That's a big question. The people who have enough to live on are really in a way walled off from the people who haven't enough to live on. I don't like that at all. What I would like is a community that is more or less self-contained, a community where the things you need are many of them produced right there. Instead, milk comes from the outside. Most vegetables come from the outside. It seems to me that all the food we eat must taste a little bit of diesel fuel.

Robert: Is it possible for young people without money to live in the country?

Malcolm: It is still possible. It is more difficult. There are no great careers open here—a career, for example, in literature. You have to be in much closer touch with the metropolitan center. And it's the same with people earning their money in any way as freelances. Even lawyers. For doctors, the country is a sort of paradise.

But there are many ways of making a marginal living. A young couple who can come out and live by doing odd jobs, which is impossible in the city. That is, if you don't have silly ideas of pride. I know a man of forty and his wife, who started out mowing lawns and doing painting jobs. He ended up by first buying a house and then having another house willed to him by a widow whose grounds he had been taken care of. So that now he is much better off than the people whose lawns he still mows.

Robert: If it's tough being young in the country, what are the problems of aging?

Malcolm: One of the great problems is expense. It costs a lot, especially if you can't drive a car any longer and have to find drivers. Or somebody to help around the house, somebody to take care of the grounds when you can't run machinery any longer. Nevertheless, you have a feeling of support. You're living in a community that knows you. To take one little example, the cars don't run you down as you pick your way across the road with a cane. Or when your wife goes shopping at the local IGA supermarket, she runs into people who know her and help her with her bundles out to the car.

Robert: How do you handle the winters?

Malcolm: You have to handle them by getting help. But if you have fuel enough, and your house is snug, then you can live as comfortably in Connecticut as you can in Florida.

Robert: Is it your impression that people who live in the country are getting older?

Malcolm: They indeed are, and that is the trouble.

Robert: How are places like Sherman trying to cope with that fact?

Malcolm: The little towns of New England are showing enterprise in taking care of their older people. They have "Over-60" centers, for example, or mini-bus service to their shopping centers, so that life does become easier. But we feel here in Sherman—or many people feel—the lack of small and limited housing for older people. One condominium for "Over-60s" would help a great deal. That's one of the points where conflict arises between the suburbanites and the

longer-time residents. The suburbanites don't want any con-
dominums in town.

Robert: Talking about all these problems, I wonder if we're
beginning to lose sight of the advantages of living in the country.
What are they?

Malcolm: Air, water, and trees. And outside of that there is a
certain largeness and leisure of life. Leisure, or the choice of what
you're going to do on any given day—that doesn't exist in the city.

Robert: What are the things that have made you happiest about
living in the country?

Malcolm: I don't know. Sometimes going out of the house and
looking at the fields or the garden and seeing how it's growing has
made me as happy as anything else. And, of course, I was crazy
about fishing when I was younger. That combines the joy of walking
with the sound of running water and the thrill of catching a fish. You
can still find places to fish, although there are too damn many No
Trespass signs. But after you become old enough you can disregard
the No Trespass signs because you know the people on the land.

Robert: Do you think that living in the country has made you a
better writer?

Malcolm: In some respects, because it has made me more
conscious of things. I like a "thingy" style, not an abstract style.
Sometimes when I read writers full of abstractions I stop and say,
"Now what the hell does he mean?" When you read something I
write you know damn well what I mean. The language is simple, and
the figures of speech have to do with actual objects, persons, and
animals.

I used to go wandering off into the woods, and after an hour or so
I would begin thinking or dreaming or reconstructing something I
wanted to write. The most grievous blow to my writing came when
my legs went bad on me and I couldn't "walk" an article any longer.

Robert: Do you think Americans sometimes oversentimentalize
living in the country?

Malcolm: It doesn't seem so to me. Of course, anybody can
oversentimentalize anything. I can't emphasize too much the beauty
of growing old in the same place you were young in, with people
you've known for half a century. That is something that Americans
often lack.

Malcolm Cowley Talks about William Faulkner

Dorys Crow Grover/1983

Unpublished interview. Reprinted by permission.

The following interview with Malcolm Cowley took place on 27 December 1983, at the 100th Anniversary Meeting of the Modern Language Association of America in New York City. I had been in correspondence with Mr. Cowley about some of the ideas discussed in this interview, and the interview further cleared some of his recollections about William Faulkner, in particular the editing of the Viking *Portable Faulkner* (1946). To begin the interview, I asked Mr. Cowley if he felt that a cultural Southern Renaissance began with Faulkner's work; that is, the emergence of so many excellent Southern fiction writers.

Cowley: No, I don't feel that. I feel that it grew up in the shadow of Faulkner's work because Faulkner had more genius than anyone else involved in it, but there were signs of a cultural Southern Renaissance before Faulkner was published. Remember that his first stories appeared in the *Times-Picayune* in New Orleans, and at that time there was quite a crowd of writers in New Orleans of whom the most prominent was the poet John McClure, and that these went along with Faulkner and sheltered him in his early work. But let us bring that down geographically and say that the Mississippi Renaissance began with William Faulkner.

Grover: Indeed, I would agree with that. What about the Fugitives at Vanderbilt?

Cowley: Yes, the Fugitives. I think it was round 1922 when they started, and it was John Crowe Ransom who inspired the group, with Allen Tate, Robert Penn Warren and Donald Davidson, as the most prominent members, as writers, but they had a lively time. Before Faulkner was printed, Nashville was a literary center. There were things going on at North Carolina, too, so we have added up now to a New Orleans, Nashville, and Chapel Hill literary renaissance, and they were all going along concomitantly. What Faulkner did was contribute genius to the Renaissance, so that one might say that every Southern writer who followed him was more or less influenced by William Faulkner.

Grover: Yes. You and I discussed this once in a letter, besides mentioning the comment he made to Joan Williams, you remember: that marvelous comment he made about his work?

Cowley: Yes. I couldn't quote that comment, but it went something like this: "It's sometimes amazing that a poor countryman like me has written those things."

Grover: Yes, you quote that whole passage in your essay "Magic in Faulkner."

Cowley: Well, you know what he revealed by that remark was, I always believed, that his writing was firmly based in his subconscious. He had genius and he had talent. I tried to distinguish between those two things. Theodore Dreiser had genius without talent, but Faulkner also had talent, by which I mean the conscious and critical application to work in general, but to his own work in particular, all methods by which it could be made intelligible to the public. Faulkner applied those methods. When you study those various drafts of *Sanctuary* that are extant—and something like "That Evening Sun" was even published in three separate drafts, each one an improvement over the preceding—they reveal that which I call talent, which he had in abundance, though as a talent he was actually not first-rate. As a genius he towered over everyone else.

Grover: There is a distinction. In your early comments in the Viking *Portable Faulkner,* you certainly brought him before the public. Do you feel that helped get him back into print?

Cowley: Oh! It did indeed! You know what I did to Faulkner, and I had done it to Hemingway before that time: I made them teachable, and they were taught. They had not been taught up to that time. For a long time the academics didn't give credit to the *Portable,* but that's what set them reading it, and what, as I say, made his work teachable.

Grover: It was a good thing to do, and I know he appreciated it, in his way—he had a unique way of showing his gratitude, didn't he?

Cowley: Yes. That is he didn't always show it so much as make you conscious that he didn't forget it. The thing he said about me that made me proudest was, "You can always depend on Malcolm Cowley."

Grover: That is a very nice thing to say. Did you ever know Caroline Gordon?

Cowley: Now, don't ask me silly questions—I went swimming with her every day—every afternoon for a month. This was in Clarksville, while Allen was absent. No—no—I'm not trying to build up a picture of a love affair here. We were friends. Caroline, I think, was one of the chastest women I have ever met, so there is no breath of scandal, as far as I know, that has ever touched her, except that somebody said she once had an affair with Ford Madox Ford. Well, that's hard to believe because—well—Ford had an attractive mind, but it stopped there. His body was dreadful (laughter). But at that time Allen Tate had started being unfaithful to Caroline. I was there during what he claimed was his first unfaithfulness.

Grover: Well, the reason I asked was that she wrote a review of the Viking *Portable Faulkner* in the *New York Times Book Review.* Remember? It was titled, "Mr. Faulkner's Southern Saga," and then Robert N. Linscott, he was a senior editor at Random House, read Gordon's essay. He said he liked her review of the Viking *Portable Faulkner,* but he told you that with the wartime paper shortage at that time . . .

Cowley: . . . they couldn't put Faulkner back into print. They only made the start of putting into production one volume, *The Sound and the Fury* and *As I Lay Dying.* But then after that they did begin putting the other fiction back into print—those books for which they had plates. This was before the days of photocopy, which they do now. But in those days, books were printed from copper plates, and Random House had melted down the copper plates of three of Faulkner's novels as its contribution to the war effort.

Grover: They could have picked someone else, couldn't they?

Cowley: They might have picked somebody else, but Linscott— he was a good friend, but he was a very solid Yankee businessman as well.

Grover: This letter from him to you is apparently in the Cowley papers (Linscott to Cowley, 31 Oct. and 8 Nov. 1944). Where are those?

Cowley: At the Newberry Library in Chicago.

Grover: I know that some of your letters and papers are there.

Cowley: I gave an enormous collection of letters to the Newberry, and new ones are still going there, under restrictions.

Grover: Has anybody published any of those, or put them together in any way?

Cowley: I am half taken with what seems to be the funniest distinction. The first, no, the second dissertation on Malcolm Cowley is being published by the Louisiana State University Press next year, and do you know what the subject is? My career up to the age of twenty-five (laughter). Now did you ever know—can you imagine that I had a career up to the age of twenty-five?

Grover: Is this the book by James Kempf?

Cowley: Yes, this is Jim Kempf.

Grover: Do you know they are running a chapter of that in a forthcoming issue of . . .

Cowley: . . .*The Southern Review,* yes.

Grover: Lewis Simpson is doing it.

Cowley: Yes.

Grover: "My Career to the Age of Twenty-Five."

Cowley: That is not the title, but it is the principal subject of the book. In a final chapter he carries me up to the age of thirty-one.

Grover: Well, your career started when you were about seventy years of age, you once said. You said in one book that you have published more books . . .

Cowley: . . . since I was seventy than in all the years before that.

Grover: That is amazing.

Cowley: I've got another one coming out. I just turned in the manuscript.

Grover: What is the title?

Cowley: The title is *The Flower and the Leaf.* It's a collection of my uncollected essays. I didn't have to do much writing.

Grover: Like Faulkner and some of his revised work.

Cowley: Yes.

Grover: Well, I thought that was interesting about Caroline Gordon's review of your Faulkner work.

Cowley: Yes. She was a Faulkner enthusiast. She also, as I say, was a good friend of mine.

Grover: Did you ever visit Faulkner when he was at Virginia?

Cowley: No, I never did. I have been in his house.

Grover: In Oxford, or in Virginia?

Cowley: In Virginia. Oh, in Oxford too.

Grover: I guess John Dos Passos became the writer in residence there (University of Virginia) after Faulkner had passed away. I didn't understand how that worked.

Cowley: It wasn't a very formal job anyway, although Faulkner took it conscientiously. And there is that book Blotner and his friend did.

Grover: Oh yes—*Faulkner in the University.* Faulkner once told you in a 1945 letter that the location of the county—Yoknapatawpha—was always shifting.

Cowley: Yes, he said it shifted. Not very far, just a few miles east.

Grover: Just a few miles east, but he did give it permanent boundaries, didn't he?

Cowley: Yes, he did, he drew a map—an imaginary map. Oxford was clearly the county seat—the seat of the University. But Frenchman's Bend, they never have been able to locate.

Grover: Really—where the Snopes . . .

Cowley: There is a very nice professor at the University of Mississippi named Evans Harrington who came near doing a thesis on the location of Frenchman's Bend. He took me around to the general store.

Grover: There is another thing I find in Faulkner—when he is very serious, he's funny sometimes; he's very humorous, understated, unconscious humor in . . .

Cowley: Unconscious! As conscious as all get out. He loves humor.

Grover: Do you think it was deliberate having his people doing those crazy things? Wasn't it just part of life?

Cowley: Which, the "Spotted Horses"? I think "Spotted Horses" is the funniest story I ever read.

Grover: So is "Was."

Cowley: Yes, all the way through.

Grover: And *As I lay Dying.*

Cowley: Yes, in places there is funny stuff in *As I Lay Dying,* but the two great stories for me as humor are "Was" and "Spotted Horses."

Grover: Well, I have always felt they are understated and, as you have said, it takes genius to do that.

Cowley: There's—I was lecturing at Stanford once and a very bright young woman in the class said, "Professor Cowley, referring to 'Spotted Horses,' why did you say this story was funny?" And I said, "I don't know what funny is, but let me read you part of this story," and I read part of it where the horses had broken loose and were running through the town and one sailed through the house over that boy, and the class was in stitches. And I said, "Now do you think it is funny?" She kind of flushed and said, "Yes."

Grover: The only person it probably wasn't funny to was Mrs. Armstid.

Cowley: Uh huh, all she had was a rolling pin. Oh! Mrs. Armstid—she didn't have anything. No, I was thinking of Mrs. Littlejohn.

Grover: Yes, and Mrs. Armstid, the poor thing, her husband got hurt and her children were hungry—poor whites.

Cowley: Yes.

Grover: Do you know Louis D. Rubin?

Cowley: No, I've been in correspondence with Rubin. He taught at Hollins College in Roanoke before I was there, and before he moved on to Chapel Hill. He does good work.

Grover: He once said that the South was a faraway country. Do you know what he might have meant? Why he would say that? Do you think New Englanders see the South differently?

Cowley: As a foreign country?

Grover: As a faraway country, he said.

Cowley: Faraway country. Well, I suppose they do. Not many of them go south except to Florida. They don't know the South, but there's another division in this country—well, there are many divisions in this country, but there is not only the north-south division, but there's also the Alleghenies that formed a great barrier to settlement. People from west of the Alleghenies—I come from western Pennsylvania—can understand Tennessee people better than they can understand Virginians; I mean, they can understand how their minds work. Then of course, when you get out to the coast it is a great amalgam of everything.

Grover: Yes, my people came from Pennsylvania, Virginia and

Iowa. But I thought it was interesting that he [Rubin] would see the South as a faraway country. I think I felt that way until I came to Texas, and Texas is not South.

Cowley: No, Texas isn't really South. Parts of it are South. East Texas is more southern than West Texas.

Grover: Yes, it is. To change the subject: what first attracted you to Faulkner's work?

Cowley: Reading it. Now, not the first work. I think the first book of Faulkner's I read was *Pylon,* and that didn't attract me very much, but I thought it was extraordinary. I found that the whole book broke down into a sort of rhythmic prose, or free verse. Try reading it. It was a manifestation of a very great talent. I couldn't say that I liked it a great deal. Then the next book of Faulkner's I read was *The Unvanquished,* which was published in the *Saturday Evening Post,* and this bears the marks of the *Saturday Evening Post,* yet at the same time it has some absolutely extraordinary passages in it; so I was more impressed. Then I read *The Wild Palms,* and the love story in *The Wild Palms* didn't move me at all, but the story of the Mississippi flood, the "Old Man" part of the book, I thought, was absolutely extraordinary. Then I next read *The Hamlet*—oh, I read *Sanctuary,* and then finally, I came to *Go Down, Moses,* and there—I wasn't swept off of my feet at first, but I began thinking about it, it seemed more and more extraordinary and it wasn't until that time that I began saying in print that here was one of the leading American writers of his generation. I still put him, at that time, after Hemingway.

Grover: Do you today?

Cowley: No, today I put Faulkner first.

Grover: I like Hemingway's work, but I put Faulkner first. I think it's because, as a woman, I cannot always relate to Hemingway. The first book of Faulkner's I read was *The Sound and the Fury,* and that was when I was in college.

Cowley: That's a tough one. You started on the first page of that and you didn't know where you were.

Grover: No, but once you realized—we had a good professor— once you realized the minds and how to go in and out of italicized parts . . .

Cowley: I think somebody analyzed thirteen time levels in . . .

Grover: In that book?

Cowley: In the Benjy character, and once you get the story behind Benjy's remarks straightened out, then they are all understandable.

Grover: But you may have to read four or five other novels.

Cowley: That's right, before you understand them.

Mr. Cowley asked that the interview end here as he was due at the Harvard Club for dinner. We are to continue the interview in Sherman, Connecticut. (This, however, has not happened.) For the record, Mr. Cowley was in good spirits and good health. He had complained about his legs, but walked well with a cane. He is taller than I, and I am five feet, eight inches tall. At age 85, he has a full head of gray hair. His eyes sparkle behind steel-rimmed glasses, and he has a ready sense of humor. He was delightful to talk to, and I was amazed at all he can recall about his friends of the past and present. He is a walking book of great dimensions.

He spoke of the recent illness of Muriel, his wife of some fifty or more years, stating how well she was recovering from a heart attack. He was carrying a briefcase, which I lugged about for him, especially when we stepped on and off the New York Hilton's escalators. He had brought it along from Sherman, Connecticut, as it contained the typescript of his new book to be published in the winter of 1985 by the Viking Press. He does not go far from home anymore, so it was a kind act to grant me the interview, for which I am truly grateful.

A Conversation with Malcolm Cowley
Donald W. Faulkner/1984

Unpublished interview. Reprinted by permission.

This interview took place on 19 November 1984 in Malcolm Cowley's home in Sherman, Connecticut. After some conversation about Faulkner's proposed edition of *The Flower and the Leaf* (1985), Faulkner suggested that the interview get underway.

Faulkner: There's a constellation of issues: you have Kenneth Lynn as a vociferous New Right critic; you have the situation in which a person could say that contemporary book reviewing has become a lot like book advertising; then there's been a movement away from the reader in this whole sense of the Yale school of criticism, of . . .

Cowley: The new French criticism.

Faulkner: And the new French criticism.

Cowley: The reader is practically abolished.

Faulkner: Is that the basic thing that you find wrong with contemporary criticism?

Cowley: Well, somebody ought to issue a call for order. The order is that criticism has gone way off the track, it seems to me. The author is abolished, the lay reader is abolished; in his place is put an all-powerful reader who manages to change everything, change the meaning of everything, totally disregarding what the author thought he was saying. And then authors begin to be affected by this, and they think, "Is what I'm writing sufficiently complex, sufficiently divided from the ordinary interests of humanity?"

Faulkner: And yet this is something you note back in 1960 when you were writing about Leslie Fiedler.

Cowley: Yes. Yes, that tendency has gone on and on and gotten stronger and stronger, so that the author, as he enters at all into criticism becomes a patient on the analyst's couch. The analyst is the wise critic. But he isn't trying to heal the author—good God, no. He's simply trying to use him as the subject for a lecture about something else. I would like to go back to simple things. And simple things, questions, are, "What is this piece of writing?" What relation does this have to the larger public, to the history of our time and to American culture?"

Faulkner: How would you respond to the person who says to the line, "What relation does it have to a larger public?" That there is no longer a larger public for writing today?

Cowley: I don't worry about that. That is more or less a sociological problem, whether the public is large or small. But the public that I was thinking of is simply the reader separate from the author and whom the author is addressing.

Faulkner: So if the author has gotten into this mire, too, that the critics have started—

Cowley: Yes, to a certain extent. The authors have let themselves be influenced by critics. Usually it's a bad influence.

Faulkner: I imagine so. How are we going to get out of that muck? It seems—

Cowley: That you can't get out of [it] except by being independent. By going somewhere into a room and sitting by yourself, walking the streets by yourself, and thinking, asking the question, "What do I really think about this?"

Faulkner: But wouldn't, at the same time, any of these critics respond by saying, especially when you hear people go on about the loneliness of the critic.

Cowley: That sounds like the loneliness of the author. The critic has pre-empted the place that authors used to have.

Faulkner: OK. I can see that. But . . .

Cowley: A little bit of humility wouldn't hurt in the least.

Faulkner: Do you think we've come to a point of criticism and writing being bedfellows too long, or whatever metaphor we might use, that perhaps we're at a point not unlike the time when, say, you and Edmund Wilson came on the scene, that in effect we've developed into another kind of genteel tradition now, this duplicitous relationship of critics and authors. That we are at a point where that whole context needs to be broken by a new generation of independent young critics? In much the same way that Wilson himself . . .

Cowley: Independent young critics and independent young authors. Both. I think the connection will be broken. We have in this country a great habit of moving in waves, like the effect of a wind over a wheat field—they all bend in one direction.

Faulkner: What would be your advice for anybody wanting to buck the flow, to stand against the wind and try somehow to change the course of the wind?

Cowley: I don't know about changing the course of the wind, but my advice is simply to say what you believe, which is not so easy because you first have to find out what you believe. And when you believe it, then say it.

Faulkner: Do you find in reading today that there are a lot of people who simply aren't doing that?

Cowley: Oh, indeed I do. I find lots of authors are already reading the reviews of their book before they write the book.

Faulkner: But it wasn't always this way. In the '20s I can imagine you could easily say the people in Paris had no sense of even the possibility of reviews. But by the '30s and the '40s and into the '50s some people of that same generation were probably doing that much the same way.

Cowley: Well, I think reviewers have helped some authors, but I think they've done in general more harm than good to authors, because the authors think too much of what the review will be. In the '20s and '30s reading reviews had a bad effect on many an author. If their first book received enthusiastic reviews then they had stage fright about writing a second book—that happened so often.

Faulkner: But then also you had—from all that I read, I get the sense that people like Hergesheimer and Cabel were the standards, were the people who were in the mainstream of writing and—there was a good sense, I suppose, of young authors really trying to develop themselves against that kind of mainstream.

Cowley: Yes, but the generational gap came in there, too. There's always a rebellion among writers, among artists in general, against the people ten or fifteen years older than they are. That's the real war of the generations. Very often a young writer or artist feels more kin with his literary grandparents than with his parents, or older brothers. Older brothers are the real . . .

Faulkner: That's a basic family trait. It's really applicable. But I just don't know what to do then in this context with, oh, the type of things I see at colleges where you have something that's quite similar to religious conversion going on, some sort of proselytizing from the pulpit or the lectern, and the young students are there as the faithful. And they become part of this new religion of criticism.

Cowley: I'm sure they are. That's a tendency that goes on in this country perhaps more than in other countries; not more than in France, but perhaps more than in England.

Faulkner: But do you have a feeling that those people, if they're smart enough, they'll find a way to outgrow that and . . .

Cowley: I think that if they're smart enough or if they have enough strength in themselves.

Faulkner: So it really does come down to a sort of individualism in the end.

Cowley: Yes, yes. I come down to admiring Emerson's essay on self-reliance. I admired Harold Bloom's essay on Emerson. I think he—did you read that? In the *New York Review of Books?*

Faulkner: Yes.

Cowley: I think he was generally right about Emerson. He is the American Writer and Critic. Not necessarily the best, but he's the seminal figure.

Faulkner: But is that a good model? I guess another thing that's an upshot of what we've been talking about is this: Isn't it important for the critic to keep his role with the writer as being—how do you put it?—the loyal opposition? That critics and writers, when they become *too* close, tend to stultify each other.

Cowley: That's true, that's true. If they become *too* close. There's not much danger of that, especially if the critics are writers themselves—which they ought to be.

Faulkner: OK. That's interesting. I thought you'd have some concerns about that issue because the sense I've always gotten from you is that no matter how close your friendship was, personal friendship was, with an author your sense of relationship to that friend as a critic to author took on professional proportions. That there's a point at which the friendship was held in abeyance, when that friendship was simply between people, so that when you're sitting at the desk with the work that's all there is. You the critic and the work.

Cowley: Yes, you can be tender toward it without being untrue, without being false. You have to come out and say what you think about this person's work. You don't always have to judge it, you don't have to *mark* it with an A or a B or a C, but you have to understand what it is. If you're a critic, you have to understand what the writer is trying to do.

Faulkner: You spend a lot more time than most of your contemporaries as a critic talking about the individual, talking about the individual's past work, talking about the context of the characters presented. In effect, you really try to place the work before you evaluate it. That seems like something that isn't being done very much. I think Updike does that to some extent.

Cowley: That is the burden of what I've been saying up until now. You ought to place it. You ask "What is this?" Also you *can* ask, and it's a very good question, "What sort of background did this work come out of? Who is this man speaking for and whom is he speaking to?"

Faulkner: OK. All right.

Cowley: Here is something else, to get off into the teaching of writing, which I've done at various times. You find that in a class there are two impulses operative. One is entirely self-enhancement, self-aggrandizement, putting down your rivals so that you will be top dog. The other is a more or less impersonal loyalty to the craft, so that instead of putting down the fellow who has written this story which has been read in class, you try to get at what he was trying to do and perhaps how he can do it more effectively. So that this is the mixture, you know—the killer instinct and the life instinct—in a class. My principle in the class was that the young writers could always learn more from other young writers than they could from the instructors. So we'd get them talking and then if you could build up the builder-uppers and put down the putter-downers, then the class would be successful. I am thinking of that class at Stanford* which was so damned talented.

Faulkner: Right, and also so aggressive from all that I've heard

*In 1960, Cowley taught a writing class at Stanford. Among its members were Ken Kesey, Larry McMurtry, Peter Beagle, C. J. Koch, Gurney Norman, James Bake Hall, Judith Rascoe, Arvin Brown, Joanna Ostrow and James D. Houston.

from people, especially that combination of Kesey and McMurtry, who seem to have been real brash characters.

Cowley: They were brash, but they were willing to help along. They fitted in quite well, both of them.

Faulkner: Well, before getting to that I have a point that I want to make about it. What you say about teaching writing and helping young writers strikes me . . .

Cowley: Helping—there's a woman in this town—she's dead now—Mrs. Osborn—with whom Muriel was talking about her attitude toward the newcomers in town. And Mrs. Osborn said, "I don't mind them as long as they don't try to *help* me." So, there's perhaps among instructors in writing too much of this feeling of wanting to help. Wanting to help in many cases means imposing your own standards on somebody else. Did you ever think for a simple principle that every gift is a command? That is, if somebody gives you such a simple thing as a jackknife, the command is, *"Use* me." And I had a friend who had that terrible impulse in his gifts. He made thoughtful gifts, but every gift was a command to me that I didn't want to obey. He gave me a compass. The command with the compass was, "Go on walks and get lost." He gave me a pruning knife. The command was, "Go out and prune your trees."

Faulkner: But isn't that twisting it just a bit?

Cowley: So that command comes into the teaching of writing.

Faulkner: What I find interesting in your description of the teaching of writing is that it seems to apply just as easily to what the good critic does. When you say the good teacher of writing takes up a student's impersonal loyalty to the craft and tries to lead the student to the point of doing it more effectively. Isn't that what the critic is also about?

Cowley: I suppose so. Yes, the critic is loyal to the ideal of writing. Then if he does give advice to the author it's always on how the author can bring his work closer to *his* ideal of writing, not necessarily the critic's.

Faulkner: OK. Now back to the '60 Stanford class quickly—the theme that I've come up with is that there was a fascinating catalyst for this in the '60's, the early '60's, when the class was. There was a big choice to be made between whether or not you left your city background and embraced a mix of rural notions and notions of just a literary world in itself. Some people had that kind of attitude and others were concerned about being raised in a rural environment, then coming to cities. Now how do these conflicts shape your writing? Collectively they seem to merge into a sense that there is a cosmopolitan world of writing—at least this is from twenty-five years of reflection on what I've gotten from people—that you were at least instrumental in pointing them toward even though you didn't force them to make those decisions. Am I a city writer who's trying to be a country writer? Am I basically a country writer who's trying to be a city writer? That those types of struggles were, as many of these people have said, part of the concerns that they brought to the class, but that you gave them some way of looking at those issues that transcended them. That's just a report from the field on things that I heard.

Cowley: I can't figure that one out, really. Perhaps I did give them an outside perspective on what they were doing. And also I do think I had this advantage in teaching that class at Stanford, that I wasn't trying to do anything for myself. I wasn't trying to put anybody down. I loved to build them up if I could, but I knew that I couldn't always. But they liked that idea of a friendly outsider.

Faulkner: That's something that they all remember. But what I was trying to get to, and now I'm turning this much more into interview material, is that there *is* a point in all this. I'd like to throw it out as a question to you. Here's what I see in that notion of the "Republic of Letters." When these people from the class twenty-five years removed say that you were pointing toward some kind of cosmopolitan integration of town and county matters, a way for them really to be what they were growing into and still make use of where they came from. It seems that it's also something that overlaps with this notion of the "Republic of Letters" that you've talked about, especially in writing on Allen Tate.

Cowley: Allen Tate and I always talked about the Republic of Letters. The Republic of Letters had a constitution. At least it had a great many laws, and the people who could observe those laws, people of a certain level of intelligence, belonged in a confraternity of writers all over the world. So that concept in the background has always been powerful. I've become less interested in them lately, but then I was.

Faulkner: It strikes me that this is something different from Writers' Congresses and things like that. It's a much more idealistic sense, that the Republic is a Republic of ideas, it's the confraternity of equal souls, and it's not something that you can really set out—

Cowley: Oh, no, you can't have a President and Board of Directors. No, you can't. It's a very loose association of people built on mutual respect and built more or less on laws that they ought to be observing.

Faulkner: When you speak of laws and a Constitution, what are some of those laws? Are they nameable?

Cowley: Some of the items in the Constitution? Articles?

Faulkner: Yes.

Cowley: Well, one of them is that your ultimate loyalty is to good work. Your ultimate respect is for people who obey these laws, but obey them freely because the laws are present in themselves. And it's very funny—there's a whole system of ethics here in which people can be unethical and even criminal by laws of citizenship, and yet obey the laws of the Republic of Letters. Then I worried about the fact that many authors would be judged by analysts to be abnormal.

Faulkner: Well, they are for the most part, aren't they?

Cowley: They *are* abnormal people. They even have, authors have, psychoses and neuroses both.

Faulkner: But this is simply by the everyday standards, so . . .

Cowley: By everyday standards.

Faulkner: These psychoses and neuroses are actually the badges of courage that are part of the Republic? Is that overstating it?

Cowley: Very often they are. That explains why many authors hate to be psychoanalyzed. They say, "My neuroses are my stock in trade. I don't want to lose them."

Faulkner: It seems true.

Cowley: But the real capital of an author, and therefore part of the unwritten Constitution of the Republic of Letters, is that, "When I say something I mean it. I don't want you to *accept* what I say, but I want you to understand it and give me credit for being honest about it."

Faulkner: Does the Republic still exist?

Cowley: The Republic of Letters? Yes, I think it still exists as an ideal. It got to be pretty shattered after World War I, and it is still convulsed with civil wars, especially between political conservatives and political radicals.

Faulkner: Should political beliefs have anything to do with the Republic of Letters?

Cowley: Why, of course they should. The Republic should have to do with everything, but the difference here is that its true members think there is a higher law of personality that transcends the political arguments. For my own part, I could get along with radicals and I could get along with conservatives so long as I respected their characters. What I hate is meanness.

Faulkner: Spite, you mean. That kind of backbiting.

Cowley: Yes.

Faulkner: This sounds like a club.

Cowley: Well, yes, it *is* a club. It is a club to which people belong or don't belong. For example, Auden belonged to the club, but I very much question that Spender does.

Faulkner: But in that way, one finds one's own citizenship in the Republic of Letters—citizenship is not conferred.

Cowley: No.

Faulkner: OK. But is there room in this Republic for the younger generation? Will they pick it up?

Cowley: I think they'll pick it up if they *want* to.

Faulkner: Should they, by your estimation?

Cowley: Oh, I think they should, yes.

Faulkner: See, this plays a lot into what I think about how the roles of critics and authors have changed. And you're talking about this "call to order" that is required. You know, let's get everybody—

Cowley: I'm talking actually about personal characteristics that are required.

Faulkner: But when you talk about the "call to order" with the current state of affairs, isn't something about resurrecting this notion, or re-presenting this notion, of the Republic of Letters one way to provide that call to order?

Cowley: It might be. I haven't figured this; I'm not an organizer.

Faulkner: I'm not asking you to. But the notion is you can present a higher ideal to people who are just squabbling with each other. You can get them to stop looking at the ends of their own noses long enough to see a star . . .

Cowley: At the present time I'm disturbed and wounded by this effort of many neo-conservative critics to make politics, bring up politics as something *more* important than literature. That was really the burden of my piece on Kenneth S. Lynn.

Faulkner: Right.

Cowley: Because mere literary standards go by the boards in his so-called criticism. But there's another effort represented by a man of more talent than Lynn, Joseph Epstein, editor of the *American Scholar.* He and some others are trying to prove that all American critics are anti-American. The answer to that, an instinctive answer is, "What the hell difference does it make?" To be a defender of American business is one thing and to be a writer is another. A writer can defend American business or he can attack American business— more or less that's his own business, but the critics ought not to judge him by how helpful his writing is to the principles of American enterprise.

Faulkner: And yet—I guess certainly the Lynn school, if you want to call it that, has justified itself in some small way by saying this is exactly what you and your contemporaries were doing in the '30s, saying that politics was perhaps more important than literature, that a critic should judge a writer in terms of his or her contribution to a larger kind of political system. That's what they're saying.

Cowley: I think, at this point, of the great old concept or question: "How much are immediate aims to be the subject of ethical discussion?" You know, for me, I think there are certain moral principles that cut across politics and antedate politics. We've called it personalism at times. I think a man's personal value is his honesty and his humility, if you want to put it there, and his kindness and certain other virtues which antedate all the political arguments. At times when I come out against the so-called neo-conservative critics, the ground on which I come out against them is simple. It's always, "Is this in terms of character good or bad?" The neo-conservatives are so often mean—that's true. I've used the word meanness more than once, and *mean* means niggling, envious and personally envious, aggressive in the sense of trying to put other people down.

Faulkner: OK. They would of course accuse you in the '30s of having been "mean," right? And they would use that self-justification, and have. Do you understand my point? That the neo-conservatives would have accused you, at least in the '30s, of being mean, just on those terms.

Cowley: I don't think they would.

Faulkner: You don't think so? OK, I think that they have.

Cowley: Oh, they accuse me, but they can't accuse me *justly* . . .

Faulkner: Oh, sure.

Cowley: For example, when I think of writers to whom I was close, younger writers to whom I was close, or whom I helped out, the first two names I think of are John Cheever and Otis Ferguson. Now, John *had* no politics and Otis had politics that were usually different from mine.

Faulkner: Oh, really?

Cowley: Yeah. We were always fighting about them but I respected him nonetheless.

Faulkner: You know, from the kinds of things you say about virtues and qualities of character this all sounds tremendously Socratic—this is the way Socrates would have talked, this is the way Socrates would have judged people, this is the way Socrates would have projected some notion like a Republic that Plato would write about . . . I mean, it sounds very much caught up in that spirit. Do you feel comfortable with that kind of connection?

Cowley: No, a little uncomfortable. The mantle is a little too large for me.

Faulkner: I wasn't asking you to run around barefoot on the Agora to talk with young slave boys—it was just an observation. OK, that helps me put a lot of that material into perspective. The other thing that I wanted to pick up on—and just do this quickly in sort of wrapping up this group of questions that I've been asking you—is something I gleaned from reading that Wilson article, "The All-Star of Literary Vaudeville." There was a section of it where he talked glowingly of Edward Arlington Robinson. Now, I'm not so much interested in it for what he had to say about Robinson, but for the way he characterized Robinson's role. He seemed to be defining what a man of letters is and what he talked about was somebody who develops fairly well a standard for the craft. And I think of your role in this throughout your life, certainly you and Wilson go kind of hand-in-hand in this effort with your whole generation. Do you think that's what a man of letters is? Somebody who sets the standard for the craft? Or by his actions, I think this is the issue here, sets the standard?

Cowley: It might be. You know, when I was writing weekly reviews for the *New Republic*—in this room, by the way—I could never finish them on time, or rather the time I *set* myself to finish them was always the time to catch the last mail train into New York. I've told that story. I could have finished them much sooner, you know, if I didn't argue with myself about what word to use in a certain place. But nevertheless I would always keep on to the very last minute. Now, was that work wasted? I don't think it was wasted. I think it wasn't wasted because I made the job harder for other people. When they start out they think the job is easy, and it is, but then they find out how hard it is and they set standards which other people have to work hard to meet. But isn't that—a psychiatrist would say that was a neurosis, that was the perfectionist neurosis. How can you do without it?

Faulkner: OK. . . .

Cowley: Yes. And . . . Edmund Wilson.

Faulkner: Can I ask you a couple of quick questions on Wilson? How—did you maintain contact with him throughout his life?

Cowley: No. We broke off contact around 1948. I got disturbed by a rather curt letter he wrote me from the *New Yorker* and I thought, hell, there's no use keeping this up. It was a close contact for a long time.

Faulkner: And he was really—he shepherded you along for a while with your early reviewing and fed you material?

Cowley: Actually he got me the job on the *New Republic*.

Faulkner: Then after that things went back and forth, especially during the late '30s. There was a lot of yelling back and forth.

Cowley: Yelling back and forth.

Cowley: He Found the Lost Generation
John King/1985

From the Los Angeles *Times*, 4 August 1985, pp. 22–24. Reprinted with the permission of John King.

In 1921 a young Greenwich Village resident named Malcolm Cowley wrote an article on "The Youngest Generation" for the New York *Evening Post's* book review section. The essay focused on the new authors who, Cowley assured readers, were soon to make their mark. If F. Scott Fitzgerald was omitted for the likes of John Dos Passos and E. E. Cummings, the reason was that Fitzgerald was already popular. Dos Passos was chiefly known in the Village and Cummings was yet to publish his poems in a book.

Fifty-two years later Cowley wrote again (this time at greater length) on the literature of that youngest generation—or, as history has christened his contemporaries, the Lost Generation. "I wonder if anyone has had the experience of writing about the same group of authors at intervals during half a century," he said in *A Second Flowering*. "The subject approaches and recedes like a landscape seen from a raft as the river sweeps by. Future appears before present, which fades into past . . . Its story is almost ended and I have other things to write about while there is time."

Twelve years later, Cowley now 86, is slowing down. He still writes, and still accepts visitors at the reconverted barn where he and his wife, Muriel, have lived since 1936, but his time must be used carefully now. "I've pretty effectively retired," he said. "I'm used to doing my writing in my head as I walked through the woods, and now that my legs don't let me do that, ideas don't come as fast."

Semi-retired might be a better description; in January of this year Viking Press published *The Flower and the Leaf* ($25), a selection of 55 essays and articles written between 1941 and 1983. It is Cowley's 14th book, the seventh since he turned seventy, and like virtually all the others it brings together literary criticism, reminiscences, politics, and an open-ended discussion of what it means to be a writer in

American society—what are the temptations, what are the respon-
sibilities. The latter question was also the center of *The Dream of the
Golden Mountains*—a memoir of the late 1930s published in 1980—
and *Exile's Return,* an account of the 1920s published in 1934.

It is hard to meet with Malcolm Cowley at his home in Sherman,
Conn., and connect this plump, friendly, near-deaf man who walks
slowly with the Dadaist poet who lived in Paris in the early '20s, or
the *New Republic* book review editor who campaigned for Communist presidential candidate William Z. Foster in 1932 and was urged
by critic Edmund Wilson in 1940 to "purge your head of politics . . .
politics is bad for you because it's not real to you."

"I was more deeply involved in the Marxist movement than I
intended to be, than I was happy about later, but there it was. It
actually happened," Cowley says now, although he was never a party
member. "In the early '30s, we (writers and intellectuals) believed
that capitalism would not survive. Then, very slowly, the emphasis
changed from revolution to preservation of our civilization against the
threat of fascism and Hitler. That was the secret of the second half of
the '30s."

The political phase of Cowley's life lasted, roughly from 1931 to
1940. Before then the classic self-confident writer who knew as early
as high school he would be a writer—a drama critic, he thought at
the time. Then he went to Harvard ("dreadfully snobbish," he
recalled) and decided poetry was his calling. After America's entry
into World War I, he drove a transport truck in France. "Instead of
coming back to Harvard after the War, I got as far as Greenwich
Village and stayed there—became a wicked villager." He eventually
got his degree from Harvard. First, however, he tried to live by his
writing in the Village, and the poet found that book reviewing—at $1
a review, with another 35¢ from the sale of the review copy to a
secondhand dealer—provided more meals.

After Cowley's studies at Harvard were finished, opportunity came
his way via a fellowship to study French literature in France. He and
his first wife were able to stay two years; the last six months in Paris
gave Cowley time to be swept into the then-new Dadaist movement.
When he returned to America at age 25, his daytime job, copywrit-
ing, was strictly for sustenance; his heart was in little magazines,
aesthetic controversies and literate speak-easies.

"It had been a good era in its fashion, full of high spirits and grand parties. . . . We had lived on the reckless margins of society and had spent our energies on our private lives," is how Cowley described the '20s in *Dream of the Golden Mountains*. The '30s, he continued, were quite different: "I wanted to live as simply as possible and turn my energies toward the world outside. I wanted to write honestly; I wanted to do my share in building a just society. . . ."

It was not an easy task, he was to learn, and for all his involvement in leftist organizations, he was most satisfied with the "living simply" part of his pledge after he and Muriel purchased a barn on seven acres of land in Sherman, a farm town 70 miles from New York. For years he spent three days a week in Manhattan while working at the *New Republic* and paying off his mortgage; he quit the magazine in 1940 and with time the poet turned book reviewer evolved into a literary critic and editor (at the Viking Press, on an advisory basis). He wrote lengthy studies of such authors as Hawthorne, Whitman, Hemingway, and Faulkner—his creation of the *Portable Faulkner* for Viking in 1946 returned an out-of-print author to the public eye, and was that author's critical rebirth. With time Cowley got into the habit of teaching one semester a year, at universities including Stanford and Berkeley. One seminar class included Ken Kesey, Larry McMurtry and Tillie Olsen among its seven members.

"On the whole I had a good time—I liked the students, and the work wasn't too hard. . . . but it didn't allow me to write," Cowley said of his brush with academia, a world toward which he has ambivalent feelings. "The experience I had supporting myself for 30 years before getting involved in university life was a good thing. . . . You have students learning writing from professors who joined the faculty as soon as they got out of graduate school. They *teach* creative writing and never do anything."

Cowley's goal for the last 50 years has been to have the writing community back in society—to have writing become something more vital than a parlor game, to have criticism play a role in the marketplace of ideas.

"Sometimes when I read writing full of abstractions, I stop and say, 'Now, what the hell does he mean?' " Cowley told his son in a 1983 interview, "When you read something I write, you know damn well what I mean. The language is simple and the figures of speech have to do with actual objects, persons and animals."

In the *Flower and the Leaf* (the title comes from one of Cowley's poems), examples of Cowley's concern with the connection of writers to the world abound. A review of French poet Louis Aragon's World War II poetry touches on much more than stylistic themes.

"The poets discovered, however, that their own medium had opportunities not granted to the others (novelists and playwrights in the unoccupied France); that with its power of allusion, it could arouse emotions and lead toward courses of action scarcely to be hinted at in prose; that poems being short, they could be copied and passed from hand to hand, even learned by heart, as Aragon's poems were learned and recited; that in short it could play the same role poetry had played in Homeric times and in the Middle Ages."

Similarly, when Cowley suggests that three of Willa Cather's novels *(Death Comes for the Archbishop, My Antonia,* and *A Lost Lady)* belong to the "small permanent body of American literature," his judgment draws on the works' impact, not just the prose. "Those three masterpieces . . . did perform services to American society even if Miss Cather was seldom consious of having social intentions," he wrote. "She made her readers feel that culture is all of a piece, depending almost as much on gardens and kitchens as on classrooms and concert halls."

At Harvard, Cowley felt, culture was treated as if it were a veneer. He believes it is to be found in any task performed with dignity, and that it should never be treated as something exclusive. For him the move to the country in 1936 was not a fashionable retreat from the metropolis (as American artists have done each generation), it was a return to a way of life he loved as a child in Belsano, Penn. "I spent long summers as a boy fishing, rambling through the woods, later on riding a horse about," he explained.

The Cowley house sits on a hill overlooking a brook, wooded hills, and the Sherman cemetery. The interior looks almost new: The walls are smooth and white, the rug spotless, the atmosphere scholarly yet free of nostalgic bric-a-brac. The pictures on display are all of family. The books piled on the glass table by the fireplace are all newly published. In a bookshelf are scrapbooks containing pictures of the Cowleys with friends like Faulkner. Cowley, though, has only one momento that he feels is worth calling attention to. It is a silver plate inscribed with the words:

TO MALCOLM COWLEY
In grateful recognition
of many hours of service
to the town of Sherman

The plate was presented to him in 1968 at the end of a 20-year stint that Cowley served as chairman of Sherman's zoning board. In a way, it is the last place one would expect to find an author, particularly a soft-spoken one; on the other hand it is a logical extension of that '30s "to do my share in building a just society."

Another way that Cowley has bridged the distance between the literary and outside worlds came in 1980 when he published a book called *The View from 80,* a belated (he was 82) reflection on what it is like to reach "the country of age. . . . The last act has begun, and it will be the test of the play." It is an upbeat work: "One's 80th birthday is a time for thinking about the future, not the past." Asked if the view from 86 would be basically the same, Cowley shook his head. "I wouldn't be able to summon up the same feeling of optimism," he said. "After 85 infirmities begin to accumulate."

Because Cowley recognizes this, and because he still has goals—specifically, a sequel to *The Dream of the Golden Mountains*—he spends his days in Sherman carefully, applying his energy to tasks no one else can do. *The Flower and the Leaf* was edited by Donald Faulkner; Cowley calls the book "a sort of genocide. . . . I wanted to have collected that which was worth reprinting." There are also journals, piles of them, with entries dating back to World War I, but Cowley has no intention of sorting through them for publication. "Let someone else do it," he said. "What I'd like to do is have time to put things in order."

F. Scott Fitzgerald once wrote that "There are no second acts in American life," but Cowley has had a third, a fourth and a fifth. All have done honor to the play as a whole.

Index

A

Accent, 39
Adventures of Augie March, The (Bellow), 46, 47
Agee, James, 70, 75
Aiken, Conrad, 11, 143–44, 152
Algren, Nelson, 105
Ambulance Service, 38, 140, 171
American Academy of Arts and Letters, 3
American Earth (Caldwell), 33
American Field Service, 20, 130, 131
American League against War and Fascism, 25
American League for Peace and Democracy, 26
American Progressives, 22
American Relief Ship for Spain, 23
American Scholar, The, 83, 91, 210
American Writers' Congress, 23, 53, 69, 74
Ames, Elizabeth, 171
Amis, Kingsley, 33
Amter, Israel, 22
Anchor Books, 101
—*And I Worked at the Writer's Trade* (Cowley), 144, 145, 150, 151, 152, 154, 156, 159, 172, 182
Anderson, Margaret, 105
Anderson, Sherwood, 124, 139
Anna Karenina (Tolstoy), 130, 162, 163
Antistory, 153, 180
Aragon, Louis, 154, 158, 174, 216
As I Lay Dying (Faulkner), 195, 197
Asch, Nathan, 8, 106, 116, 169, 170, 171
Asch, Scholem, 106–7, 170
Atlantic Monthly, 38, 102
Auden, W. H., 36, 105, 209
Authors Union, 20

B

Baker, Carlos, 110, 113, 114, 115, 116
Baker, George Pierce, 29
Barnes, Edna, 190
Barrès, Maurice, 174
Barthelme, Donald, 157
Bastard, The (Caldwell), 33
Baudelaire, 174
Bear, The (Faulkner), 108–9, 159, 173
Beat Generation, 180
Bellow, Saul, 33, 45, 46, 47, 50, 92, 166
Bennington College, 86
Benton, Tom, 68
Berger, Thomas, 45
Berryman, John, 166
Best, Marshall, 13
Biggs, John, 154
Bishop, John Peale, 154
Bloom, Harold, 204
Blotner, Joseph L., 109, 197
Blue Juniata (Cowley), 5, 123, 130, 138, 161, 183
Blume, Peter, 164, 165, 168, 171, 187
Bogan, Louise, 158
Bowen, Stella, 7
Boyle, Kay, 9
Breton, Andre, 138
Brian, Denis, 113
Bridge of San Luis Rey, 169
Bridge, The (Crane), 176, 179
Broom, 40, 120, 138, 142
Broth, John, 115
Brown, Bill, 169
Brown, Slater, 8, 164, 169, 186
Burke, Kenneth, 12, 58, 59, 70, 75, 88, 105, 123, 127, 153, 155, 168, 169, 171
Burroughs, William, 45, 48

C

Caldwell, Erskine, 32, 33, 84, 160
Canby, Henry Seidel, 125
Cantwell, Robert, 84
Capote, Truman, 98, 103
Carnegie Hall, 24
Catch-22 (Heller), 46
Catcher in the Rye, The (Salinger), 46
Cather, Willa, 139, 157, 216
Cézanne, 29

Chapin, Henry, 154
Cheever, John, 11, 45, 120, 180, 211
Chicago World's Fair, 83
Citizens Committee for the Election of Israel
    Amter, 22
Clark, Eleanor, 77
Coates, Robert M., 105, 106, 140, 143, 169,
    170, 171
Colliers, 40
Comintern, 58, 75
Commentary, 170
Committee for Technical Aid to Spanish De-
    mocracy, 26
Committee to Organize a Congress against
    War, 26
Communism, 19, 20, 23, 57, 121
Communist International, 57
Communist Party, 25, 26, 54, 56, 58, 59, 61,
    65, 66, 67, 68, 69, 70, 77, 80, 83, 84, 87
Compass, 101
Congress of American Revolutionary Writers,
    23, 54
Congress of the International, 57
Covici, Pat, 17
Cowley, Muriel, 3, 18, 118, 139, 164, 187,
    200, 206, 213, 215
Cozzens, James Gould, 51, 94
Crane, Hart, 8, 9, 37, 44, 111, 105, 118, 124,
    138, 139, 146, 168, 169, 176, 179
Criticism, 42, 94, 97, 122, 201–2, 204, 205
Crosby, Harry, 171–72
Crowell-Collier, Publishers, 40
Cummings, E. E., 4, 38, 105, 106, 118, 124,
    125, 130, 138, 139, 140, 155, 168, 213

D

Dadaists, 214
Daily Worker, 26, 57
Damon, S. Foster, 152
Darwin, 66
Davidson, Donald, 193
Day, Dorothy, 169
Death Comes for the Archbishop (Cather),
    216
Deconstructionists, 168
Depression, the, 125
Dial, The, 4, 125
Dickens, Charles, 163
Dictionary of Literary Biography's Update,
    165
Didion, Joan, 158

Dimitrov, 57
Donleavy, J. P., 45, 46, 47, 50
Dos Passos, John, 6, 15, 32, 33, 38, 51, 106,
    124, 138, 139, 140, 155, 197, 213
Doubleday, 101
Dream of the Golden Mountains, The (Cow-
    ley), 121, 167, 182, 214, 215, 217
Dreiser, Theodore, 37, 124, 194
Dupee, Fred, 77, 79, 80, 81

E

East of Eden (Steinbeck), 17
Eastman, Max, 55, 56
Ebony, 32
Eisenberg, Diane U., 129–30, 151
Eliot, T. S., 4, 88, 168, 176
Elizabethan drama, 7, 142
Emerson, Ralph Waldo, 30, 97, 137, 141,
    174, 175, 176, 204
Engle, Paul, 68
Epstein, Jason, 101
Epstein, Joseph, 210
Ernest Hemingway: A Life Story (Baker), 110,
    113
Ethan Frome, 182
Exile's Return (Cowley), 18, 61, 95, 103, 118,
    125, 129, 131, 138, 146, 147, 156, 161, 165,
    171, 182, 214

F

Faber and Faber Publishers, 4
Far Side of Paradise, The (Mizener), 110
Farewell to Arms, A (Hemingway), 110
Farrell, James T., 75, 76, 84
Fascism, 26, 57, 58, 59, 60, 68, 69, 72, 149,
    214
Faulkner in the University (Blotner), 197
Faulkner, Donald, 217
Faulkner, William, 9, 11, 13, 31, 32, 43, 49,
    93, 105, 106, 107, 108, 109, 110, 118, 124,
    125, 127, 138, 140, 144, 145, 149, 158,
    159, 162, 173, 174, 176, 177, 193, 194,
    195, 197, 198, 215, 216
Faulkner-Cowley File, The, 13, 106, 109
Ferguson, Otis, 84, 211
Fiedler, Leslie, 116, 201
First Writers' Congress, 84
Fischer, Marjorie, 85
Fitzgerald, F. Scott, 4, 6, 10, 33, 38, 44, 92,
    101, 105, 106, 108, 136, 146, 213, 217
Fitzgerald, Zelda, 10, 115

Flaubert, Gustave, 130, 141, 154, 174
Flower and the Leaf, The (Cowley), 196, 213, 217
For Whom the Bell Tolls (Hemingway), 108
Ford, Ford Madox, 7, 138, 195
Fortune, 80
Foster and Ford candidacy, 64, 68
Foster, William Z., 214
France, 6, 7, 20, 45, 116–17, 125, 130, 132, 140, 171, 174, 181, 203
Frank, Waldo, 73, 85
Franklin, Benjamin, 37
Freeman, Joe, 73, 75, 76, 77
Freud, 43, 66
Frost, Robert, 4, 36, 97
Fugitives, 193

G

Gargoyle, 6
Georgia Boy (Caldwell), 33
Gilliam, Florence, 6
Ginger Man, The (Donleavy), 46, 47, 50
Glasgow, John, 148
Go Down, Moses (Faulkner), 199
Gold, Mike, 73
Golden Notebook, The (Lessing), 112, 158
Golden Spur, The (Powell), 169
Gone with the Wind (Mitchell), 9
Gordon, Caroline, 11, 13, 159, 164, 167, 169, 171, 195, 196
Grapes of Wrath (Steinbeck), 31, 108
Great Gatsby, The (Fitzgerald), 10, 101, 108, 146
Great Scenes from Great Novels, 130
Greenberg, Clem, 88
Greenwich Village, 4, 6, 95, 96, 138, 169, 213, 214
Guggenheim Foundation Fellowships, 4, 98, 100
Guinzburg, Thomas H., 3
Guthrie, Ramon, 106, 170

H

Hamlet, The (Faulkner), 199
Hammerstein, Oscar II, 4, 36
Harcourt Brace, 101
Harper's, 102
Harrington, Evans, 197
Hart, Henry, 53
Harte, Bret, 37

Harvard, 29, 30, 36, 97, 125, 130, 135, 138, 155, 171, 175, 214, 216
Harvard Advocate, 120
Harvard Club, 3, 151, 200
Harvard Poetry Society, 131
Hathaway, Clarence, 57
Hawks, Howard, 11
Hawthorne, Nathaniel 51, 52, 141, 215
Haydn, Hiram 89
Hayes, Alfred, 84
Heggens, Thomas, 10
Hemingway, Ernest, 7, 11–12, 14, 15, 24, 31, 32, 35, 37, 38, 44, 45, 47, 49, 92, 105, 106, 107, 108, 110, 113, 114–19 passim, 124, 125, 127, 138–40 passim, 142, 143, 145, 147, 157, 170, 171, 173, 178, 179, 194, 199, 215
Hemingway, John 113
Hemingway, Mary, 113
Herbst, Josephine, 8, 170
Herman, John 170
Hermann, John, 8
Herzog (Bellow), 45
Hicks, Granville, 44, 68, 79
Hillard, Robert, 155
Hitler, 24, 31, 57, 58, 59, 60, 72, 214
Hooks, Sidney, 55, 56
Hopwood Prizes, 39
Hopwood, Avery, 39
Hotchner, A. E., 113, 114, 115
Howe, Irving, 91
Howells, William Dean, 37
Hudson Review, 39
Humboldt's Gift (Bellow), 166
Hynan, Patrick, 139

I

"I Am Expelled from Prep School" (Cheever), 120
Ibsen, Henrik, 136
In Cold Blood (Capote), 98
International Publishers, 53, 54
International Writers' Congress for the Defense of Culture, 158
Invisible Man (Ellison), 46

J

Jarrell, Randall, 166
Jewish novelists, 92
John Reed Clubs, 55, 56, 78, 82
Jolas, Eugene, 7

Jones, James, 38
Josephson, Matthew, 6, 12, 129, 155, 158, 169, 171
Journeyman (Caldwell), 33
Joyce, James, 99, 109
Jung, Carl, 43

K

Kazin, Alfred, 84, 160
Kempf, James, 196
Kenyon Review, 39
Kerouac, Jack, 105, 111, 180
Kesey, Ken, 45, 101, 111, 180, 206, 215
Knopf, 101, 111
Kunitz, Joshua, 61

L

Lamont, Corliss, 23
Lanham, Buck, 115
Lawson, John Howard, 73
Le Mortre D'Arthur, 15
League of American Writers, 20, 26, 27, 28, 64, 76, 78, 85, 86, 90
League of Professional Groups for Foster and Ford, 21, 25
Let Us Now Praise Famous Men (Agee), 70
Letters (Hemingway), 171
Lewis, Sinclair, 139, 157, 124
Life, 30, 31, 32, 33, 114
Life of Harry Crosby (Wolf), 141
Light, James, 136, 169
Linscott, Robert N., 195
Literary Review, The, 125
Literary Situation, The (Cowley), 44, 92, 100, 107
Literary prizes, 38–39
Little Review (Anderson), 105
Lockridge, Ross, 10
London, Jack, 37, 102
Lost Lady, A (Cather), 216
Lost generation, 6, 37, 123, 125, 129, 130, 133, 134, 136, 137, 138, 157, 165, 213
Love in Chartres (Asch), 170
Lowell, Robert, 166
Loyalist cause, 71
Lynn, Kenneth, 201, 210
Lytton Strachey (Holroyd), 110

M

Macdonald, Dwight, 77, 78, 80, 81

Macleish, Archibald, 138, 149
Madame Bovary (Flaubert), 130
Mailer, Norman, 33, 144, 157
Making It (Podhoretz), 111
Malcolm Cowley: A Checklist of His Writings (1916–1973) (Eisenberg), 130, 151
Man in the Gray Flannel Suit, The, (Wilson), 30
Man's Fate (Malraux), 70
Manhattan Transfer (Dos Passos), 31
Mann, Thomas, 24, 109
Marx, Karl, 66, 67, 90
Marxism, 21, 65, 214
Matthiessen, F. O., 77
McCarthy era, 86, 141
McCarthy, Mary, 77, 78, 80, 81
McClure, John, 193
McComb, Dudley, 155
McMurtry, Larry, 206, 215
Mecca Temple, 55
Medical Bureau, 26
Mellon, Mary, 12
Mellon, Paul, 12
Melville, Herman, 141, 176
Memoirs of Montparnasse (Glasgow), 148
Mencken, H. L., 157
Michigan, University of, 38
Midwestern novelists, 92, 94
Milburn, George, 12
Milford, Nancy, 110
Mill on the Floss (Eliot), 101
Miller, Henry, 48
Minnesota, University of, 106
Miss Lonelyhearts (West), 130
Moby Dick (Melville), 175, 176
Modern Language Association, 193
Morris, George, 80
Moss, Arthur, 6
Moveable Feast, A (Hemingway), 115
Mr. Faulkner's Southern Saga (Gordon), 195
Mr. Roberts (Heggens), 10
Munson, Gorham D., 6
Munzenberg, Willi, 58
My Antonia (Cather), 216
My Old Man (Hemingway), 113

N

Narrow Covering, The (Siebel), 35
Nation, 16
National Committee for People's Rights, 23
National Committee for the Defense of Political Prisoners, 25
National Endowment for the Arts, 103

National Institute of Arts and Letters, 3
National Writers' Congress, 24
Negativism, 30–31
Negro writers, 49, 51, 92
New Critics, 43, 94
New Deal, 68, 69
New Left, 65, 66, 90, 91
New Masses, 26, 75, 79, 81, 87
New Republic, 4, 13, 16, 20, 22, 24, 40, 78,
  109, 120, 125, 130, 131, 139, 148, 162, 171,
  212, 214, 215
New School, 77
New Statesman, 48
New World Writing, 39
New York City, 4, 25, 140, 151, 160, 182,
  187, 188, 193, 215
New York Review of Books, 16, 204
New York Times, 13, 91, 109, 121
New York Times Book Review, 195
New Yorker, 12, 45, 113, 114, 153, 161
Newberry Library, 72, 105, 121, 195, 196
Newspaper Guild, 37
Newsweek, 102
Nordhoff, 38
Norris, Frank, 37
North American Committee to Aid Spanish
  Democracy, 26
North of Boston (Frost), 4
NOT-writer, 98

Parker, Dorothy, 170
Partisan Review, 39, 77, 78, 79, 80, 81, 82,
  87, 89
Pay-Day (Asch), 170
Pennsylvania, 50
People's Front, 57
Perkins, Maxwell, 11, 17, 115
Phillips, William, 77, 78, 82, 83
Philosophy of Literary Form (Burke), 88
Plimpton, George, 113, 116
Podhoretz, Norman, 111
Poe, Edgar Allen, 137, 141
Poetry, 95, 103, 104, 120, 124, 128, 129, 161,
  184
Popular Front, 57, 58, 61
Portable Faulkner, 12, 13, 44, 109, 139, 144,
  158–59, 177, 194, 195, 215
Portable Hemingway, 12, 139, 178
Porter, Allen, 75
Porter, Katherine Anne, 36, 99, 105, 158
Positivism, 30–31
Pound, Ezra, 7, 44, 105, 106, 138, 142
Powell, Dawn, 169–70
Powers, J. F., 36
Prince Edward Island, 50, 51
Prohibition, 141
Proust, 109, 141, 142, 154
Provincetown Players, 136, 169
Putnam, Phelps, 106
Pylon (Faulkner), 199

O

O'Hara, John, 94
O'Neill, Eugene, 29, 105, 124, 169
Oates, Joyce Carol, 112, 159
Office of Facts and Figures, 19
Office, The (Asch), 170
Old Left, 64, 66
Old Man and the Sea, The (Hemingway), 31
Olson, Tilly, 35, 215
On Moral Fiction (Gardner), 16
On the Road (Kerouac), 111, 180
One Flew Over the Cuckoo's Nest (Kesey),
  46, 180
Orwell, George, 71

P

Papa Hemingway (Hotchner), 113
Paperbacks, 100, 101, 102
Paris Review, 111, 113

R

Racine, 174
Racine (Cowley), 130
Raintree County (Lockridge), 10
Random House, 11, 195
Ransom, John Crowe, 36, 193
Rascoe, Burton, 105
Renoir, Jean, 11, 107
Reporter, 101
Republic of Letters, 207–9
Rexroth, Kenneth, 95
Richardson, Samuel, 48
Road, The (Asch), 170
Robinson, Edward Arlington, 211
Rockefeller Foundation, 98
Rodman, Selden, 15
Roethke, Theodore, 166
Roosevelt, Franklin, 65, 70, 167
Rorty, James, 55
Rosenberg, Harold, 74, 85
Ross, Lillian, 113, 114, 116
Rubin, Louis D., 198

Rukeyser, Muriel, 53

S

Sala, Tristan, 138
Salinger, J. D., 33, 46
Sanctuary (Faulkner), 9, 11, 31, 32, 194, 199
Saroyan, William, 84
Saturday Evening Post, 4, 9, 153, 199
Schneider, Isidor, 85
Schwartz, Delmore, 166
Scientism, 43
Scribner's, 11, 178
Scribner, Charlie, 101
Secession, 40, 120, 138
*A Second Flowering: Works and Days of the
     Lost Generation* (Cowley), 118, 123, 124,
     172, 213
Second Writers' Congress, 77, 81
Seghers, Anna, 158
Selde, Gilbert, 10
Self-subsistence, 126, 127, 185, 190
Seward, William, 113
Shakespeare, 63
Shaw, Bernard, 136
Sheean, Vincent, 24
Sherman, (Conn.), 3, 19, 129, 139, 164, 169,
     182, 183, 186–91 passim, 200, 201, 214–17
     passim
Shipman, Evan, 171
Siebel, Julia, 35
Simpson, Lewis, 196
Social novels, 51–52, 94
Socialist writers, 59
The Sound and the Fury (Faulkner), 177, 195,
     199
Southern Renaissance, 193, 194
Southern Review, 196
Southern novelists, 92, 93
Southerner, The 11, 107
Soviet Russia Today, 24
Soviet writers, 71
Spanish Civil War, 110
Spanish-American War, 183
Spender, Stephen, 105, 209
"Spotted Horses" (Faulkner), 108–9, 197
Stalin, 55
Stalin-Hitler Pact, 26, 166
Stanford University, 30, 34, 198, 205, 206,
     207, 215
Stein, Gertrude, 6, 138, 142–43
Steinbeck, John, 105, 108
Structuralists, 168
Sun Also Rises, The (Hemingway), 108

Sweep, 142
Sweet's Architectural Catalogue, 20
Sweet's Catalogue Service, 20

T

Tate, Allen, 8, 49, 123, 141, 164, 169, 195,
     207
Tender is the Night (Fitzgerald), 108
That Evening Sun (Faulkner), 194
Them (Oates), 112
Third Writers' Congress, 24, 84
This Quarter, 7, 142
This Side of Paradise, (Fitzgerald) 38, 146
Thornton Wilder Trio, A, 130
Thurber, James, 105, 125, 143
Time, 102
Times-Picayune, 193
Trachtenberg, Alexander, 54, 57, 61, 62, 78
Tradition and the Individual Talent (Eliot), 88
Transatlantic Review, The, 7
Transition, 7
Trollope, Anthony, 9, 52, 162, 163
Trotskyites/Trotskyists, 80, 84
True Confessions, 17
Turner, Addie, 8, 164, 171
Twain, Mark, 37

U

Ulysses (Joyce), 99
University teaching, 34
University writing programs, 36, 96
The Unvanquished (Faulkner), 199
Updike, John, 205

V

Valley of Decisions (Davenport), 17
Valley, The (Asch), 170
Venetian State Papers, 7
Vergilian literature, 30
Vietnam, 69, 89, 96, 126
View from 80, The (Cowley), 167, 179, 182,
     217
Viking Press, 3, 12, 13, 17, 18, 101, 111, 139,
     178, 180, 200, 213, 215
Vintage, 101

W

Wall Street Crash, 9, 166, 167

Walsh, Ernest, 7
Wapshot Chronicle, The (Cheever), 45
Wapshot Scandal, The (Cheever), 45
Warner Bros., 11, 107
Warren, Robert Penn, 11, 13, 109, 139, 145, 159, 193
"Was" (Faulkner), 197
Washington Post, 121
Washington, University of, 126
Weeks, Ted, 38
Wells, H. G., 60
Wescott, Glenway, 106, 134, 135
Western Review, 28, 39
Wheelwright, John Brooks, 106, 169, 171
Whipple, T. K., 154
Whitman, Walt, 37, 141, 168, 215
Whittier, John Greenleaf, 137, 141
Wicked Pavilion, The (Powell), 169
The Wild Palms (Faulkner), 199
Wilde, Oscar, 137
Wilder, Thornton, 33, 38, 106, 118, 124, 138, 168
Williams, Joan, 194
Williams, William Carlos, 105
Wilson, Edmund, 5, 11, 105, 138, 148, 149, 154, 155, 162, 202, 211, 212, 214
Wolf, Friedich, 73, 75
Wolfe, Thomas, 32, 33, 49, 105, 106, 118, 124, 138, 180

Wood, Grant, 68
World War I, 38, 96, 97, 118, 124, 129, 134, 140, 141, 148, 150, 165, 167, 173, 208
World War II, 11, 38, 97, 106, 107, 120, 124, 125, 130, 157, 161, 166, 214, 216
Wouk, Herman 30
Writers at Work, 106
Writers' colonies, 8
Writing, alcohol and, 8, 10
Writing, essays, 10
Writing, market for, 39–40
Writing, poetry, 4, 10
Writing, process of, 10, 42, 162, 179, 192
Writing, propaganda, 31
Writing, revision of, 18, 160–61
Writing, teaching of, 4, 29, 35, 37, 42, 205–6

Y

Yaddo, 171
Yet Other Waters (Farrell), 75, 76
Young, Stanley, 12

Z

Zelda (Nancy Milford), 110